ASIAN BUSINESS

CUSTOMS & MANNERS

Mary Murray Bosrock

Meadowbrook Press
Distributed by Simon & Schuster
New York

Library of Congress Cataloging-in-Publication Data

Bosrock, Mary Murray.
  Asian business customs & manners : a country-by-country guide / by Mary
Murray Bosrock.
      p. cm.
  Includes bibliographical references and index.
  ISBN10 0-88166-525-8, ISBN13 978-0-88166-525-3 (Meadowbrook);
  ISBN10 0-684-05200-8, ISBN13 978-0-684-05200-7 (Simon & Schuster)
  1. Business etiquette—Asia. I. Title.
  HF5389.3.A78B67 2007
  395.5'2095—dc22

                              2006030289

Editor: Megan McGinnis
Editor and Researcher: Catherine A. H. Walker
Proofreader: Alicia Ester
Production Manager: Paul Woods
Graphic Design Manager: Tamara Peterson
Desktop Publisher: Danielle White
Cover Photo: Val Escher; Globe in image © 2006 by George F. Cram Co., 4719
    W. 62nd Street, Indianapolis, IN 46268, 800-227-4199, ext. 3715
Index: Beverlee Day

Published by Meadowbrook Press, 5451 Smetana Drive, Minnetonka,
Minnesota 55343

www.meadowbrookpress.com

BOOK TRADE DISTRIBUTION by Simon and Schuster, a division of Simon
and Schuster, Inc., 1230 Avenue of the Americas, New York, New York 10020

10 09 08 07 10 9 8 7 6 5 4 3 2 1

Printed in the United States of America

To Ron, who has given me the world:
our sons, Matt and Steve.
To Matt and Steve, who have given me my girls:
Monique and Leslie
Alyssa, Isabella, Juliana, Alexandra, and Anna.

CONTENTS

Part II: Country Information

PREFACE

The world isn't globalizing—it's already global. To many, globalization has meant that old systems and ways of thinking no longer work. Goods, money, and people now cross borders at astonishing speeds. While globalization didn't create many of today's economic problems and cultural clashes, it made us aware of them, which has made many people feel helpless to solve them.

This book will help you gain control as you do business internationally. It's not about manners, etiquette, or how to hold your fork. It's about survival—for our companies, economy, and way of life. To survive, we must compete in a global economy. And to compete effectively, we must understand other countries, cultures, and ways of doing business. Intercultural understanding was once a luxury for the idle rich, but no longer. Ignoring cultural differences isn't innovative or clever; it's arrogant and bad for business.

What Asia Can Offer American Businesses

As both producer and consumer, the Asian market has enormous potential. With dozens of independent countries and a number of dependencies, Asia is the world's largest continent (almost one-third of the world's land surface) with the largest population (in 2000, roughly three-fifths of the world's population was Asian).

In the last several decades, the world has watched a number of Asian countries develop into economic powerhouses. In the 1950s, Korea was Asia's third-poorest nation, heavily dependent on foreign aid; in 2004, South Korea was the world's eleventh-largest economy. That same year, the economies of China, India, and Japan ranked in the world's top twenty.

In fact, today China's economy is surpassing the United Kingdom's, and by 2040, leading global financial firm Goldman Sachs predicts it'll exceed the United States'. Similarly, by 2032 India's economy is on target to surpass Japan's.

With this information in hand, no company can afford to ignore the Asian market. Yet many Western companies, especially small and medium-size ones, are reluctant to plunge into it. Why? To many, Asia seems so *foreign*—and thus intimidating. Its cultures and customs differ dramatically from those of the West (and almost as dramatically among countries within its borders).

Thanks to the worldwide distribution of Western films, TV programs, and media, Asians know a lot about Western culture—much more so than Westerners know about Asian culture. Many Westerners can't distinguish Hong Kong from Singapore, Indonesia from Malaysia, or Taiwan from

Thailand. Not surprisingly, most lack even a basic understanding of Asia's widely varying histories, cultures, and social customs.

For example, many Westerners don't realize that Asia is a *continent*, not a *country*. Each Asian nation has its own unique history, cultures, languages, religious traditions, and cuisines. Furthermore, Asians aren't "all the same." The Chinese, Japanese, Koreans, Indians, and Indonesians aren't interchangeable, and thinking so is ignorant and insulting to Asians.

Although doing business in Asia and with Asians can be a culturally complex undertaking, it's one with potentially rich rewards for those willing to learn just the basic facts of the people and their countries. This knowledge is crucial to successfully doing business in Asia.

This book includes information everyone should know when interacting with Asians, whether as a host or guest. When you're the host, you expect your Asian guest to know your country's basic customs; the more knowledgeable your guest, the more favorably you view him or her. Similarly, the more you know about your Asian host's culture, the better the impression you'll make and the faster you can discuss business.

Although it's designed as a resource for businesspeople, this book is also helpful to leisure travelers, students, teachers, travel and hospitality professionals, and hosts who regularly entertain Asian visitors. Keep this book on your desk or tuck it in your briefcase. I've organized it with your busy schedule in mind.

In Part I, I discuss the most basic rules for communicating with someone from another culture. I also include important customs that are practiced in nearly every Asian country. In Part II, I provide details on communication and behavior in fourteen Asian nations plus brief overviews of Australia and New Zealand. Before you meet or talk with an Asian, you can quickly learn or review important facts about his or her culture that'll help you communicate clearly.

Asia is changing just as the rest of the world is. While researching information for this book, I met a lovely young Indian woman who's studying in the United States. I asked her a few questions about Indian culture, and she promised to get back to me soon.

Eight hours later, she forwarded me an e-mail from her parents, who live in India. They'd fully answered my questions. When I started working in international business thirty years ago, receiving this kind of response from half way around the world might have taken eight days!

The information in this book isn't just "nice to know." It's vital to your success and that of your company if you want to do business in Asia or with Asians. Knowing this information can lead to increased earnings for your company. In short, what you learn in this book will go straight to your bottom line.

The World According to Me

As you read this book, please understand that it reflects my experiences as an international businessperson. I'm simply telling it as I see it. All of us personalize our observations, no matter where we are in the world. A half-dozen people on a street corner in Dayton, Ohio, will tell six different stories about the traffic accident they just witnessed. A half-dozen people in Delhi will do the same.

I base my discussion of each country not only on personal observations but also on meetings with people from that country: diplomats, doctors, lawyers, businesspeople, teachers, and students. My goal is to pass on what I've learned and what other people with significant international experience have deemed important to know about Asians.

Letter from Asia

During the past several years, as I've collected information for this book, I've asked Asians for their views of Americans and what they'd like to tell Americans planning to visit Asia. The following is a compilation of some of their more significant comments.

Dear American Friends:

We like you and your country—we truly do. We appreciate and envy many things about you. You are free to move around, change directions, express yourselves as individuals, and be whoever and whatever you want.

We enjoy sharing our cultures with you because your reactions are enthusiastic, spontaneous, and natural. We feel less inhibited just being with you. From blue jeans and cosmetics to music and movies, American products are known for quality and value—and they heavily influence our changing lifestyles.

We admire your country's leadership in higher education. In fact, many of the young leaders shaping Asia's future have been educated in your colleges and universities.

Unlike in Western nations, a cultural dichotomy thrives in our countries. Our millennia-old morals and mores, art and architecture, language and literature coexist with computers and credit cards, sleek cars and trendy fashions, music videos and fast food. We are determined to embrace modernity while holding on to our traditions.

Despite our affinity for the United States and its people, we sometimes feel that Americans take us for granted. We work hard to understand your history, language, and culture; too often it seems as if you make little effort to understand ours.

In fact, most of us believe Americans do not know anything about the rest of the world—and you do not want to learn. We are frustrated when we meet Americans, including graduates of prestigious universities, who believe Hong Kong is a city in Japan and all Chinese wear Mao suits, and who have no idea that Indonesia has the world's largest Muslim population.

To us, globalization must not mean Americanization. We—like everyone, everywhere—want the material things you take for granted: drinkable water, ample food, and comfortable homes. But these wants do not mean we want to be like you.

Unlike Westerners, we emphasize the importance of the group, not the individual. We conduct business, make decisions, and socialize as a group. On your first visit, do not expect to walk in, slap us on the back, and sign a contract. If you want to establish a business relationship with us, visit often, enjoy our countries, and get to know us. Be patient.

When you visit us, it is more important than ever that you respect our ways. They are no better or worse than yours—they are just different and are based on millennia of tradition. Do not preach to us about human rights, women's rights, or Christianity. Unless you have studied our cultures in great depth, you are in no position to judge.

We do not expect you to know Ramadan as well as we know Christmas, or to be as accustomed to pad thai or kushiyaki as we are to pizza and cheeseburgers. But we do expect you to respect and appreciate everything our cultures offer. We are honored to serve you and introduce you to our ways. If you refuse our hospitality, we lose face.

When you dine with us, attend business meetings, or visit our sacred places, please respect the appropriate etiquette and dress. You should try to blend in; do not call attention to yourself. Always dress neatly and conservatively. Men should consider shaving off beards, and women should consider wearing their hair up or pulled back and avoid wearing bright colors and excessive makeup.

We are happy to talk with you in your language; indeed, most business discussions will be in English. In business meetings, use simple, straightforward language; avoid using jargon and idioms. But do not talk to us as though we were small children. We are well educated, sophisticated internationalists who have built thriving economies from our understanding of export markets. Many of the items that make your everyday lives more productive and enjoyable are made in our countries.

If our English is sometimes less than perfect, remember that we are making a great effort to communicate in your language. If you think you may become impatient with our English skills, feel free to learn our languages.

Please visit us, but come informed and with an open mind. If you want to lead the world, you have to know something about every part of it. So try our food, visit our ancient temples and mosques, and participate in our festivals. We are proud of our homes, traditions, and countries. We hope you will enjoy and appreciate them.

Respectfully,

Your Asian Friends

ACKNOWLEDGMENTS

For their valuable contributions, I'd like to thank the following people:

Sukri Abu Bakar, Director, Malaysian Industrial Development Authority, Chicago

Steve Banner

Jodi Boerner

Nicole Botsman

Brad Brennan

Inke Brons

Woodrow W. Byun

Byung Moon Kim

Michael Caldrone

Wilson Chu

Brad and Doris Davis

Dhama Dhamavasi, Consul, Royal Thai Consulate-General, Chicago

Jennifer Wu Dunn

Robin Elsham

Matt and Holly Bennett Etzell

Maureen Gergely

Alan Griffiths

Jinny Han

Sumita K. Harle

Dell Jariwala

Tammy Jih

Father James Vinh Le

Tyler Le

Peter Lefferts

Yana Lin

Lita Malicsi

Vincent Mar

Alison Mercer, Honorary Consul General of South Korea

Zelinda Murphy

Philip Pillai

Hjayceelyn Quintana, First Secretary and Consul, Embassy of the Philippines

Steve Reidel

Robin Rix

Eleanor K. Sequeira

Martin and Barbara Spurling

Pamela Pappas Stanoch

William R. Strang, Honorary Consul General of Japan

Tami Sulistyo

Mike Sullivan

Evan Williams, Honorary Consul General of Japan (retired)

Hong Yang

Stephen Young

Xiao Zhang

My special thanks to everyone at the embassies, consulates, tourist boards, and trade commissions who contributed their invaluable experience and advice.

Warmest thanks to my husband, Ronald M. Bosrock, Honorary Consul General of Austria, who has supported this book in many ways from its inception.

And to all the others who helped and encouraged me in ways large and small, my sincere thanks.

Mary Murray Bosrock

Mary Murray Bosrock
Saint Paul, Minnesota

Part I

GETTING STARTED

HOW TO GO INTERNATIONAL

In Asia, there's a sharp difference between public and private behavior. This book describes public behavior. In business situations, Asians always behave formally and properly—and you should, too. Once you've formed a relationship with an Asian colleague, casual behavior is acceptable. When you've reached that stage, you've gained a friend for life.

Avoid Generalizations

Just when you're tempted to generalize about an Asian, you'll meet an atheist Filipina, a sloppy Singaporean, a blunt Indonesian, a rude Japanese, an idle Korean, or a fussy Thai—and all your generalizations will go out the window.

Even though people from the same country often look alike, speak the same language, eat the same foods, and practice the same religion, each one is different. Uniqueness is what makes international travel so much fun. I've listened to people of the same nationality debate a particular custom or behavior —and they rarely agreed. Women disagreed with men. Older people disagreed with younger ones. Sometimes there was general disagreement. Each person had a unique way of behaving and unique way of interpreting others' actions, which often led to miscommunication.

If people who share a culture sometimes have trouble communicating, then is communication *impossible* for a business traveler? Certainly not. Although you'll probably never meet a Thai who has every quality I describe in the chapter on Thailand, my three decades' experience in Asia has

"Your competition isn't necessarily the person at the next desk, but the woman in India or the man in China. We're looking for bright, imaginative, and dedicated talent able to work well with other people, often people not like themselves. And we can hunt for those sorts of people all over the world! So it pays to develop competencies that support global business. Things like cross-cultural awareness, flexibility, language skills, sensitivity, the ability to value differences in people, and the ability to understand nonverbal communications styles."

—Robert W. Lane, Chairman & Chief Executive Officer, Deere & Company

shown that there are certain common customs and characteristics you'll encounter when dealing with people from a particular country. Knowing these commonalities will help you understand Asians and feel more comfortable with them. It'll help you avoid misunderstandings and communicate clearly and effectively so you can establish productive business relationships—and possibly friendships.

> "The people of the world are bigoted and unenlightened: Invariably they regard what is like them as right, and what is different from them as wrong, resulting in mutual recrimination.... They do not realize that the types of humanity are not uniform and that their customs are also not one, that it is not only impossible to force people to become different but also impossible to force them to become alike."
>
> —Yung-cheng, emperor of China, in 1727

There isn't a country I've worked or traveled in that I haven't enjoyed. Regardless of how dynamic the business environment or how beautiful the countryside, it's always the people—the thousands of individuals—who hold my interest and eventually win my heart.

Don't Be the Ugly American

The term *the ugly American* was introduced as the title of a 1958 novel by William J. Lederer and Eugene Burdick about an ignorant, incompetent U.S. ambassador to a fictional Southeast Asian country. The term became widely known after the film based on the novel was released in 1963, and it quickly became an epithet for rude, self-centered people who roamed the world with utter disregard—even disdain—for other cultures.

Many of the Americans I work with and meet on my travels aren't ugly—just uninformed. They want to understand and appreciate other cultures, but they have little experience or exposure to customs different from their own. In the continental United States, we can travel thousands of miles in several directions without encountering significant cultural or linguistic differences. In Asia, a journey of thousands of miles can take you through several countries, cultures, and languages. It's no surprise that international travel can befuddle Americans!

Most of us don't have the time or ability to learn the numerous languages and customs of cultures around the world. So how can we begin to communicate with our international business associates? By being willing to make mistakes. Sensitive imperfection can be endearing.

For example, an ambassador I know says his wife always learns the language of a country faster than he does. Why? Because she tries to speak the language as she shops, tours, visits, and dines—and she doesn't worry when she makes mistakes. Her earnest attempts to speak the language charm the local people, who encourage her communication efforts. The ambassador—with an official position to uphold—never speaks the language unless he's certain he can speak it correctly. He doesn't get the practice and encouragement his wife does, and thus he doesn't learn the language as quickly.

Be aware that there are good mistakes and bad mistakes. Good mistakes, like those the ambassador's wife makes, clearly convey the message "I care, I'm trying, I'm sorry if I got it wrong." Bad mistakes, like dressing sloppily or asking inappropriate questions, shout, "I don't care, I won't try, and I'm not one bit sorry if I don't understand you." These are mistakes that give international visitors a black eye.

Approach international travel as if it were an invitation to a party at your boss's home. At such an event, you'd behave with the goal of a raise or promotion in mind. You'd be sensitive, dress appropriately, and bring a suitable gift. When visiting a host country, adopt the same attitude and take the time beforehand to learn the customs and behaviors that'll make you a gracious guest.

Show Consideration and Respect

Consideration and respect are the qualities you need most for successful international travel. I base every suggested behavior in this book on these qualities. You can't show others respect and consideration without first learning about them and their culture.

But doing your homework before you visit a country is just part of the task; once you're in the country, you must keep learning. You can learn a lot about appropriate behavior by observing, asking, listening, and—the best method—trial and error. Trying shows your vulnerability and humanity, and it can excuse numerous communication errors. We all make mistakes when communicating in our own culture, so we certainly can't expect perfection when communicating in another.

When interacting with Asians, ask yourself, "Are my actions considerate and respectful?" Following are the most important ways you can learn appropriate behavior so your consideration and respect won't go unnoticed or misinterpreted:

- Observe how the local people behave. This is one of the easiest, safest ways to learn appropriate behavior. Note what others wear, how they greet one another, how they eat. Follow their example, and you'll usually be correct.
- Whenever communication or expected behavior is unclear, quietly and politely ask your host or business associate, the hotel concierge, or a shop clerk what to do or say. You may feel foolish, but people will appreciate that you're trying to learn. Here's information you'll want to ask about if it's not absolutely clear:
  * What's the expected attire for an event?
  * What's the proper pronunciation of a name?
  * What tip is expected?
  * What's an appropriate gift for the occasion?
  * What's the proper way of wrapping and presenting a gift?
  * What flowers are appropriate for an occasion?
  * When and where may I smoke?
  * What time does an invitation really mean?

Listen carefully and write down necessary information. For example, when a person says his or her name, listen carefully to the pronunciation and write down the name phonetically to help you recall the name later. Note any titles given.

- During meetings or presentations, listen closely to your hosts and take careful notes. Doing so signals your sincerity. If your hosts speak English as a courtesy to you, remember that English may be their second or third language, and you may need to listen even more closely. (If you get impatient, be empathetic. Think how well *you'd* express yourself in your second or third language.) If you're not sure what's been said or what's expected of you, politely ask for clarification. It's better to ask a question than risk misunderstanding.

- At social functions, listen carefully to what local people say to you and to one another. Ask informed questions; your genuine interest will always be

> Young Asians are embracing Western customs, clothing, food, and attitudes. Movies, TV programs, the Internet, and increased international travel are making young people across the continent more westernized than their parents.
>
> Nevertheless, even young Asians expect visiting Westerners to treat Asian cultures with respect.

appreciated. What you learn about a country and culture from these exchanges will come in handy in future conversations.

Showing consideration and respect will never steer you wrong, and even small gestures carry a lot of weight. Try to speak a few words of the host country's language, use chopsticks (when appropriate), taste the local food, greet people properly, learn from others' behaviors, and you'll successfully build business relationships and friendships.

The Ten Commandments of Visiting Asia

1. Do your homework. A basic knowledge of each country's culture and history will greatly benefit you.
2. Take your time and be patient. Asians develop relationships slowly.
3. Always be sincere. Building a relationship requires trust, and trust requires sincerity.
4. Never embarrass anyone publicly or make anyone lose face. Doing so will end a relationship.
5. Use a softer speaking voice than you'd normally use. Never raise your voice to try to overcome language difficulties.
6. Show respect for other cultures, even if they seem strange to you. Asian cultures were highly developed when European cultures were still in their infancy.
7. Ask, look, and listen! Asians are proud of their cultures and enjoy teaching others about their ways. They'll appreciate a respectful interest.
8. Learn what behavior your Asian colleagues expect, and be aware of the image you're projecting at all times.
9. Make friends. When Asians like you, they'll forgive just about anything you may do wrong.
10. Assume the best about people and their actions. When problems arise, assume miscommunication is the cause. Most behavior is rational once we understand its rationale.

THE FACTS OF ASIA

Asia: A Continent of Contrasts

Nowhere else in the world are there such dramatic differences as in Asia. From land size, geography, and climate, to population, standard of living, and form of government, each Asian country is unique. Here are some examples of the contrasts:

Land Size
Singapore is approximately the size of Chicago. China is the fourth-largest country in the world, covering nearly four million square miles.

Geography
Pakistan has some of the world's highest mountains, including K2 in the Himalayas. Most of Bangladesh lies less than fifty feet above sea level.

Climate
Winters in Seoul and Beijing are snowy with freezing temperatures. Indonesia, Singapore, and Malaysia have steamy, tropical weather year-round.

Population
India is about a third the size of the United States, but has nearly four times the population—just over a billion people. The Maldives is nearly twice the size of Washington DC, but has about two-thirds the population.

Urbanization
Most people in Japan, Taiwan, and South Korea are urban dwellers. Fewer than one third of Thais and Bangladeshis live in cities.

Ethnicity
Japan is largely homogeneous, with one dominant culture and one dominant language. Indonesia contains more than three hundred ethnic groups who speak more than three hundred languages.

Culture
Although Asian countries share a common set of basic values, each has a unique national culture and several distinct local cultures.

Furthermore, as political borders drop, cultural borders rise. People are more determined than ever to hold on to their cultural distinctness (language, food, religion, and customs), even as they enjoy and anticipate the benefits of globalization.

Religion

In Asian cultures, religious beliefs are closely interwoven with social life and business life. Depending on the country, the Islamic, Buddhist, Hindu, Shinto, and Christian faiths have large numbers of followers.

Furthermore, Taoist and Confucian philosophies influence many Asian cultures.

Government

China is a Communist state with a tightly controlled media; its citizens don't enjoy many of the rights that Americans take for granted. Japan is a constitutional monarchy with a parliamentary government that allows a diverse and flourishing free press. Japanese citizens enjoy the same basic rights as Americans do.

Standard of Living

The gross domestic product (GDP) of Japan is US $41,480 per person. Bangladesh's GDP is US $2,100 per capita.

A well-traveled senior executive of a Fortune 500 company once told me, with a good deal of embarrassment, about his visit several years ago to Indonesia to negotiate a multimillion-dollar contract with the government.

Feeling confident that his product was superior to that of his competitors, he arrived for his meeting with an Indonesian government minister. Greetings were warm and the conversation friendly until the participants got down to business. The minister said, "We welcome you to Indonesia. Now please tell us what you know about our country."

The visiting executive had been prepared to talk extensively about his company and his product. He was forced to admit that he knew very little about Indonesia.

The minister replied, "You have come half way around the world to ask my government to purchase a multimillion-dollar system that virtually every person in our country will use for many years. Yet you know nothing about us or our country. How could you possibly meet our needs? I suggest you go home, learn something about us, and then come back to us with your product."

The visitor did just that and eventually got the contract, but the delay was costly and a seasoned international executive should have known better. Don't make his mistake in your international travels.

Given the wide range of variations, it's easy to see why it's important to learn at least a country's basic facts before visiting it. Being familiar with China doesn't automatically mean you're familiar with Taiwan. Similarly, learning about Indonesia doesn't mean you're learning about India or Pakistan.

Always remember that each country in Asia is unique. Take the time to learn its vital statistics.

Challenges Facing Asia

Poverty

Asia's fight against poverty is making progress, quite remarkably in some nations. In 2002, the Asian Development Bank (ADB) reported that roughly one out of five Asians—about 690 million people—lived on less than one U.S. dollar a day. While the statistic is appalling by American standards, in 1990 one out of *three* Asians lived on that amount. If current economic growth continues, the number of Asians living in extreme poverty could drop to 150 million by 2015.

But Asian countries have a long way to go to meet this prediction. Although wealthy Asian nations give aid to poorer ones (for moral reasons as well as to help secure regional stability), keeping the poverty rate low depends on the entire Asian economy growing. According to the ADB, if the current growth rate slips

Asians know education can help alleviate poverty, and many work hard to learn new skills. For example, UNICEF recounted this story in the August/September 2003 issue of *Reading Today*:

"Ten years ago, Hira Akhtar and her husband, Moslem Uddin, lived in a simple hut in the village of Baniyar Kandar in Bangladesh. It was all they could afford on her husband's income of a thousand taka (seventeen U.S. dollars) a month from his work as a sharecropper.

"Today they live in a spacious, red-brick bungalow, complete with a brand-new corrugated iron roof and a broad veranda. Inside, the sleeping mat has been replaced by a wooden-framed double bed, and they even own a television.

"The difference: Hira now earns four thousand taka a month from a sewing business she developed using skills she learned in literacy classes given by Dhaka Ahsania Mission (DAM), a nongovernmental organization and the winner of the 2003 International Reading Association Literacy Prize (sponsored by UNESCO)."

by even one percentage point, the number of Asians living in extreme poverty could drop to only 429 million.

Furthermore, while the poverty rate is dropping, the ADB also warns that the gap between the rich and poor is widening. As that gap widens, the poor benefit less and less from any economic growth.

Recent natural disasters—notably, the Indian Ocean tsunami of 2004 and the Pakistan earthquake of 2005—hurt people already living in desperate poverty. The recovery from these tragedies has strained resources and will set back the area's financial development for years to come.

Declining Population

While many Americans think all Asia is as populous as the teeming cities of India and China, they're wrong. In fact, at least since late 2004 Chinese factories have faced a labor shortage.

Although many believe Asia is the epicenter of the "Population Bomb," some analysts assert that Asia's population growth in the twentieth century was really a "health explosion." In other words, mortality rates declined as life expectancy improved. The fact remains, however, that Asia's population growth is slowing.

China and India are the world's most populous nations, but the fertility rates of these and other Asian countries have been dropping in recent decades. For a population to grow by reproduction, its replacement level must be more than two to one—that is, on average each woman must bear at least two children.

India's fertility level is likely still above replacement level, but it has dropped by nearly half since the 1950s. Some Indian states and major urban areas are below replacement level. Vietnam's fertility level may be just at replacement level, but Bangladesh's reproduction growth has slowed. The fertility levels of China, Hong Kong, Japan, Macao, South Korea, Singapore, Taiwan, and Thailand are currently below replacement level.

As Asia's population ages, the implications of this decline will be far reaching, affecting health care systems, pension systems, family structure, labor force, migration (importing labor), and myriad other policy issues.

Disease

HIV/AIDS
Increased HIV rates will worsen life expectancy and put terrible pressures on national economies.

At the end of 2005, over eight million Asians were HIV positive—two-thirds of them in India alone. Although rates of infected people have declined in Cambodia and Thailand as well as in four Indian states, rates have increased in China, Indonesia, and Vietnam. Outbreaks may occur in Bangladesh and Pakistan.

Some estimates for future cases are grim. One study projects that by 2010, between ten and fifteen million Chinese and between twenty and twenty-five million Indians will be HIV positive.

SARS

The 2002–2003 SARS (severe acute respiratory syndrome) epidemic caused significant economic damage in Asia. The epidemic began in China and spread by international travel to twenty-nine countries. In a nine-month period, more than eight thousand people world wide were infected, and nearly one out of ten of them died.

Although there hasn't been an outbreak since 2003, the SARS epidemic proved how vulnerable economies become once a contagious disease spreads.

Avian Influenza (Bird Flu)

Between 2003 and 2006, all but fifteen of the more than two hundred cases of avian influenza were in Asia. Of all the cases, 58 percent were fatal—a shocking statistic.

Avian influenza has already damaged the Asian economy. Tens of millions of chickens and ducks in Asia were killed in order to prevent the spread of the disease. Furthermore, the World Bank's predictions of the effect of a world-wide pandemic on the global economy are dire.

Environment

Economic success in Asia hasn't come without a price. Asian nations must now face environmental problems like water and air pollution, deforestation, soil erosion, loss of land and marine habitats, acid rain, and oil spills.

Environmental degradation can be life threatening. For example, deforestation likely caused—or at least worsened—landslides in Indonesia and the Philippines that led to hundreds of deaths. India's poor air quality has caused thousands of premature deaths.

In some areas, growing populations have led to more sewage, more vehicle emissions, and more habitats cleared for agriculture. In some developing countries, industrialization has required more energy use, and these nations can't always afford to invest in clean technologies.

Asians know that pollution crosses national borders. For instance, Japan must deal with acid rain made from pollution generated in South Korea, as well as oil spills from tankers traversing the Sea of Japan.

Asian countries are starting to work with one another and with global agencies to solve environmental problems, but progress has been slow.

Traffic

The traffic problem seems out of control in many Asian cities, which are densely popu- lated and were built long before the invention of motor- ized vehicles. Cities from Beijing to Bangkok are strug- gling with clogged streets, air pollution, and scarce parking.

> In 2003, the demand for vehicles in China increased 75 percent. Despite newly tight- ened rules for credit on vehicle purchases, experts predict vehicle sales to increase between 10 and 20 percent annually for several years. The inevitable result will be increased gridlock and traffic fatalities.

(Parking is not only nearly impossible to find, but also extraordinarily expen- sive.) Avoid driving entirely, if possible. High speeds and (in some countries) sweeping disregard for road rules make driving hazardous. Use trains and mass transit systems, which are generally very good.

Discrimination and Prejudice

Religious

Violent religious extremists are causing serious problems for many Asian nations. The Philippines, Indonesia, Thailand, and India are currently con- tending with radical Islamic groups that are terrorizing those lands.

India is also trying to contain the continued violence between Muslims and Hindus. Meanwhile, Pakistan is struggling between adhering to tradi- tional Islamic law (*Shari'a*) and yielding to pressures to modernize—a conflict that has led to violence.

Not all religious conflicts are violent, but overt discrimination does pre- vail in Asian countries. For instance, in China the state persecutes people who worship in churches it doesn't sanction and control. Following one tenet of the Hindu faith, many Indians tolerate caste-based discrimination. The largely Catholic Filipino culture often marginalizes Muslims.

Ethnic

Many Asian nations must deal with conflicts among ethnic groups—a daunt- ing problem for countries that may each have dozens of different ethnic groups. For example, China has over fifty official ethnic groups, each with its own culture, identity, and (in some cases) language.

Many nations face scrutiny for their poor treatment of ethnic minorities, but in some cases, the powerful minorities may control majorities. In Indonesia, for example, ethnic Chinese are a very small minority but hold a disproportionate amount of the country's wealth. Taiwan's official language is Mandarin (a Chinese language), but the majority of people speak Taiwanese, which was banned in schools for many decades.

Caste-Based

Although the caste system is weakening, caste discrimination is an ongoing problem in several Asian nations. Laws exist to protect Dalits (Untouchables) in India, but the government doesn't always enforce the laws.

Also, few people outside Japan know of its caste system; the Buraku (a minority of up to three million people) endure discrimination in education, employment, and marriage.

Sex-Based

Across Asia, the traditional preference for sons won't be easily overcome. Selective abortions of female fetuses, female infanticide, inadequate nutrition and health care for girls, and neglect of girls' education are common practices in many Asian nations.

Violence against women is also a problem in Asia. From groping on Japanese commuter trains to honor killings (when a man kills a female relative for bringing perceived shame upon the family) in Pakistan, social acceptance of abuse challenges many Asian women's quality of life.

In some Asian nations, women face discrimination in inheritance laws: a daughter inherits only a half share, while a son inherits a full share. Only in 2005 did India guarantee a daughter's right to a full share of an inheritance.

Discrimination in the workforce is widespread, from South Korea to Indonesia. Many Asian nations also face low numbers of female judges and elected officials.

Asian nations, especially developing countries, know they must address these problems in order to compete in the global market. They can't afford to waste the lives and potential of half their populations.

GENERAL RULES: WHAT TO KNOW AND HOW TO BEHAVE

Basic Facts and Statistics

In late 2005, the National Geographic Society began conducting a survey designed to test the geographic skills and knowledge of American young adults. The discouraging results were published in early 2006. Here are just a few examples:

- Of those surveyed, 75 percent couldn't find Indonesia on a map—despite the devastating tsunami in 2004 that made headlines for weeks. Only 25 percent knew that Indonesia's population is largely Muslim.
- Three-quarters believed English is the world's most commonly spoken native language. (It's Mandarin, a Chinese language.)
- Seven out of ten couldn't find North Korea on a map, and more than two-thirds didn't know that the border between North and South Korea is the most heavily fortified in the world.

Other countries often complain about Americans' ignorance. Americans seem to know nothing about the people and places beyond U.S. borders. What's worse, they don't demonstrate much interest in learning.

For international business success, you don't need extensive training or experience in foreign languages. You simply need to take the time necessary to develop a basic knowledge of your host country and its culture. Without this knowledge, you'll appear not only ignorant, but also arrogant.

Here are the basic facts you should know when visiting a country:

- Its official name
- The collective name of its people
- The language(s) spoken
- Its president or prime minister's name
- Its political system
- Its currency

- Main events of the past century, including border disputes and recent allies and enemies (The more details you know, the better your conversation will be.)
- Current issues and events

Meeting and Greeting

First impressions are powerful! Good first impressions create the expectation of positive relationships. Bad first impressions require a lot of work and time to overcome—if such an opportunity even arises. When you've traveled thousands of miles and spent a lot of money in hope of developing a new business relationship, you need to make the best possible first impression.

Your chances of making a good first impression improve enormously if you know what to expect when meeting a person or group. Doing your homework lets you relax and project a positive attitude. In addition, exercising restraint, common sense, and good taste will help ensure that a relationship gets off to a good start.

First impressions are especially important to Asians. When two Asians meet for the first time, each immediately appraises the other's language, deference, formality, posture, manners, degree of bow or *wai*, eye contact, education, age, company, and position. (Many Asian languages contain honorific pronouns that reflect the level of these qualities.) In general, an Asian won't speak to a stranger without first knowing this information about him or her. A relationship can develop only after each knows and approves the other's status.

This greeting ritual may make it difficult for Westerners to make positive first impressions in Asia. They're unaware of or insensitive to the fact that backslapping (or any touching) and sloppy posture, dress, or speech—as well as flagrant displays of individuality, loudness, arrogance, or aggressiveness— offend or embarrass Asians.

You may be uncomfortable with formal behavior. Or you may regard greeting rituals as a waste of time and unnecessary to accomplish your business objectives. If these are your thoughts, you'd better stay home. You won't seal any deals with that attitude.

Your host may appear in a three-piece pinstripe suit, shake hands, smile, and say, "How do you do?" If he does, consider yourself lucky.

If, however, he appears wearing native attire and observing local meeting customs, your chances of making a good first impression improve enormously if you're prepared to bow (or *wai*, *namaste*, or salaam), appropriately exchange business cards, make (or not make) eye contact, and speak a phrase or two in the local language. Preparation will let you respond graciously and comfortably, regardless of the greeting offered.

Restraint, common sense, and good taste will also serve you well. The "how y'all doing?" greeting combined with a knuckle-crushing, arm-pumping handshake isn't common in Asia. Polite reserve combined with an open, friendly attitude is much more likely to get a relationship off to a good start.

General Rules

- Be yourself, but be prepared to observe local greeting customs. Bow, *wai*, *namaste*, or salaam as appropriate. Asians don't expect these greetings from foreigners, but they'll appreciate them.
- If possible, have a respected, well-connected third party introduce you.
- Don't stand too closely to anyone.
- Don't try to maintain eye contact.
- Stand or sit up straight.
- Don't touch or backslap anyone.

Handshakes

Most Asians greet Westerners with a handshake, and Japanese and Korean businesspeople may also bow slightly. Don't attempt a full-fledged bow with all its nuances unless you've learned how to bow properly in that culture (a skill mastered only with extensive experience). Lacking this knowledge, shake hands and bow slightly instead. Here are tips for shaking hands:

- In many countries, be prepared to give and receive a lighter, less firm handshake than you would in the United States.
- In business, extend your hand to the most senior-ranking person first.
- If you're a man, wait for a woman to initiate a handshake. There may be cultural or religious taboos against women shaking hands with men outside the family. If a woman nods, smiles, or otherwise indicates a greeting without extending her hand, do the same and consider yourself greeted.
- If you're a woman, don't be offended if a man declines to shake your hand. Some cultures have taboos against physical contact between the sexes.
- Shake hands at business and social functions.
- Be sure to stand before shaking hands.
- Always remove gloves before shaking hands.
- Never shake hands with one hand in your pocket.

Traditional Greetings

Style	Location	Instructions
Bow	Korea and Japan; to a lesser extent, China and Taiwan	The depth of the bow depends upon the relationship between the people involved, the situation in which bows are exchanged, and the country in which you're bowing. The bow imbues an encounter with formality and can express gratitude, devotion, sympathy, loyalty, apology, congratulations, or a simple hello or goodbye. It's a highly regarded way to show respect.
Namaste (pronounced "nah-mah-STAY")	India	Hold hands at chest level with palms pressed together and fingers pointing up, then bow slightly.
Salaam (pronounced "seh-LAHM")	Bangladesh, Malaysia, and Pakistan	Raise right hand to the forehead with hand slightly cupped (as though giving a relaxed salute) and bow slightly.
Wai (pronounced "why")	Thailand	Keeping fingers together and pointed up, press palms together close to the chest, then bow slightly. The higher one places the hands, the more respect he or she shows. Subordinates might raise fingers to nose level; however, fingertips should never extend above eye level.

Names and Titles

To Asians, a person's name and title express a wealth of information about family history, education, profession, reputation, and personal achievement. Names and titles are sources of pride; foreign visitors must understand that the correct use of a person's name and title shows respect. Incorrect use is an insult.

In the United States, people shift from using last names (surnames) to first names (given names) almost immediately after meeting. Americans consider it warm and friendly to do so and think everyone believes the same—not true. Using first names makes many Asians uncomfortable.

Most Asians address one another by last name indefinitely. In general, Asians don't want to call you by your first name, and—except in Thailand and Indonesia, where last names are long and difficult to pronounce—they don't want you to call them by theirs.

Name use is slowly changing in Asia. Young people, international businesspeople, and people educated in Europe or the United States may begin using first names more quickly than more traditional Asians. Visitors, however, shouldn't use first names until their hosts and colleagues explicitly invite them to do so.

Using names and titles correctly is one of the most complicated tasks for an international traveler, even an experienced one. Last names, middle names, and first names appear in different orders, and different rules apply to their proper usage. Specifics about correct usage vary among countries; consult each country's chapter to learn the etiquette for name and title usage in that nation. Knowing the specifics is worthwhile: Proper use of someone's name and title can lead to a successful negotiation, while misuse may end a business relationship.

> A young American's middle-aged Chinese secretary always called him "boss." He was younger than thirty, and this address made him uncomfortable. He repeatedly asked the woman to call him "Bill." She always replied, "Bill is too hard to pronounce."
>
> She didn't really have a pronunciation problem—the explanation was just an indirect way for her to say she couldn't bring herself to call her boss by his first name.

General Rules

Think of the following rules as tools for establishing a cultural comfort zone. If you want to make your colleagues comfortable and amenable to doing business, respect their cultural comfort zone for using names and titles.

- Know each country's rules for name and title usage. Each Asian country has distinct rules.
- Always establish and use a person's correct name. When someone is introduced to you, listen carefully to the name's pronunciation. Try to avoid asking him or her to repeat the name (the request suggests you weren't paying attention), but do so if necessary. Asking someone to repeat a name is better than getting the name wrong.
- As soon as possible, write down the name phonetically so you remember the pronunciation later.

- Ask each person by what name he or she prefers to be addressed. Remember, many (perhaps most) Asian women keep their maiden names when married.
- Always use last names until you're invited to use first names, or until others repeatedly use your first name.
- Ask for a person's business card so you can see the correct spelling of the name and the correct title.
- When in doubt, use a title. Always use the title on someone's business card or the title used upon introduction.
- If someone has more than one title and you're uncertain which title to use, use the higher title. Err on the side of formality.
- When conversing or corresponding with someone in English, it's acceptable to use English professional titles (*Doctor*, *Professor*, and so on).
- Never give anyone a nickname or joke about his or her name.
- Many Asians who do international business take common Western first names for themselves as a way to simplify pronunciation. But never bestow a Western name on an Asian.
- Younger people may use first names more quickly than older people; nonetheless, wait for an invitation to use first names.
- Introduce yourself properly. Say your full name slowly and pronounce it clearly, then give your title, job description, and company name.
- If necessary, help the introducer or host with your name's pronunciation.

Face

The Asian concept of face combines the Western notions of honor, integrity, respect, and reputation. The more face one has, the better his or her reputation is, the more power and prestige he or she has, and the more respect and deference others show him or her.

Saving face means avoiding embarrassment, failure, and defeat. Losing face shames the person, the family, the company—even the country. To save face, a person acts consistently, avoids giving inherently contradictory ideas or statements, and strives to achieve group harmony.

Asians are extremely sensitive to criticism, especially public criticism. Because the culture focuses on the group, Asians go to great lengths to save face for themselves or others. For example, superiors often minimize, cover up, or ignore mistakes subordinates make. They never criticize subordinates in front of fellow workers. Doing so makes the subordinates lose face and essentially makes them ineffective members of the group. For their part, subordinates work hard to avoid making mistakes that could embarrass superiors. They know losing face may mean ostracism.

To further evade conflict and disharmony, Asians cover up disagreement with vague, ambiguous, or overly polite responses. For example, if you propose a plan to your Asian colleagues and they request further study or reply with "maybe," they mean "no." Their indecisiveness is an attempt to save face—yours.

Asians place more importance on face than Americans give the Western equivalents of the concept. Thus it's crucial to never do or say anything that may make an Asian lose face. If you do, you'll almost certainly end a relationship. Here are some tips:

- Follow the local protocol for bowing, apologizing, deferring, toasting, gift giving, and so on.
- Respect a person's rank or status.
- Use titles properly.
- Never reprimand or criticize anyone publicly.
- Never make statements that may embarrass or offend someone.
- Resolve problems and conflicts privately.
- Never ask questions that may cause loss of face if answered honestly. For example, don't ask, "Are you having trouble learning the new software?" Instead, say, "Here's where I've put the manual for the new software. The technical support number is written on the inside front cover."

An American acquaintance of mine once had dinner with new Malaysian friends. They served him a wonderful meal, and he praised it effusively—which surprised and pleased the Malays.

The American asked his hosts, "What would you say if you really liked a meal that I served you?" They replied, "'I think this is very good.'" When he asked what they'd say if they didn't like the meal, they smiled and said, "'I think this is very good.'"

Humility, fear of bad luck, and saving face explain the Malays' ambiguous "compliment."

Language

Speaking a host country's language is the best way to win friends for yourself, your company, and your country. Nothing better conveys the message "I care about you, your culture, and your country" than taking the time to learn the native language. The warm appreciation and welcome you'll receive are incomparable.

Realistically, however, most of us don't have the time to become fluent in other languages—and what languages would we learn if we did? For example, India alone has twenty-two official languages and several hundred more that don't have official status.

> Zhao Yuanren, a Chinese linguist, wrote the ninety-three-word "Story of Shi Eating the Lions" using only Chinese characters that are pronounced "shi." His goal was to show how difficult it is to transliterate Chinese characters into phonetic spellings and preserve the meaning. He succeeded!

Although more people in the world speak Mandarin as a first language than any other language, the Chinese government estimates that only half its citizens speak it. There may be as many as 1,500 Chinese dialects, including Cantonese, the most widely spoken dialect in Hong Kong.

In addition, some Asian languages are difficult for native English speakers to learn. Many Asian languages are tonal; that is, words with the same pronunciations have completely different meanings when spoken with a rising, falling, or level pitch.

Asians also use silence in conversation to respectfully contemplate what each person has said. Silence makes many Americans uncomfortable, and they tend to fill gaps in conversation. When they do speak, Asians use delicate nuances and talk softly with courtesy and respect.

Asians often communicate indirectly and vaguely, with many sentences left unfinished and thoughts unspoken. "Yes"

> Transliterating Chinese or Japanese ideograms (characters) and Arabic or Sanskrit words into English is a purely phonetic task that can lead to multiple spellings. Here are just a few examples:
> - *hadj, hajj, haj* = a Muslim's pilgrimage to Mecca
> - *Lao Tzu, Lao-tsu, Lao-tse* = a Chinese philosopher
> - *Mao Zedong, Mao Tse-tung* = a Chinese political leader

often means "I'm listening" or "I understand," rather than "I agree." Conversely, "let's wait and see" or "I'll try, but it could be difficult" usually means "no."

A task-oriented, time-conscious, frank, and aggressive Westerner may find communicating with Asians frustrating and difficult. The face-conscious Asian, however, won't likely do business with someone he or she considers blunt, crude, or confrontational.

So what's the best approach? Learn a few simple, polite phrases—enough to show you're trying. Learn how to greet and thank your hosts. Learn a short toast; you don't have to say it perfectly, and your hosts will greatly appreciate your effort. Remember: mistakes made from trying are good mistakes. When you speak at least a few words in your host country's language, you express a positive attitude toward the country and its people.

English as a Second Language

Due partly to Britain's colonial influence and partly to American postwar success, English is a common second language spoken in Asia. Many to most businesspeople speak English; however, English is likely their second or third language. If your hosts speak English with you, they're probably doing so as a courtesy. Don't assume English is your host's native language, and don't take the arrogant "everyone should speak English" attitude. Instead, to avoid misunderstandings, do the following:

- Speak slowly and clearly.
- Use the simplest words possible (without being condescending).
- Never assume the listener understands your meaning; if there's any doubt, repeat what you said in different ways until you're sure the listener understands you.
- Never use slang terms, idioms, sports analogies, or colloquialisms, such as:
    * "I was tickled to death."
    * "We've got you covered."
    * "You can count on it."
    * "I got a kick out of it."
    * "We're batting a thousand."
- Always be patient and leave room for error.
- Never correct an Asian's English pronunciation. Doing so will cause embarrassment and loss of face, jeopardizing a promising relationship.
- Nod to convey "I understand," not "I agree."
- Assume the best; never jump to conclusions.

Pronunciation

A friend told me that when he visits his native country after a long absence, his family sometimes has trouble understanding him when he speaks the native language. He, in turn, has difficulty understanding regional dialects from other parts of the same country.

If it's hard for my friend to properly pronounce the language he learned as a child, what hope is there for those trying to speak a few polite phrases learned as adults? The good news is that most people will be pleased with your attempts to speak the local language. Saying *hello, please,* and *thank you* in the host language will make you friends, even if you butcher the pronunciations.

For each country I discuss in Part II, I provide a list of basic phrases in the primary language of that country. Please understand, however, that pronunciations are approximate. Only by listening to fluent speakers can one know a language's true pronunciation.

Also, just as in the United States, regional dialects can greatly change a word's pronunciation. Imagine a person from Massachusetts creating a pronunciation guide of English phrases; it'd differ considerably from the same guide made by a Texan.

Speaking Volume

In Asia, the higher a person's status, the softer he or she speaks. Asians also lower their voices to emphasize a point or when conversations become intense. They consider raised voices and loudness crass behavior.

Americans, in particular, seem to raise their voices when they aren't being understood or getting their way. A persistent worldwide criticism of Americans is that they're too loud and boisterous. Such behavior could make an Asian withdraw from a discussion in an effort to evade confrontation.

To avoid offending Asians, use a moderate tone and volume when speaking with them.

Using Interpreters

You've hired an interpreter and you think your communication problems are solved. Watch out! Your problems may just be starting. Clearly communicating ideas in business negotiations is difficult, even when parties speak a common tongue. When using more than one language to conduct business, misunderstandings are inevitable, which means an effective interpreter is crucial for clear communication. Here are some tips for using an interpreter:

- Ask your interpreter to advise you on meeting protocol—punctuality, preliminary small talk, when to begin discussing major issues, identification of participants, and so on.
- Before a meeting, discuss with your interpreter the meeting's objective and the main points you plan to make.
- Never place the interpreter between you and your colleagues. Address your remarks to your colleagues, not the interpreter.
- Apologize to your counterparts for your inability to converse in their language.
- Take your time; speak slowly and clearly.
- Keep language simple and direct.
- Pause frequently to allow for interpretation—after every verbal "paragraph" or, when the matter is especially important or complicated, after every sentence.
- As your discussion proceeds, ask your colleagues questions and get their feedback.
- Repeat main points.
- Assume your colleagues can understand English, even if they're using an interpreter; never say anything you don't want others to hear.
- Follow up with a written summary of what was said and agreed upon.

Conversation

There's no better way to get to know people than to engage in warm, friendly conversation. In Asia conversation is an art, and Asians pride themselves on their conversation skills. Most are well informed about American current events and enjoy asking questions about the United States.

With that said, Asians often won't engage in lively conversation soon after meeting new people. Unlike Westerners, who are often eager to forge friendships and make business deals quickly, Asians remain formal and impersonal until they've established trust.

Once they extend their friendship, however, Asians will talk about nearly anything: their businesses, families, private lives, even intimate thoughts and feelings. When an Asian offers this level of confidence, the recipient must take the friendship seriously. Casualness and insensitivity could destroy a budding relationship.

To help your conversation skills, brush up on history, art, literature, and culture so you can contribute intelligently when conversing with your Asian colleagues. And the best tip is to ask questions. People everywhere are proud of their countries and love to talk about them. (*Note:* Some cultures prefer quiet or little conversation at the dinner table. Take your cues from your hosts and the other guests.)

The following sections are general guides for acceptable conversation topics, unacceptable topics, and topics that require sensitivity.

Acceptable Topics

- History of the host country: Ask respectful questions and make only complimentary remarks.
- Art and architecture
- Music
- Beauty of the host country
- Food and drink—local, regional, and global
- Cars
- Local attractions, places of historical interest, restaurants, and so on

Unacceptable Topics

- Business talk at social events (unless your Asian colleagues initiate it)
- Comparisons of anything in Asia to its American counterpart
- Personal questions. That is, don't ask about a person's:
  * Occupation
  * Income
  * Marital status
  * Education level
  * Place of residence
  * Health (This topic, however, is acceptable in some Asian nations.)
- Money (yours or your colleagues')
- Human rights
- Jokes: Jokes don't translate well, even if your colleagues speak English. Each culture has its own

A friend of mine once worked as a cashier in her college cafeteria. One of her professors, a Korean, ate his lunch in the cafeteria every day. They'd chat pleasantly for a few moments as he paid her for his meal.

One day, as he handed her the money, my friend teased, "If I let you go through without paying, will you give me an A on the test tomorrow?" To her surprise, he didn't laugh. Instead, he flushed and stammered, "No, no, that wouldn't be fair to the other students."

It took her several minutes to convince him that she was joking. Although the professor spoke perfect English and had been in the United States for a long time, the joke didn't translate for him.

sense of humor. Also, jokes often depend on double meanings of words or phrases that don't exist in another language.

Topics That Require Sensitivity

Each culture has its sensitive topics, those that can make emotions run high. For example, many Asians harbor strong feelings about World War II and its aftermath. There hasn't been a war on American soil for more than a century, and never a war of such destruction as WWII. Americans may not fully understand why the topic is so sensitive, and want to learn more about it.

When conversing with your hosts, the following topics may arise. If they do, ask sensitive, general questions, but don't offer your opinion unless you're extremely well informed. Your hosts may eagerly discuss these issues with you, but note their tone and body language. If they seem upset or uncomfortable discussing a topic, drop it and change the subject.

- World War II
- Communism
- Imperialism
- Terrorism
- Politics
- Religion
- Feminism
- Ethnic tensions
- Class systems
- Relations and tensions among Asian nations

The American view of events may differ markedly from the Asian perspective. A fairly recent example was the North Atlantic Treaty Organisation (NATO) bombing of the Chinese embassy in Belgrade in May 1999.

Tens of thousands of angry Chinese demonstrated at the time, and the Chinese still don't believe NATO Secretary-General Javier Solana's assertion that the bombing in the former Yugoslavian city was an accident.

If you were to argue for NATO's position with a Chinese colleague, you likely wouldn't win the argument—so don't try.

In April 2006, when Chinese President Hu Jintao was visiting the White House, a protester shouted at him from the crowd, and it took several minutes to restrain her. President Bush apologized, and Chinese television blacked out the incident.

Nonetheless, President Hu lost face, and the Chinese viewed the incident as an attempt to humiliate them.

Written Communication

Many Asians read and write English better than they speak it. They may prefer to communicate by e-mail, which is less formal and has looser rules about punctuation and sentence structure than formal letter writing.

- Never base your opinions of your colleagues' intelligence on their English-language skills. Remember that English may be their second or third language.
- Correspond in English, unless you can have your correspondence translated perfectly into the local language.
- With that said, try using your colleagues' language in salutations and closings. Use a personal closing.
- Always have business documents translated into the local language.
- Don't use common acronyms (like FYI or ASAP) or abbreviations (nite/night, 4/for, or U/you), especially in e-mails. North Americans regularly use these informal shortcuts in electronic communication, but Asians may not understand them.
- Never use red ink. In several Asian nations, red ink is used only to write the names of the dead (for a funeral, for example). Writing a living person's name in red is tantamount to hexing him or her.
- If a message upsets you, calm yourself completely before responding—or telephone the sender for clarification. Verbal communication can help prevent "nasty-gram" correspondence.
- If in doubt, use a formal writing style rather than an informal one.
- Know an organization's hierarchy and who should receive copies of your letters and e-mail messages. Ask if you don't know. Don't use preset copy lists; send copies of correspondence only to people who should receive them.

Thank-You Notes

Promptly write a thank-you note to anyone who hosted you for dinner, who entertained you, or who gave you a gift. Include a personal note about the gift or event.

When you next write to or see someone who's given you a gift, mention or wear/display the gift. For example, wear the scarf a colleague gave you when next meeting with him or her, or display the crystal bowl prominently in your home when the giver visits.

Although you should send a formal thank-you note whenever you receive a gift, be aware that many Asians don't routinely send thank-you notes. If your recipient doesn't acknowledge your gift, assume he or she appreciates it and continue giving gifts when appropriate. If you stop giving gifts, you risk ending a relationship.

General Rules of Correspondence

Salutation
- Dear (Sir/Madam)
- Dear (title) + last name

Closing
- Yours truly
- Sincerely
- Yours sincerely
- Very truly

Envelope address

First line:	Recipient's name
Second line:	Building and block address
Third line:	District and postal service
Fourth line:	City
Fifth line:	Country (spelled out in full in block capital letters)

Example	Yo Mijoshi
	3-8 Kanda Wishikicho
	Minato-ku 106
	Tokyo
	JAPAN

Dates
In Asia, the day generally precedes the month.

United States	Asia
April 5, 2008	5 April 2008
4/5/08	5/4/08 or 5.04.08

In some countries, the format may be year, month, day.

United States	Asia
April 5, 2008	2008-04-05

Always verify dates. You don't want to arrive on April 5, 2008, for a meeting that doesn't take place until May 4, 2008, because you misunderstood 4/5/08.

Time

Asians generally use the twenty-four-hour clock. 2:00 PM, for example, is 14:00; 6:30 PM is 18:30; and 10:00 PM is 22:00. To get afternoon and evening times using this system, just add twelve hours to the time on your watch. Or to convert afternoon and evening times expressed in the Asian system to the American system, subtract twelve hours. Both systems express morning times the same.

Metric Conversion Chart

When you know	Multiply by	To find
inches	25	millimeters
feet	30	centimeters
yards	0.9	meters
miles	1.6	kilometers
centimeters	0.393	inches
meters	1.1	yards
kilometers	0.6	miles
ounces	28	grams
pounds	0.45	kilograms
grams	0.035	ounces
kilograms	2.2	pounds
fluid ounces	30	milliliters
pints, U.S.	0.47	liters
quarts, U.S.	0.95	liters
gallons, U.S.	3.8	liters
liters	2.1	pints, U.S.
liters	1.06	quarts, U.S.
liters	0.26	gallons, U.S.

Floors

In some Asian countries, the "first floor" is generally a building's second level. The ground level is labeled "0" or "ground floor." The second level is labeled "1," the third level is labeled "2," and so on. For superstitious reasons, some Asian buildings label fourth floors or thirteenth floors with other numbers (see page 88).

Body Language

Eye contact; posture; placement of hands, feet, arms, legs—these body movements send positive or negative messages to other people. We misread these signals constantly within our own culture. Imagine the mixed signals we send and receive when dealing with another culture.

Asians use body language prominently, and they tend to manipulate their facial expressions for effect. As a result, Americans often misunderstand Asians' nonverbal signals.

Behavioral scientists say people make seven hundred thousand signals through body language. What one person views as proper behavior, another may consider an affront. "Surely," you might say, "there must be some common ground. How about a smile? It's the universally understood gesture, right?" Not quite. Even a smile can be misunderstood.

It's true that smiling warms any environment, so smile if the occasion calls for one. But be aware that your smile may not be returned. In some cultures, people don't smile at strangers.

Also, a smile has different meanings in different cultures. In Asia, a smile or laugh can mean fear, humiliation, anger, or an apology. For example, when Americans want to make a serious point, their faces normally become stern. Asians, however, may smile or laugh in order to reduce the tension or soften bad news. It wouldn't be unusual for an Asian to tell you with a smile that his father just died of lung cancer. Although it's likely off-putting to see such an expression accompanying grave news, always be sensitive to the context and respond appropriately.

General Rules

- Be reserved in everything—speech, comportment, and attire. Save your friendly, exuberant personality for later meetings, when you're more acquainted with your colleagues.
- Never stare at anyone.
- Proper posture is a must. To Asians, sloppy posture indicates a disrespectful person. Sit with your back straight and your legs crossed at the knee or knees together. Don't sit with legs spread.
- Never mimic anyone's body language.
- Never mimic what you think is a national gesture.
- Never slap people on the back.
- Don't display affection in public.
- Keep your hands out of your pockets when speaking to or greeting someone.
- Never use toothpicks, nail clippers, or combs in public.

- Cover your mouth when you yawn.
- Don't chew gum in public.
- Don't point or beckon with your index finger.
- Don't scratch in public.
- Stand tall when a country's national anthem is playing. Never talk, laugh, or shuffle your feet.

Common Gesture, Uncommon Meanings

Many gestures have different meanings in different countries. A gesture that may be appropriate in one country may be rude or have a completely different meaning in another. Such gestures include the "okay" sign, the thumbs-up gesture, the hand wave, and even the seemingly innocuous nod. For example, in Asia nodding may mean "I understand" or "I hear you" rather than "I agree."

Because gestures can be so easily misunderstood, the best approach is to avoid them entirely. Alternatively, learn in advance the local meanings of any gestures you consider essential to your business.

Touching

For the most part, Asians aren't "touchers." Spouses don't show affection in public. Even children, upon returning from long absences, stand three feet away from their parents and bow.

- Most Asians are uncomfortable with being hugged or slapped on the back.
- Asian men don't touch foreign women. Don't touch an Asian of the opposite sex unless you've established a close friendship.
- Asians revere the head as the seat of the soul. Never touch an Asian's head, especially a child's.
- During drinking sessions, persons of the same sex may pat one another on the back, drape an arm around another's shoulder, or make other friendly gestures.

Eye contact

When meeting, greeting, and conversing, people in the United States generally look into one another's eyes. Americans believe a person who doesn't make eye contact is untrustworthy. Asians don't share this belief. Many Asians learn from an early age that continued, direct eye contact is rude and threatening. In fact, Japanese parents scold their children with a long, hard stare.

When conversing with Asians, don't think they aren't listening or paying attention if they don't look you in the eye. On the contrary, lack of eye contact (as well as silence) usually means they're listening intently and are quite interested in what you have to say.

Feet

Asians believe feet are unclean because they're the lowest parts of the body.

- Never point or gesture your feet at anyone or anything.
- Don't tap your feet on the floor.
- Don't swing a crossed leg; it's too easy to accidentally point your sole at someone.
- Keep feet on the floor; never prop them on furniture.
- Don't talk about feet, including foot ailments (fallen arches, corns, bunions, and so on).
- Don't touch or move things with your feet, especially someone else's belongings.

Hands and Arms

Asians consider talking with arms and hands unrefined behavior. When conversing, don't put your hands in your pockets, don't rest your hands on your hips, and don't fold your arms across your chest. Instead, rest your hands in your lap.

Use both hands to give and receive all objects, especially business cards. Passing objects with one hand is disrespectful. In some Asian countries, it's customary to use the right hand to pass objects

A young American woman recently told me about her first business trip to Japan: "I made a presentation to a group of Japanese men and was offended at what I considered their rudeness. As I spoke, they refused to look into my eyes. They never made eye contact with me. Every time I tried to engage someone with my eyes, he'd look away. I didn't understand then that these gentlemen were showing the highest respect for me by averting their eyes. They honored me as a teacher as well as a person of authority, and they were humbling themselves in my presence."

An American flight attendant once told me of a cultural mistake that nearly turned into an international incident.

After the plane departed en route to Korea, she proceeded to fetch the drink cart. A piece of luggage was partially blocking the aisle, and she used her foot to gently push it farther under the seat. Her wholly innocent action, however, enraged the Korean gentleman whose bag she'd moved.

To him, it was as if she'd spat on his bag. It took some time to calm him down, largely because the flight attendant didn't understand why her moving his bag with her foot had upset him so.

while grasping the right forearm with the left hand. Some Asians, however, give and receive objects with the right hand only. They consider the left hand unclean because it's used for personal cleansing.

Dining

How you eat and respond to food are essential for diplomacy. Your table manners can quickly make or lose foreign friends. When your hosts offer a local delicacy or a national specialty, they're extending a sample of their culture as well as their friendship. If you reject the offering, which is often the best they have, you reject them, their culture, and their friendship—not an effective way to begin a mutually beneficial relationship.

When dining in Asia, be prepared for surprises. You may be offered dog or snake meat, sea slugs, chicken blood, raw fish, monkey brains, or a thousand-day-old egg. Regardless of whether the food on your plate once swam, crawled, or flew, taste it. You may like it. Even if you don't, eat a reasonable portion anyway. I've eaten dozens of exotic dishes all around the world—a number of which I wouldn't choose to serve in my own home. And I survived. You'll survive, too.

So try what you're served; tasting those monkey brains or those sea slugs just might seal the big deal and lead to a fruitful friendship.

> Before you book a table at a restaurant, check whether it accepts credit cards. Some don't accept any credit cards; others may accept ones from only one or two companies. This practice is true not only in small towns and villages, but also in larger cities.
>
> Also, call your credit card company before traveling to Asia to alert them that you'll be charging in foreign cities. Otherwise, your card may be refused. Credit card theft is a growing problem in Asia.

General Rules

- If you have special dietary restrictions, tell your host ahead of time.
- Don't appear overly concerned about the cleanliness of dishes, utensils, or the kitchen—even if you are.
- Never complain or joke about the food served.
- Be aware of the number of courses served and pace your eating. Many of us have thought an appetizer was the main course. By the time the main course arrived, we were too full to eat it.

- At restaurants, the person who extended the invitation pays the bill. There's no "Dutch treat" in Asia.
- In some restaurants and homes, men and women may dine in separate rooms.
- Forget your mom's admonition to "clean your plate." Always leave at least a small amount of food on your plate when you've finished each dish or course. If you clean your plate, your host will refill it.
- After a meal at someone's home or after someone has bought you a meal, always send a thank-you note promptly.
- Don't ask to have your leftovers boxed to take with you.
- Don't eat while walking on streets.

Remember *The Five Chinese Brothers* by Claire Huchet Bishop? In the story, one of the brothers could hold the entire sea in his mouth. During our first visit to China, I thought my husband would become the sixth Chinese brother—the one who could hold all the rice in China in his mouth.

During a twelve-course dinner, my husband told our Chinese hosts that fried rice—the eighth course—was his favorite dish, and he polished off his serving. Our polite hosts kept refilling his plate, and he politely cleaned it each time.

I don't remember who quit first—my husband because he was full or the hosts because there was no more rice to serve. But now I know why my husband always gains five pounds on his trips to Asia!

Table Manners

- Before sitting at the table, wait for your host to designate your seat and invite you to sit.
- Hosts serve the guest(s) of honor first.
- Try every dish served to you. You needn't eat a lot, but a taste is polite.
- Eat slowly; you'll insult your host if you finish a course first. Having an empty plate in front of you implies the host gave you a stingy portion.
- You may slurp soup and smack your lips when eating noodles. Your hosts will consider the noises a compliment.
- Never take the last portion of food from a serving platter.
- Don't refill your own glass. Refill your neighbors' glasses; they'll refill yours.
- Cover your mouth with your hand when using a toothpick.
- Don't smoke at the table unless your hosts do so, which is likely. They'll offer you a cigarette when they light up. Offer a cigarette to everyone present each time you light up.

- Don't get up from the table until the hostess does.
- With that said, leave the table to blow your nose.
- Thank the hostess before leaving the table.

Banquets

Banquets are a way to honor guests, especially the guest of honor. They also provide a way to network and make personal connections (the goals of business entertaining everywhere), as well as to bring people together to enjoy good food and good company.

Banquets focus on social status and etiquette. They show that hosts can entertain lavishly. The more elegant and abundant the food, the more resources guests assume the host has. Furthermore, attending a banquet incurs a degree of obligation: If you're the guest of honor at a banquet, you're in the host's social debt.

While an ordinary business dinner may have three to four courses or a large variety of dishes, a formal banquet may have more than a dozen courses. The higher the guest of honor's rank is, the more courses the banquet is likely to have.

Banquets begin at 6:30 or 7:00 PM and last between two and two-and-a-half hours. Tables are generally large and round with a turntable in the center for serving.

Banquet Etiquette

- When hosting a banquet, invite your guests first by phone. Send formal written invitations after you've set the date.
- Choose a restaurant that's acceptable to and convenient for your guests. Check with the hotel concierge or a knowledgeable colleague for restaurant recommendations.
- If you're reciprocating a banquet, keep the number and lavishness of the courses similar to those of your hosts' banquet. Don't try to outdo your hosts, but don't skimp, either.
- Always be on time or a little early for a banquet.
- Hosts always greet their guests upon arrival.
- The guest of honor enters the dining room first. If you're the host, insist that your guests enter first.
- Guests wait for the host to tell them where to sit.
- Seating assignments vary among countries. If you're hosting a banquet, ask a knowledgeable colleague to help you arrange the seating assignments.
- To start the meal, the host places food on the guests' plates.

- Never refuse any food. Pace yourself; slowly eat small amounts of each course served. Always leave some food on your plate as you finish each course; otherwise, your hosts will refill your plate. If you enjoy the early courses too much, eating the later ones will be trying.
- The host invariably makes the first toast shortly after the banquet begins. Don't drink until after he or she has made the toast.
- Hosts expect the guest of honor to make a short toast immediately after the initial toast, or after one or two courses have been served. (See page 43.)
- You may offer toasts to the entire table or just to those sitting near you.
- Guests may toast with water, juice, or soft drinks if they don't drink alcohol.
- Hosts and guests may applaud you after an introduction or toast. If they do, join in the applause to express your thanks.
- Asians serve beer and tea with the meal, and they serve tea again after the meal. They may serve mao-tai or other local liquor sometime during the meal.
- While many Asians accept intoxication, they frown upon it at formal dinners. Take care not to become obviously drunk.
- Hosts expect the guest of honor and his or her party to leave a banquet first.

Eating Styles

Although people in China, Hong Kong, Japan, Korea, and Taiwan generally use chopsticks to eat, keep in mind that not all Asians do. People in Indonesia, the Philippines, and Thailand use forks and spoons. Those in Singapore use either chopsticks or forks and spoons, and the Vietnamese use either chopsticks or spoons. In Malaysia, ethnic Chinese use chopsticks, while Malays use their right hands with or without forks and spoons. In Bangladesh and Pakistan, people use right hands and spoons, while Indians use just their right hands. Some westernized Pakistanis and Indians, however, may use utensils.

Eating with Your Hands

Specific customs for eating with your hands vary among regions even within the same country. When eating in this style, discreetly watch what others are doing and do the same. Never make fun of eating with your hands or hint that it isn't polite or cultured behavior. Here are other general guidelines to follow:
- Expect drips and spills; wear wash-and-wear clothing.
- Wash your hands before a meal. Many restaurants have sinks in the dining area for washing hands. Some have wait staff who bring a pitcher and bowl to tables. In this situation, place your hands over the bowl and let the server pour water over them. The server will then provide a cloth for drying. If

your hosts participate in a washing ceremony, join them. In some cultures, people rinse their mouths along with washing hands.

- Always use your right hand to place food in your mouth. You may use both hands to do some tasks, like tearing bread, but watch what others do before using both hands.

- Be especially careful not to use your left hand to pass or receive food; however, watch what others do. In some cases, people may use both hands to do some tasks, like holding the sides of a heavy bowl. Or they may hold the side of the bowl with the right hand and place the left hand underneath to support it.

- Don't take food from a serving dish and put it directly in your mouth. Put it on your plate or in your bowl first.

- Don't use your whole hand to eat; use your fingers only.

- Don't put your fingers in your mouth when eating. Use your thumb to push food into your mouth.

- Don't offer anyone food from your plate.

- Wash your hands after eating.

> Eating with hands isn't a "low-class" custom—it's a cultural practice. In fact, some Asians think that spearing food with sharp implements is barbaric!
>
> Affluent and refined Asians eat with their hands in even the most expensive restaurants. A friend of mine once told me about the first time he ate with the cosmopolitan mother of his Indian friend: "She was dripping in diamonds," he said, "and ate elegantly with her fingers."

Eating Banana Leaf Rice

In traditional Bangladeshi and Pakistani Muslim homes and restaurants, people may eat banana leaf rice: vegetable and meat curries served with rice and sauce on a large banana leaf. Many of these dishes are vegan.

To eat this dish, reach into the rice bowl with your right hand, take a small amount with your fingers, and roll it into a ball between your thumb and middle and index fingers. Never roll it in your palm. Dip the rice ball into the sauce on the banana leaf. Gently roll in a piece of chicken or a vegetable and put it all in your mouth.

To show you're finished eating, fold the banana leaf in half with the fold toward you.

Eating with Chopsticks

It's a good idea to practice eating with chopsticks before your trip. Mastering them takes a bit of time, but it's a skill you'll likely never forget. Even if you don't master this eating style, your hosts will appreciate your efforts and will overlook any clumsiness.

When visiting people who use chopsticks, don't ask for Western eating utensils until you've at least tried to use chopsticks.

- Pick up chopsticks with your right hand, then transfer them to your left hand. Then use the fingers of your right hand to grip the chopsticks properly.
- Hold the chopsticks between your fingers, never in your fist.
- When you're not using them, always place your chopsticks on the chopstick rest with the tips (the ends that go into your mouth) pointing to your left. Never place them across the top of the rice bowl.
- Don't plant your chopsticks in the rice. (That's how Buddhists offer rice to deceased ancestors.)
- Don't point or gesture with chopsticks.
- Never cross your chopsticks.
- Don't tap or drum on the table with your chopsticks.
- Never use a chopstick to spear food.
- Don't lick the tips of chopsticks.
- Don't push food around with chopsticks.
- Don't pick out the tastiest morsels with your chopsticks.
- Don't use the hand that holds chopsticks to pick up a dish when you're holding the utensils.
- Don't use the tips of chopsticks to take food from the serving dish; use the other ends.
- Don't put food taken from the serving dish directly into your mouth. Place it first on your plate.
- Lift your rice bowl (set at your left) to your mouth, then use your chopsticks to eat the rice. Never mix food in with your rice.
- Eat the solid morsels in your soup bowl (set at your right) first, before drinking the broth directly from the bowl. Most Asians eat noodles by bringing the bowl to their mouths and slurping them from the chopsticks. Replace the soup bowl lid when you've finished.
- Sauces are for dipping food, not for dunking, soaking, or pouring over rice.
- When finished eating, place your chopsticks neatly on the table or on the chopstick rest (tips pointing to the left).

- Many Asians consider it distasteful to touch food with one's hands, or to touch one's mouth with one's hands. Don't pick up dropped food with your hands and pop it into your mouth.

How to Eat Food You'd Rather Not

For the most part Asian food is marvelous to Americans, and most of us find limiting how much we eat abroad a major challenge. (My experience certainly can attest to both claims!) But many Asians eat animal organs, some eat horse meat, others pork tartare—these and other dishes might be difficult for Americans to digest. If you have a weak stomach or dislike the food served, here are some helpful hints:

- Before you leave for the meal, prepare yourself mentally for the unexpected and take a dose of Pepto-Bismol.
- Never ask what a dish is until you've finished eating it.
- Cut the food into small pieces.
- Don't chew particularly unpleasant food, just swallow fast. Sometimes the texture is worse than the taste.
- Taste everything, and try to eat at least a little of it. If you just can't eat something, taking a taste is considered polite behavior.
- Never criticize, joke, or make a face about what's served.
- To distract yourself from the food and to pass the time until the next course is served, converse with your dining partners.
- When offered seconds of something you don't like, say, "Thank you, but let me finish this portion first." Then eat slower and talk more.
- If you're truly worried a dish may make you ill, decline politely. A refusal is certainly preferable to gagging at the table.

Drinking

Across much of the continent, drinking is a national pastime and many Asians expect visitors to participate. They view drinking as a social event that provides the opportunity to converse on a more personal level.

In Japan and Korea, an evening of social drinking may end in intoxication. On such occasions, the Japanese and Koreans accept drunkenness as normal behavior. If your colleagues become drunk, never criticize or call attention to them, or show pity or disapproval, even if someone falls over in front of you.

Not all Asians approve of drinking alcohol or drunkenness. Devout Muslims don't drink it (or smoke tobacco, for that matter); neither do some devout Buddhist Thais. People in Malaysia, Indonesia, and the Philippines don't tolerate public drunkenness. Filipinos view drunkenness as crude, greedy, and self-indulgent behavior. If your Asian colleagues abstain from drinking alcohol, you should do likewise.

Also, Western women shouldn't drink alcohol (or smoke tobacco) in bars or other public places unless Asian women are doing so. It's a chauvinistic tradition, but ignoring it will garner a great deal of unwanted attention.

When in Asia, never flatly decline an offer for any beverage. Your refusal could make the person extending the offer lose face. Try—or pretend to drink—beverages offered to you. Asians are proud of their local beverages, like sake in Japan, *soju* in Korea, and mao-tai in China.

Here are some other tips to consider:

- If you can't drink alcohol, tell your host ahead of time. Perhaps say you have a stomach ailment or other medical problem, and ask for a soft drink or fruit juice instead. Alternatively, don't tell your host anything, accept the alcoholic beverage, and pretend to drink it.
- Be careful when drinking alcoholic beverages in Asia. In some, the alcohol content is higher than in comparable drinks in the United States.
- Never drink and drive. The drunk-driving laws in many Asian countries are strict and the punishments severe.
- If you're hosting Asian guests, make sure to have nonalcoholic drinks available for those who don't drink alcohol for health, cultural, or religious reasons.

Toasting

In most Asian countries, toasting is an important part of entertaining. Be prepared to make a toast to friendship, your hosts, their country, or other appropriate subjects.

Use toasts to establish a closer, more friendly relationship. You should enjoy toasting and being toasted. It's an offer of friendship. Here are some tips for toasting:

- Make your toast short.
- If possible, make a toast in your host's or guest's language. Even if it isn't perfect, your Asian colleagues will enjoy and appreciate it.
- Your colleagues will generally appreciate an accompanying story (short and in English), but don't tell jokes—they seldom cross cultural lines.
- In general, women don't make toasts.

Entertaining Foreign Guests

To Asians, dining in your city's best restaurants can't compare to eating a meal served in your home. Visitors always enjoy seeing how you live, how you decorate your home, what music and art you enjoy, and—especially—meeting your family. An invitation to your home is a gesture your guests won't soon forget. Some points to remember:

- Check whether your guests have any dietary restrictions.
- Avoid huge, American-size servings of meat. Most Asians (and others, too) eat much smaller portions of meat than Americans do.
- It's important to provide at least one vegetarian option when hosting an event. For religious reasons, some Asians are vegetarians. Asians who aren't vegetarians but abstain from eating pork or beef will appreciate a meatless dish.
- Don't offer guests a tour of bedrooms or other private areas of your home. They'll be more comfortable in "public" rooms like the living room, dining room, and den.
- Use the proper glasses for whiskey, wine, and beer. Never serve drinks in paper cups or serve food on paper plates with paper napkins.
- If taking Asian colleagues to a restaurant, keep in mind that many Asians prefer their own cuisine. Ask your guests beforehand whether they'd like to eat in a restaurant that doesn't serve Asian food.
- Always ask your guests if they'd like to experience a particular event while in your area. Here are some suggestions:
  * Picnic or barbecue
  * Baseball or American football game
  * Concert or theater performance
  * Museum visit
  * Shopping
  * Hiking
  * Sightseeing
  * Boating or sailing
  * Playing golf or tennis

Tipping

Americans are among the most generous people on earth. When Americans visit another country and generously tip service people, they're trying to be kind and appreciative, not abrasive or arrogant. But they often create the impression that they're boorishly flaunting their wealth—or worse, trying to take over the country.

Everybody has a sense of personal worth, even if he or she isn't wealthy. You can violate that sense of worth by giving a tip that's inappropriately large or small. Tip too little, and service people are likely to feel cheated out of fair compensation for their work. Tip too much, and they can feel as though you consider them charity cases. But if you tip fairly and appropriately, they'll appreciate it without feeling demeaned.

> Although Part II includes guidelines for tipping in each country, it's crucial to ask a knowledgeable colleague or your hotel concierge for the current tipping practice for any service. This simple step can save you considerable embarrassment.

In the past, tipping wasn't common in Asia. In fact, the Chinese considered all tips an insult; for years, it was illegal to even accept a tip. Instead, servers accepted a positive comment in the guest register or a small gift as thanks for excellent service.

Today, for cultural reasons many Asians give good service without expecting a tip. To them, giving poor service means losing face. Nonetheless, tipping is becoming more common, but appropriate tips are modest. They rarely amount to 15 to 20 percent of the bill, as they do in the West.

General Rules

Rules for tipping vary among countries and even among regions in countries. For example, workers in tourist areas may expect tips, while workers in the rest of the country may not. Inflation, fluctuating currency exchange rates, and rapidly changing local attitudes all affect appropriate tipping practices.

- Keep in mind that service people are often from another country and may not speak English or the local language.
- If someone has performed an exceptional service, you may put an appropriate amount of local currency in an envelope (a "red envelope" is often appropriate; see page 58), write the server's name on it, and quietly give

it to the server or leave it where he or she will receive it (your hotel room or the front desk, for example).

- Many hotels and restaurants in Asia include a 10 or 15 percent service charge. Servers and staff don't expect an additional tip; in fact, they may even reject it if offered.

    With that said, it's worth noting that service personnel in hotels and restaurants that cater primarily to Americans may expect larger tips.

Manners

As prehistoric people began to interact with one another, they learned to behave in ways that made life easier and more pleasant. As cultures developed, they created their own rules for social behavior.

Asian manners often differ dramatically from Western manners. For example, Asians traditionally greet one another without physical contact, while Westerners traditionally shake hands.

The following are some general guidelines on Asian manners. (See Part II for information on manners specific to each country.)

General Rules
- Show respect for others' habits and customs.
- Respect others' privacy and dignity at all times; when in doubt, put yourself in their place and act accordingly.
- Asians always appreciate quiet, modest behavior.
- Always say "please" and "thank you"—in the local language, if possible.
- Turn off your cell phone in restaurants, theaters, museums, places of worship, or anyplace else where cell phone use is disruptive.
- When answering your cell phone, speak quietly and excuse yourself to finish the call.
- Never use profanity.
- Never extend an invitation you don't intend to honor. It's an American custom to casually say "Let's have lunch sometime" with no intention (or obligation) of following through. If you make such an invitation to Asians, they expect you to honor it.

- For mixed couples, each country has different rules about whether the man or woman should enter a building first. Be prepared to follow the locals' example.

Respect for Elders

Asians honor the aged; they treat elders deferentially, even reverently. Visitors should strictly observe this tradition under all circumstances. By treating an older person without proper respect, visitors risk losing their Asian colleagues' respect and ending the relationship on the spot. Always follow these guidelines when in the company of older people:

- Greet elders before all others and use the traditional greetings appropriate to the culture.
- Pay attention to and converse with older people.
- Stand when an older person enters the room.
- Give your seat to an older person.
- Never raise your voice in an older person's presence.
- Always remove sunglasses when speaking to older people.
- When with older people, maintain good posture and keep your feet on the floor and knees together when seated.
- Ask permission before smoking or drinking in the company of older people.

Smoking Etiquette

Attitudes toward smoking are changing world wide, as are the circumstances under which smoking is acceptable. Compared to Americans, Asians smoke in large numbers. But they do know the health hazards associated with smoking and secondhand smoke, and more and more of them are taking the warnings seriously. If you smoke, follow these guidelines:

- Always be considerate of your Asian hosts or colleagues.
- Discreetly observe when and where others smoke.
- At meals, don't smoke at the table unless you see others smoking. Even then, ask the people around you whether they mind if you smoke.

If you don't smoke, more and more Asian hotels offer nonsmoking rooms, and more and more restaurants offer nonsmoking sections. Ask before you book a room or table whether nonsmoking areas are available.

Punctuality

In countries where punctuality is expected, lateness says you:

- Lack respect.
- Have sloppy, undisciplined personal habits.
- Are potentially unreliable as a business partner or supplier.

If you're an "Oh well, what's a few minutes late?" person, I suggest you become an on-time person when traveling abroad. Punctuality shows that you understand local customs and can follow them. In general, Asians in some countries (especially Hong Kong, Japan, and Singapore) expect foreigners to be on time for appointments, banquets, and other social functions. In those nations, it's best to arrive early.

Although they expect foreigners to be on time, some Asians aren't punctual themselves. For example, be prepared for Malays, Thais, and Filipinos to be late, especially for social occasions.

In Part II, I cover each country's generally accepted attitude toward punctuality. Follow this guide. If uncertain about the attitude toward punctuality, ask your host, a colleague, or the hotel concierge. To be safe, always be on time for meetings, but be patient if your hosts are a bit late.

> Traffic congestion is horrendous in Asia's major cities. I once waited more than two hours for a friend to make his way from Bangkok's famed Oriental Hotel to a restaurant only a couple of miles away. Stuck in traffic, he reported his progress—or lack of it—to me by cell phone.
>
> And even when traffic isn't an issue, addresses in some cities can be difficult to find, even for local taxi drivers. Many Americans have returned from Japan with stories of how their cab drivers patiently drove up and down a street while they peered at each building, searching for the right address. In Japan, few streets have names and few buildings are numbered sequentially.

Pace

One of the greatest challenges in doing international business is understanding and accepting the local pace—that sense of urgency (or lack thereof) with making or postponing decisions, keeping promises, meeting deadlines, and getting the job done. To foreign colleagues, the local pace may be faster or slower than what they're used to; but to local colleagues, the pace is natural and reflects cultural habits and attitudes.

It's important to understand that one pace isn't necessarily better or worse than another—it's just different. If local colleagues aren't advancing a project as quickly as foreign colleagues would like, the locals' perceived slowness doesn't reflect malice or incompetence; they just operate more slowly in their culture. And the foreign colleagues must learn to understand and accept that fact.

As Asia modernizes, its economies are growing quickly. Skyscrapers are sprouting in Hong Kong, Shanghai, Bangkok, and Singapore. Frenetic economic activity abounds in Asia's financial centers. But despite these similarities to Western culture, Asians operate at a different pace than Westerners do.

To understand the Asian sense of pace, it's essential to understand that Asians see themselves as part of a culture that has endured for thousands of years and will continue for thousands more. If one generation doesn't achieve its goals, the next one—or the one after it—will. Obstacles like famine, disease, or war eventually pass, as they have before. Families, nations, and cultures endure.

This mindset explains why, during the French and U.S. occupations during the last century, the Vietnamese were prepared to fight, suffer, and die to achieve their objectives—for generations, if necessary. The French and Americans didn't share the same level of commitment and fortitude, and they grossly underestimated it in their opponents.

> Chinese schoolchildren learn about fatalism from the story of the farmer who has both of life's most precious possessions: a son and a horse. One day, the horse runs away, and the neighbors pity the farmer. "Never mind," the farmer says, "You never know what happens." Sure enough, two days later the horse returns, bringing a pack of wild horses with him. This time his neighbors congratulate him on his good fortune. The farmer's response is the same: "You never know what happens."
>
> A few days later, his son breaks both his legs in a fall from a wild horse. The neighbors once again commiserate, and once again the farmer says, "You never know what happens."
>
> Then a group of the emperor's soldiers ride through the town, taking every able young man with them to fight in a border war. The farmer's son, temporarily disabled, gets to stay home.
>
> You never know what happens.

Asians also believe that life brings endless change, which provides numerous opportunities. This sense of fatalism tends to make Asians ready to turn a seeming disaster into a business opportunity. They're prepared to patiently await the best moment to take advantage of opportunities; they don't force the moment.

To Westerners generally, and Americans in particular, if something can't get done now, today, this week, this month, this year—certainly in a lifetime—then it's not worth doing. A Westerner who wants to successfully do business in Asia needs to do three things:

1. Cultivate patience and flexibility.
2. Pursue relationships, not transactions.
3. Focus on long-term gains, not quick profits.

As one veteran China trader said: "If you are the kind of person who has trouble waiting for a red light to change, then China is not for you."

Dress

Dressing appropriately and attractively has two rewards. First, your appearance should convey that you've made an effort; dressing properly creates an opportunity for you to project that you're someone with whom others want to do business. Second, and perhaps more important, your appearance affects your behavior. Dress well, and you behave well and project confidence.

Conversely, there's no worse feeling than sticking out because your dress and appearance don't conform to local standards. Calling attention to yourself makes you uncomfortable, and you'll generally project that discomfort to others.

Asians judge people on their appearance. They believe how you dress indicates your education, status, and class. They expect Americans to dress as Americans—but within certain bounds of taste. So dress like an American—a clean, neat, pressed, polished one with classic, conservative tastes in styles and colors.

> Upon arrival on his first trip to Indonesia, the vice president of a large American company immediately purchased a batik shirt. Because the weather was oppressively hot, he was certain a batik shirt and slacks would be appropriate for his meeting.
>
> As he entered the office of his prospective customers, he was embarrassed to find himself facing three gentlemen wearing dark suits, white shirts with French cuffs, and silk ties!

General Rules

- Always dress conservatively and modestly. The traditional business suit for men and a simple, elegant dress for women are appropriate everywhere in Asia. Although many young Asians wear current Western fashions, experienced businesspeople dress conservatively, and so should you.
- Never wear sloppy, dirty clothing and shoes; always wear high-quality clothing and shoes. Asians will judge you on the quality of your attire.
- Don't go native. Nothing will make you look sillier or feel more self-conscious than trying to dress like a local and failing. Don't wear a kimono, sarong, or other traditional Asian garment unless you know when, how, and where to wear it.
- Make sure your shoes are clean and polished. Never wear scuffed or unfashionable shoes.
- Be aware: Asians remove shoes upon entering many restaurants, homes, and temples. Wear shoes without laces to make removal easy. Always wear clean socks without holes.
- If you're unsure of the appropriate clothing for a particular occasion, ask a knowledgeable colleague. When in doubt, always dress more formally than casually.
- Good grooming is vital. Make sure your nails are clean and manicured.
- Many Asians consider facial hair on men ugly and barbaric. Men should consider shaving off beards, or at least keep them closely and neatly trimmed.

Appearance is so important to Asians that many spend a lot of time and money trying to "improve" their looks. Once taboo, plastic surgery is now common in many countries, but less drastic (and less expensive) methods are even more widespread.

For example, many Asians consider light-colored skin beautiful, and women spend vast amounts of money to achieve it. Perhaps the desire for white skin comes from a need to look educated and wealthy (only the skin of laborers and peasants is tanned because of exposure to the sun). Or maybe it's a lingering imperialist attitude, which equates light skin with power.

Whatever the explanation, one market research company estimates that 40 percent of women in Hong Kong, Malaysia, the Philippines, South Korea, and Taiwan use skin-whitening creams, despite the fact that some are dangerous.

- Invitations specifying "formalwear" usually mean full eveningwear.
- Invitations specifying "informal" or "casual" mean "smart casual"—which means a nicely coordinated, stylish, elegant outfit. Men wear linen blazers, pleated pants, or stylish designer jeans. Women wear fashionable slacks or skirts and matching blouses.
- Regardless of the heat, don't wear tank tops or shorts in the cities, and never wear shorts, sundresses, or sleeveless tops when visiting temples or mosques.
- Wear shorts only at the beach or pool and jeans only for rugged outdoor activities.
- Wear cotton and other natural fibers in hot, humid areas. You'll be more comfortable wearing these fabrics than polyester and other synthetics.
- Be sure to take a sweater, wrap, or jacket whenever you go out. Shops, restaurants, and offices are often over air-conditioned, sometimes uncomfortably so.
- Unless you're engaging in athletic activities, don't wear athletic shoes and sweat suits. Never wear this attire in restaurants or shops, or for any business occasion. Asians don't consider it casual wear.

Indonesia, Pakistan, Bangladesh, and India have the world's largest Muslim populations. Most Asian Muslim women dress very conservatively, and many wear their own ethnic styles of veils and headscarves. Although this tradition may seem oppressive to Americans, visitors must understand that many Asian women prefer to wear traditional attire—and even feel more free than they imagine American women are.

In a 1984 issue of *Mahjubah: The Magazine for Muslim Women*, one Muslim woman explains the appeal of traditional attire:

"If women living in Western societies took an honest look at themselves, such a question (why Muslim women cover themselves) would not arise. They are the slaves of appearance and the puppets of a male chauvinistic society: Every magazine and news medium tells them how they should look and behave. They should wear glamorous clothes and make themselves beautiful for strange men to gaze and gloat over them. So the question is not why Muslim women wear a hijab, but why women in the West, who think they are so liberated, do not wear a hijab."

- Avoid wearing:
  * Funny hats or T-shirts
  * Country club attire (golf shorts, tennis clothes, and so on)
  * Any clothing in loud, flashy colors (brightly colored plaid pants or sport coats)

Finally, if your dress and appearance don't pass muster, relax. Note any errors for future reference, and then carry on with your business. If you conduct yourself with dignity, good taste, and consideration for others, your behavior will overcome any sartorial deficiency.

Dress Tips

Men

- For formal occasions, a dark suit and tie with dress shoes are always appropriate. Wear this outfit for all first business meetings, banquets, and all formal dinners.
- For informal occasions, wear blazers or conservative sport coats, slacks, sport shirts, and dress shoes or dressy casual shoes.

Women

- It's always best to dress conservatively. Never wear tight or low-cut clothing. Although younger Asian women may dress in provocative fashions, you won't inspire confidence in your senior male colleagues if you follow their lead. Make sure your shoulders are covered and skirt hemlines fall at least to the knee.
- Be aware: Especially in restaurants or homes in Japan, you may be seated on tatami mats on the floor. If you're wearing tight and/or short skirts, sitting will be difficult.
- Wear suits, dresses, skirts, and blouses in subdued colors. In many major Asian cities, women dress elegantly whenever they're in public—and they're setting the standard they'll expect you to meet.
- The "little black dress" (but not too little) is appropriate to attend a dinner, opera, theater performance, or concert.
- Accessories are important. Wear a high-quality scarf, jewelry, and shoes, and carry a stylish purse.

Gifts

At all levels of Asian society, giving gifts is obligatory. Each country has occasions when exchanging gifts is expected, like Chinese New Year, Christmas, and national days. In some countries, people expect to receive a proper gift before they'll begin or continue a relationship. An improper gift—or giving a gift at the wrong time—may be an insult.

Furthermore, any gift or favor carries with it an obligation to reciprocate. Not reciprocating jeopardizes the relationship, because everyone keeps track of gifts and favors given and owed.

Asians don't expect Westerners to understand gift-

> As Asians interact more with Western society, gift-giving customs are relaxing rapidly in many Asian countries. Nonetheless, it's best to understand and follow the traditional rules when visiting a country. As always, err on the side of formality.

giving customs and follow them to the level that Asians do. Nonetheless, a vital part of developing a friendship or business relationship in Asia is knowing what gift to give and to whom, when to give it and under what circumstances, and how to present it. It'd be a shame to inadvertently insult someone you're trying to impress by giving the wrong gift or giving it incorrectly.

Gift giving may seem like a complicated, often intimidating task, but don't despair. When considering gifts, always take the time to consult a knowledgeable person, like a local colleague or your hotel concierge. In addition, using courtesy and common sense—as well as the following guidelines and the gift-giving information in each country chapter—will give you a good foundation.

General Rules

In general, gifts should:
- Never be cheap or tacky.
- Be of high quality, but not ostentatious. Look for brand names with international prestige.
- Never be intimate items.
- Never be practical items.
- Never violate a tradition or religion (see pages 76–89 for gift suggestions for members of various religions).
- Never be vulgar or insulting.
- Be appropriate to the relationship and culture.
- Be comparable in value to the gifts you receive.

When you receive a gift

- Accept it graciously. Refusing to accept a gift can insult the giver.
- Open it according to custom. In most Asian cultures, people don't open gifts in the giver's presence in order to save face for both the giver and receiver if the gift is inappropriate. Upon receiving a gift, don't open it unless asked to do so; never ask to open it. Instead, receive the gift with both hands, thank the giver, and place it next to you to open later.
- If you're invited to open a gift (which isn't likely), do so graciously. Don't toss the card aside carelessly and rip off the gift-wrap. Instead, read the card with interest and nod your acceptance, then carefully open the gift. After discreetly examining the present, quietly thank the giver with an appropriate comment on the gift.
- Always record the gift on the giver's business card, in your address book, or in a file.
- Wear or display the gift when you next meet with the giver. Comment on its usefulness or how much enjoyment it's given you.
- Send a thank-you note promptly. (See page 30–31.)

When you give a gift

- Never give a gift unexpectedly. Ask a knowledgeable colleague whether the event calls for a gift. Or call the secretary of the person you're meeting beforehand (while confirming the meeting, for example) and mention that you'd like to give a gift as a gesture of friendship.
- Personalize a gift whenever possible. There's no nicer gift than one that shows you took the time to find something that reflects the recipient's tastes, interests, and personality.
- Always record a gift you give to prevent giving it again to the same person.
- Always wrap a gift before giving it. In fact, consider having it professionally wrapped; tell the wrapper what the occasion is and who the recipient is, and you'll be sure your gift is wrapped correctly. In some Asian countries, how you wrap and present a gift is as important as the gift itself.
- Know the significance of a color. Some colors have certain positive or negative meanings in different cultures (see page 89 and the gift section of each country chapter). For example, avoid using white gift-wrap. (White is the color of mourning.)
- Enclose a signed card.
- Never use red ink on a card or a gift; doing so will sever a relationship. Traditionally, Asians write only the names of the deceased in red. Writing a living person's name in red is like putting a curse on him or her.

- In some Asian cultures, it's polite to refuse a gift once or twice. If your Asian colleague declines a gift, keep politely insisting that he or she accept it.
- With that said, don't urge your recipients to open their gifts. Remember that many Asian cultures don't permit opening gifts in the giver's presence.

General gifts to consider giving
- Arts and crafts from your home state or region
- Native American arts and crafts
- American-made chocolates or candy made in your region
- Photo books of your city, state, or region
- High-quality fountain or ballpoint pens
- Smoked salmon from the Pacific Northwest or Alaska
- Amish handmade products
- Fine American or European whiskeys, liqueurs, or wines (except in Muslim countries). More and more Asians are acquiring a taste for these beverages, but it's best to make sure your colleagues prefer such gifts before giving them.
- Ginseng, an important root in traditional Chinese herbal medicine with many therapeutic properties. Many Asians consider North American ginseng an excellent gift.
- Small gifts for children (if visiting a colleague's home). Toys, coloring books, children's books from your country or region, and sweets are appropriate gifts. Teens will enjoy T-shirts or sweatshirts from universities or sports teams in your state.

General gifts to avoid giving

There's no other area of the world where you can get in more trouble by giving the wrong gift than Asia. There are many taboos based on the cultural meaning of certain colors, numbers, and items.

My consulting company once worked with an organization that was preparing to sign a joint venture with a Chinese company. Our client ordered thirty expensive clocks to be engraved and given to all the Chinese partners—a big mistake, because the Chinese associate clocks with death. Fortunately, we found out about this plan before the engraving took place, and our client canceled the order.

Before visiting a country, make sure you read the gift section in its chapter and follow the advice. Here are a few general examples of gifts to avoid giving:

- Items that number thirteen (a taboo in most Asian cultures)
- Even numbers of gift items, especially pairs or groups of fours (considered unlucky in some areas)
- Clocks (associated with death in many Asian countries)
- Sharp objects (knives, scissors, letter openers, and so on—they traditionally connote the severing of a relationship.)

> A Japanese businessperson once told me that he was on a Western airline's inaugural flight of a new route to Japan. As the passengers boarded, a flight attendant greeted each one with a smile and a white carnation. My Japanese acquaintance said, "It was as if everyone were preparing for a funeral as we got on the plane. It made me very nervous!" White carnations are funeral flowers in Japan; they symbolize death.

Gifts of Appropriate Value

Always give a gift that's comparable in value to the one you received. If you give a gift that's noticeably more or less valuable than the one you received, you risk making the recipient lose face—and possibly ruining your relationship.

When giving gifts, never try to outdo your Asian colleague. The lavishness of gifts will steadily escalate, and you'll lose—always.

If you're working with people at different levels of an Asian company, you'll need to give gifts of different values. For example, you might give the chief negotiator in your joint venture discussions a high-quality pen set and the factory manager a less-expensive appointment calendar or notebook. If you were to give the factory manager the same gift as the executive, you'd demean the executive and embarrass the factory manager.

Hostess Gifts

Asians do most entertaining in restaurants. When invited to someone's home, however, always bring an appropriate, wrapped gift for the hostess and present it correctly (see pages 55–56).

> Flowers are usually a lovely hostess gift, but don't give them without first checking local customs. Certain numbers, colors, or types of flowers have special meanings—sorrow, death, anger, courtship—that vary among countries. Ask a florist to recommend appropriate flowers for an occasion.

Consider giving

- Pastries
- High-quality chocolates
- Books
- Recordings of music

Don't give

- Clothing
- Perfume
- Jewelry
- Personal items
- Any of the general items to avoid giving listed on pages 56–57

Business Gifts

Asians maintain business relationships at all social levels through gift giving. They most often give business gifts at meetings—sometimes at the first meeting, sometimes at the successful conclusion of negotiations, sometimes just to continue a relationship. Some exchange gifts before meetings; others exchange them afterward.

While gift giving is less important than it once was, be prepared to follow these guidelines:

- Let the host present a gift first. If you give a gift first, you risk making your hosts lose face if they have nothing to give you.
- When given a gift, always be ready to reciprocate. Before traveling to Asia, pack several gifts of different values, have them professionally

At Chinese New Year, the Chinese give *hong bao* ("lucky money") in special red envelopes to children and to people who have provided a service or special assistance during the year: garbage collectors, doormen, maids, and so on.

"Red envelopes" are also appropriate for other occasions, including gifts for children and for newlyweds. Employers give red envelopes to employees, often as year-end bonuses that may be as much as a whole month's salary. The amount given depends on the closeness of the relationship.

Many Chinese carry red envelopes and *hong bao* with them in case a situation that calls for such a gift arises. For example, if someone visits a colleague's home for dinner and learns that it's the birthday of one of the family's children, giving *hong bao* in a red envelope is a nice gesture.

Giving red envelopes incorrectly is bad luck, so ask a knowledgeable colleague for advice about appropriate amounts. For red envelopes for children, an amount around the equivalent of US $10 is usually appropriate. Bills for *hong bao* should be new and in even denominations.

One last word of advice: never give red envelopes to government officials.

wrapped upon arrival, and carry them in your briefcase so you'll always be prepared if given a gift in a factory, home, or office.

- If there are several people present, wait until the recipient is alone to give your gift. Or give one group gift or identical gifts to each member of the group.
- Give group gifts during a scheduled meeting.
- Present a group gift to the leader of the group.
- Don't include your business card with a gift.
- If you're a man who's giving a gift to a Asian woman, tell her you're giving it on behalf of your wife, secretary, or other appropriate woman. Doing so says the gesture isn't a romantic one.
- Don't give gifts to government officials.

Consider giving
- Practical, high-quality office items
  * Fine pen and pencil sets
  * Business cardholders
  * Leather briefcases and portfolios (but avoid giving leather to Hindus and pigskin products to Muslims).
- Electronic items
  * Laser pointers
  * Calculators
  * PDAs
- Cigarette lighters (if you know the recipient smokes)
- Items that aren't noticeably inferior or superior to the gifts you've received (Recipients in some nations where corruption is a problem may perceive obviously expensive gifts as bribes.)

Don't give
- Literature or artwork from a country with whom the host country has a strained relationship (for example, don't give a Chinese colleague a gift from Japan). In fact, if possible, avoid gifts altogether that are made in Asia (although Asian-made electronic items are acceptable).

It's always a good idea to ask a knowledgeable colleague or a shop clerk about the appropriateness of any gifts you plan to purchase. For example, it'd be a grave mistake to give out promotional green baseball caps to your Chinese colleagues. In Chinese culture, wearing a green hat means someone in your family is an adulterer.

- Items in colors that have negative meanings in the host country or are associated with political beliefs (for example, red for Communism)
- Obviously expensive items that your colleagues may interpret as bribes
- Any of the general items to avoid giving listed on pages 56–57

Health and Safety

Health

Asia has endemic diseases that most Westerners don't commonly encounter, like malaria, cholera, plague, typhoid fever, hepatitis A, and parasitic infections. See the list of resources on page 373 to help you learn about recommended vaccinations and health precautions.

- Before your trip, visit a travel clinic if possible. Most primary care physicians don't know enough about health risks in Asian countries. Many university hospitals and major metropolitan medical centers have travel clinics.
- Check your health insurance policy before you travel. Make certain it covers emergency care in a foreign country. If it doesn't, buy a rider for coverage.
- If you'll be in an area where medical facilities don't meet Western standards, also purchase supplemental insurance for emergency medical evacuation. In general, don't trust the blood supply in Asia. If you're in an accident, emergency medical evacuation insurance prevents your getting blood transfusions with possibly tainted blood in substandard facilities. (Of course, if you're unconscious or treatment simply can't wait, you'll have to hope for the best and then get checked for blood-borne diseases as soon as you return to your home country.)

  Know that Rh-negative blood is virtually impossible to find in China (less than 1 percent of ethnic Han, the majority in China, has this blood type).
- For easier customs processing, keep medication in original, labeled containers. Pack all medication in your carryon luggage. That way, if your checked luggage goes astray, you've still got your medication.
- Pack a small first-aid kit.
- Take your physician's phone number with you.
- Wash your hands with soap before touching your mouth or eating.
- Avoid eating dairy products unless you're certain they've been pasteurized.
- Eating at sidewalk or roadside food stalls is risky at best. Contaminated or improperly prepared food can carry bacteria, viruses, or parasites. Diseases like hepatitis A and typhoid are also spread this way.

- Even in major hotels and first-class restaurants, be wary of eating raw or unpeeled cooked fruits or vegetables. They may be contaminated.
- To reduce exposure to schistosomiasis and other parasitic diseases, always wear shoes, sandals, or shower shoes. Never walk barefoot on grass, pavement, or beaches; keep feet covered even when walking in your hotel room. Also avoid swimming in freshwater lakes or streams. Swimming in saltwater is generally safe, but major harbors and surrounding waters are often polluted.
- To avoid contracting malaria, wear insect repellent whenever you're on an outing outside a major city.
- When traveling in tropical or subtropical areas, use sunscreen regularly. A nasty sunburn is a real distraction when negotiating!
- In the last decade, more than two hundred people (mostly Asians) have died of complications from avian influenza. While visitors aren't likely to contract the bird flu, avoid live poultry and poultry feces (on farms or at markets), and eat only fully cooked poultry and eggs.

Drinking Water

The quality of drinking water varies drastically in Asia. In some countries, water purification systems are among the world's best, while in others (or regions within them) all tap water is undrinkable. To play it safe, follow these tips:

- Try to drink only bottled or boiled water. Even if a country's tap water meets international standards, the chemicals used to purify it may make you ill.
- Don't even brush your teeth with tap water.
- At restaurants, drink a bottled beverage only after watching the server open the bottle in front of you.
- Don't put ice in your drinks.

Hospitals and Clinics

The standard of care at Asian hospitals varies from excellent to nonexistent. For minor medical or dental problems, your hotel can refer you to an English-speaking physician or dentist.

If, however, you even suspect your problem is serious, check with your country's nearest embassy or consulate before seeking treatment. But don't wait until the problem is severe before getting help. If your problem is critical, you may be evacuated to another country for emergency care.

Know that many Asian hospitals and providers may require immediate cash payment for services.

Restrooms

Asia has some of the world's finest restaurants and hotels—all with excellent "Western" toilet facilities familiar to Americans. In rural areas and older buildings, however, you'll likely encounter squat toilets.

A squat toilet may be a hole in the ground, or it may be a porcelain fixture with "footprints" flanking the aperture and perhaps a cover. Whatever its form, be prepared to squat while facing the wall or hooded end of the fixture.

To make squatting easier, avoid wearing high heels, pantyhose, tight pants and other clothing that restricts your ability to squat, or any

> Many places in Asia designate women's and men's restrooms with the appropriate symbol of a woman or man. If restrooms don't have these symbols, simply ask someone to point them out.

clothing you don't want touching a not-so-clean floor. You may want to remove your pants or skirt until you master squatting (don't worry—you will). You may need to hold on to something to steady yourself.

Many facilities sell toilet paper in small packets, so always carry small change. Also, many plumbing systems can't discard toilet paper. In those cases, a notice will be posted; discard used toilet paper in the wastebasket.

Not all facilities offer toilet paper. Some provide a hose with running water. Others provide a barrel of clean water with a ladle or bowl in it. In these facilities, people use the water and their left hands to cleanse themselves (hence the widespread revulsion for using the left hand for eating). They never put their hands directly in the barrel; instead, they ladle water over them outside the barrel. They also use the ladle to pour water into the toilet to cleanse it.

> If you find using a squat toilet difficult, console yourself with the knowledge that some Asian experts say if you haven't used a squat toilet, you haven't really been to Asia.

Always take premoistened towelettes, hand sanitizer, and tissues or toilet paper with you. The one time you don't is when you'll find yourself in a public restroom that doesn't have toilet paper, sinks, running water, soap, or towels.

Safety

When traveling abroad, take the same safety precautions you would when traveling in the United States. Follow these additional guidelines to keep safe when visiting Asia:

- See the list of resources on page 373 to help you plan a safe trip.
- The time to make important decisions is *not* after traveling seven to ten hours in a crowded plane. Jetlag—plus strange sights, sounds, smells, and customs—can confuse you, making it easier for others to victimize you.
- Whenever possible, explore new places with a local escort.
- Know how to use public phones, and learn key phrases (such as "I need help.") in the local language so you can communicate with the police if necessary.
- At all times, have on hand the phone numbers and home addresses of your employer's local representatives, the nearest American embassy or consulate, and your principal business contacts.
- Always carry your passport, airline tickets, credit cards, and other valuables on your person—not in a briefcase or purse. Or leave them in a reputable hotel's safe.
- Credit card and ATM fraud in some Asian countries is increasing. Before traveling to an Asian country, let your credit card company know you'll be using your card there. Also be aware of others around you when using your card. Don't leave the card on display (on a store counter, for example); thieves may try to memorize the number.
- Don't carry documents or packages for anyone, and store your own important papers in the hotel safe.
- Make photocopies of your passport's identification pages and keep one copy in a place separate from where you store your passport. Travel with several extra passport photos. The photos and copy of the identification pages will make it much easier to replace your passport if the original is lost or stolen.
- Don't carry papers that link you with the American government or the military. A terrorist could misinterpret even a card stating you're an "Honorary Kentucky Colonel."
- Don't wear a money belt or pouch outside your clothing or hung visibly around your neck. It could make you a target.
- Don't set your bag at your feet while checking schedules or using a phone. It might get snatched.
- Don't leave your drink or food unattended. Unscrupulous people may drug the food or beverages of victims, then rob them.

Hotel Safety

- Pack a small flashlight in case the hallways and stairwells are dark, or the hotel loses power.
- Take note of fire exits.
- Upon entering your room, make sure the phone line to the front desk works. Note emergency phone numbers.
- Keep your door—including those to connecting rooms—locked at all times, even when you're in your room. Secure sliding doors and windows.
- Verify who's at your door before opening it.
- Never leave cash, jewelry, or other valuables in plain sight. Store them in the room safe or in a safe-deposit box at the hotel's front desk.
- Always enter the hotel through the well-lit main entrance.
- Be especially careful in parking lots and ramps; use an escort service if available.

Driving

Driving in a foreign country is always difficult and nerve-racking. Make every attempt to avoid driving in Asia. Large Asian cities have very heavy traffic, and their traffic rules differ from American cities'. In some areas, local drivers largely ignore the rules. In others, you have no legal rights if you're in a traffic accident.

For your safety, use public transportation, hire a driver (the safest option if you can afford it), or take a taxi. Here are a few tips for hiring a taxi:

- Ask your hotel to recommend a reputable taxi company. Hotel staff should also tell you how and where to get a taxi and the approximate cost to your destination. Generally, a hotel will phone a taxi for you.
- Before you enter a taxi, verify that the driver knows how to get to your destination and ask for the cost.
- Always carry bills in small denominations. Taxi drivers (as well as vendors) may not accept bills in large denominations, and some who do may give change in counterfeit bills.

Corporate Culture

Your company has asked you to go to abroad. Are you lucky? You bet you are! Someone thinks you have a skill worth exporting or an ability to sell your company's services or products in another country. You're on your way to becoming an international business traveler, a role many businesspeople dream of but never get to play.

Are you nervous? I hope so. Nervousness means you won't be arrogant. Arrogance is the worst potential pitfall for the international business traveler. Acting arrogantly

> Peter Drucker, the management guru, said, "Be ready or be lost. If you don't think globally, you deserve to be unemployed and you will be."

says, "I'll do it my way. I'm paying the bill; let them adjust to me."

Nervousness also means you might make the effort necessary to combine sound business practices with basic local knowledge (that is, learning the basic facts of the countries you'll visit and a few basic phrases in their languages).

Businesspeople with decades of experience in Asia have repeatedly told me this fact: Business success means learning as much as possible about the history, culture, and customs of the region. Always remember that people have fought wars to preserve their ways and beliefs.

Never ignore the differences among Asian countries. Doing so risks offending your potential colleague or customer and embarrassing yourself and your company. Recognize and respect each country's languages, cultures, and attitudes; they affect every facet of business practice.

The number of business opportunities in Asia is enormous—and more and more Western companies are taking advantage of them. Make sure you take the necessary steps to ensure your company's success.

General Rules

Like everything else in Asia, corporate culture differs among countries. Never lump people together, assuming that their cultures and experiences are similar. The following general rules apply to doing business in most Asian companies:

- Adjust to—or at least respect—the Asian style of doing business. Unlike Americans, Asians (especially followers of Confucius) emphasize group welfare, are often ambiguous, and prize rituals, etiquette, and ceremonies.
- Be patient. Asians make decisions by consensus (which means slowly). Once Asians decide to implement a decision, however, they often do so rapidly, even by Western standards.
- Be prepared to commit time, energy, and money to any project in Asia.
- Be ready to move quickly as opportunities arise. To beat the competition, don't wait for a project's formal announcement.
- Networking is essential. In Asia, whom you know is more important than what you know. Also, Asians may suspect that Americans intend to cheat

them. To build a business relationship, you'll have to let people get to know and trust you.

- Be careful about doing business with people you don't know or for whom you can't get good references.
- Meet your prospective business colleagues face to face.
- Asians take introductions seriously. Have a respected third party speak for you before your arrival, then have him or her introduce you. This arrangement establishes your credibility. If the introducer doubted your credibility, he or she wouldn't risk losing face by introducing you.
- Appearance and status count! Your Asian colleagues will carefully note how you dress, where you stay, where you dine, and how you travel. From this information they'll decide whether they should take you seriously.
- Don't argue or be too blunt or aggressive. Asians highly value saving face and achieving harmony.
- Gathering accurate information may be difficult in Asia. Asians prefer not to answer pointed questions honestly. They may answer with what they think the asker wants to hear.
- Never ask yes-or-no questions that may cause someone to lose face if answered honestly. For example, don't ask someone in a meeting, "Can you finish this project by the end of the month?" Rather, ask open-ended questions such as, "When is the earliest you can have the project finished?"
- Never assume that the person who speaks the best English is the best employee.

> With nearly one million lawyers, the United States is by far the world's most litigious society. Americans thrive on conflict, and some companies regard it as a creative, constructive force. Colleagues, friends—even strangers—openly debate almost any issue that arises. Many people consider conflict the fun of conversation.
>
> Not so in Asia. In a society that's group oriented, people solve problems by consensus without confrontation. They may respond to conflict by smiling and changing the subject. If someone keeps pushing the subject, Asians may eventually withdraw from the discussion and ultimately end the relationship.
>
> Furthermore, if you openly criticize an Asian's idea, the person will consider it a personal attack, which may make him or her lose face and may doom the relationship.

Part I: Getting Started

- Make sure your product or service is high quality, readily available, appropriate for the market, and meets local standards.

> Be skeptical of statistics and facts your Asian colleagues provide. Asians invariably strive to present themselves, their company, and country in the best possible light.

- Have an intermediary or lower-ranking staff member discuss money issues.
- To make a deal, you may have to meet with government officials as well as business associates. Hire an agent (a person or company knowledgeable in local laws and customs) to help you navigate the bureaucracy and business regulations. An agent will also be invaluable as you negotiate contracts, research and visit local plant sites, and so on.
- Know that Asians may consider contracts statements of intent, not iron-clad promises.
- Have your correspondence translated into your colleagues' language by a reputable translator. It's worth the expense.
- Don't attempt to Americanize the workplace. You'll have far more success if you adapt to the local culture. Respect local customs, traditions, and work ethics.
- Let buyers tell you what they need. Know that many Asian companies face a shortage of startup capital.
- Establish and maintain a local presence.
- Be flexible and willing to operate within the existing business and political structures.
- Be prepared for perception gaps. Ways of thinking and approaches to life and business may differ from yours.
- Emphasize compatibility.
- Schedule appointments at least two weeks in advance.

> To promote its ethical business practices, a group of American and European businesspeople once sent a delegation to meet with distinguished Chinese officials.
>
> After finishing the presentation for instilling a new global economy, the visiting leader asked the Chinese leader what he thought of the principles. The Chinese official simply said, "Very good, yes, very good."
>
> The visiting leader then asked, "When do you plan to adopt them?" The Chinese official responded, "When we are as rich as the United States and Europe."

- Localize your marketing effort. What sells in Seattle doesn't necessarily sell in Singapore, and the ads that work in Boise don't necessarily work in Bangalore.
- Make sure focus groups include people of the same business or social level. If you include people of different levels in a focus group, those of lower status will defer to those of higher status.
- Use a local sales force—you'll generally have more success this way. Local people understand the market better and have better connections than outsiders.
- Strive to improve the quality of your employees' lives and make them glad they work for you.
- Be aware: Corruption, theft, racketeering, and weak judiciary systems are problems in some Asian nations.

Names and Titles

All general rules about using names and titles (see pages 21–22) apply in business—only they're twice as important. Remember:
- Never use first names until invited to do so.
- Learn the correct pronunciation of names and use them often.
- Ask a person what name and title he or she prefers.
- Use a person's proper title.
- If possible, learn proper pronunciation and usage of names before you meet. Write down this information and underline the name you should use in conversation.

Business Cards

The business card is an important communication tool in Asia. It can be one of your most valuable resources when meeting people.

Your Business Card
- To show your commitment and respect for the culture, have your business card printed in the local language on one side and in English on the other. Be aware that you may encounter at least two forms of written Chinese: People in Taiwan, Malaysia, Macao, and Hong Kong use classical (complex) characters, while those in China use simplified characters.
- Make sure your formal title appears on your card.
- If you hold any postgraduate degrees, include that information.

- If your company is more than fifty years old, put the founding year on your card. Longevity adds esteem.
- Travel with plenty of business cards—everyone exchanges them in Asia.
- Enclose your business card in all correspondence. Don't, however, enclose one in a card accompanying a gift.

How to Exchange Business Cards

Many Asians exchange business cards with great ceremony. Although the rituals vary among countries, the following rules will serve you well in most places. Remember: This is your first opportunity to make a good impression.

1. Before exchanging your card, make sure the Asian-language side is face-up and position the text so the recipient can read it.
2. Present the card with both hands, holding it so the recipient can read the information. At the same time, bow slightly and say your name.
3. When a person hands you his or her card, bow and receive it with both hands.
4. Study the information. Then nod in recognition.
5. Politely ask a question or make a comment. For example, "I notice you're the director of quality control. I'm eager to learn about your experiences."
6. At meetings, arrange the cards in front of you in the same order as the people are seated. This "seating chart" will help you remember names.
7. After meetings, place cards carefully in your briefcase. (You should put away a business card upon receipt only at occasions during which everyone stands, like a reception. Even then, carefully study the card and comment on it before respectfully tucking it in your briefcase.)
8. Never write on your card or anyone else's in front of others. Doing so is disrespectful.

Meetings

Here's some general information about meetings in Asia:

- A meeting's primary purpose may be to get to know and evaluate one another, to gain trust, or to check out the chemistry of participants. Know the meeting's purpose and come prepared.
- In some countries, meetings open with business discussions. In others, they begin with small talk.
- Take careful notes during meetings and presentations. Doing so signals your sincerity.

- Always remember that Asians prefer to speak indirectly. "That may be difficult" or "I'll try" probably means "no." They'll also avoid conflict to save face. If someone is giving elusive answers, you're likely asking questions that are too direct.
- Although your Asian colleagues may be indirect, be precise yourself.
- Don't assume anything about promises made during a meeting. Write down everything said and schedule time at the end of the meeting to review. After the meeting, send participants a written summary of all decisions made.

Presentations

- Learn a little about what your audience expects from a presentation. This knowledge will be invaluable.
- Some Asians (particularly the Chinese) read their presentations, because they're not trained in public speaking and don't want to make mistakes. Although there isn't a specific protocol in Asia for giving presentations, Westerners should do their best to avoid using notes, thus appearing knowledgeable and in command.
- Dress professionally for a presentation. Asians consider informal clothing disrespectful. (See pages 51–53.)
- In the United States, an enthusiastic presentation is almost required. In many Asian countries, such a presentation is considered phony or crude. When giving a presentation, be energetic yet professionally reserved.
- Be especially careful of your word choice in presentations, even if the audience understands English.
- If possible, use visual aids in the local language (PowerPoint presentations, handouts, meeting outlines/agendas, and so on).
- Don't expect Asians to participate in audience activities. Be especially careful never to make anyone look foolish.
- Keep your hands out of your pockets and maintain good posture. To your Asian colleagues, sloppy body language indicates sloppy business practices.
- In the United States, we say, "There's no such thing as a stupid question." But Asians won't ask a question that may make them look silly or ill informed, especially in front of a group. Keep this in mind during question-and-answer periods. Always answer questions seriously and respectfully.
- It's rude to respond to someone brusquely or contentiously. To attack a person's idea is to attack him or her personally. Be respectful at all times.
- Know how to graciously accept a gift (see page 55) if you receive one at the end of the presentation.

Socializing

When establishing, renewing, or continuing a business relationship in Asia, be prepared to socialize. This is no time to decline invitations. Remember, most Asians do business only with people they trust, and they get to know potential partners and suppliers through business entertaining. So whether you're invited to a Chinese banquet, drinks at a karaoke bar, or a quiet meal in a restaurant or home, accept the invitation. The time, money, and energy you spend socializing will pay big dividends. Here are some general tips for socializing in Asia:

- While business breakfasts are becoming common, Asians prefer business lunches. Many still consider business breakfasts uncivilized.

> "A role for chief executives is to look at spreadsheets but also to look in the eyes of the people you are going to deal with."
> —Sir Anthony "Tony" O'Reilly, Irish businessman and former CEO and Chairman of H. J. Heinz Company

- Enjoy the local food—leave your diet at home as much as possible.
- Appreciate and participate in drinking rituals—but pace yourself. When drinks are served, take one, even if you only sip it or pretend to drink it.
- Be prepared to make a toast for every occasion.
- Don't talk business at dinner unless your host initiates the conversation.
- Be prepared for long evenings and late hours. Asians often make or break business deals at these times.
- Participate in whatever you're invited to do, and be prepared to perform if asked. You may even have to sing a song—perhaps your college fight song. You might expand your repertoire with "Jingle Bells" or any Frank Sinatra tune.
- If invited to a banquet, reciprocate by hosting a banquet of comparable quality before you leave.

Personalizing Relationships

In Asia, the "Hi, how are you? Let's sign the contract" approach never works. If you want to succeed in Asia, prepare to take the time to personalize your relationships. Here are some tips:

- Make it clear to people with whom you hope to do business that you're there for the long haul. Americans have a reputation for disappearing, so visit potential colleagues or customers—especially high-level ones—as often as possible.

- Stay in touch; phone, write, and e-mail often.
- Contribute to local charities.
- Join appropriate associations in the local community.

> "In good times, we do business with friends. In bad times, we do business with friends. *Make friends!*"
>
> —Reportedly said by August A. Busch III, Chairman of the Board, Anheuser-Busch Companies, Inc.

- Spend time discussing local issues. (Be sure to brush up on them beforehand.) Any knowledge or interest you show in the local culture will help build closer and stronger business relationships.
- Don't come on too fast or too strong. Maintain a low-key approach and adjust your pace, if necessary.
- Allow time to build your potential colleague's or customer's confidence in the relationship.
- Be yourself—warm and friendly but initially more formal than you'd be at home.

Especially for Women

Many Westerners believe that because many Asian traditions lack gender equality, Asian societies don't welcome businesswomen.

For example, Confucian doctrine dictates women are subservient to men. One principal states: "The virtue of a woman lies in the three obediences: obedience to the father, husband, and son."

Obviously, such traditions don't promote the same educational and professional opportunities for women as they do for men. But attitudes are changing rapidly in most Asian countries. Women are moving into leadership positions, although they're still rare in some business circles.

Asians direct much of their resistance toward businesswomen at local women, not Westerners. While doing business in Asia, I've generally found that women have an advantage over men and it's sometimes easier for women to gain access to companies. When it comes to having the following desirable abilities, Asians believe that women are at least the equal of men.

- Reading nonverbal cues
- Speaking in a soft, well-modulated voice
- Listening to all opinions
- Exploring common ground and clients' needs
- Making an effort to build bridges

- Taking time to build consensus
- Never trying to rush a decision
- Showing interest in people and their lifestyles

By demonstrating these abilities, women increase their chances of business success in Asia.

General Rules

- Research local customs toward women and respect them—even if you think they're outrageous.
- Define your role clearly, and establish your position and ability immediately. Before your visit, send prospective colleagues notice of your educational background, professional experience, honors and awards, titles, and current responsibilities.
- To establish credibility, have a mutually respected person introduce you.
- Offer your hand first upon meeting or greeting a man, but don't be offended if a man doesn't take it. Some cultures allow touching between members of the opposite sex only if they're relatives.
- Never lose your cool.
- Respond gracefully when men open doors for you, stand for you, or otherwise exhibit chivalry.
- Don't be embarrassed or angry if someone treats you in a sexist manner.
- Speak softly and behave calmly. Many Asian cultures consider aggressive behavior repugnant, especially in women.
- Dress conservatively and modestly but femininely—and never with sexual overtones.
- Do nothing that another could misinterpret as a sexual invitation. If you want to use a wedding ring to ward off advances, know that many Asian women wear their wedding rings on their right hands.
- Enter meetings with confidence. Stand tall (even if you're not). Asians will judge your expertise by your body language.

> Many Asian men have formed their image of Western women from films, TV ads, and other media. As a result, an American woman—especially a blue-eyed blond—may suddenly find herself in the limelight, whether or not she wants to be. Dress modestly and behave conservatively to help prevent unwanted attention. Make it clear from the outset that establishing a business relationship is your only interest.

- Expect cultural misunderstandings. If you feel someone has insulted you, ask for clarification. Chances are, you've misunderstood the action or statement.
- Be patient. It may be a new experience for some people to do business with women.
- Roll with the punches. If you're clearly dealing with someone incapable of working with a woman, consider

> Before I was granted an interview with Lee Kuan Yew when he was prime minister of Singapore, I was asked to submit a written request accompanied by a curriculum vitae specifying the college I attended, the undergraduate degree I received, the graduate work I completed, as well as my professional experience. The Singaporeans didn't care that I was a woman—they just wanted to be certain I was qualified to speak with their prime minister!

asking a male colleague to join you or to handle that particular detail.

Holidays and Festivals

Each Asian country and many regions within each country have holidays and festivals during which businesses are closed. Here's some general information you should know:
- Before planning your trip, check the holiday schedules for the countries you're going to visit. It may be impossible to do business during the days near some holidays, like Chinese New Year, Ramadan, Christmas, and the week preceding Easter.
- Also be aware of regional and local holidays and festivals. If you plan to visit customers or shop in cities, a little-known holiday could ruin your plans.
- Ask about school holidays. Many people travel with their families during these breaks, and cities may be more crowded.

Interfaith Etiquette

From the Shinto priest presiding over the opening of a fast-food restaurant in Tokyo to the feng shui master giving construction advice for a bank's new headquarters, faith and ritual are inseparable from business and everyday life in Asia.

To establish any business or personal relationship in Asia, you must show respect for a person's beliefs—and you can't show respect for something unless you know at least a little about it.

This section provides basic information on Asia's major religions and philosophies as well as etiquette tips for interacting with their followers. Here are a few general tips:

- Respect others' beliefs at all times. If you're invited to a service at a temple, mosque, or church, ask about the correct protocol for dress and behavior. Each religion has rules that are sacred to its traditions.
- Always dress formally when visiting a house of worship.
- Women should carry a shawl or large scarf with them in case a house of worship requires a covered head and/or shoulders.
- Always learn and use the correct title for a clergy member or religious leader.
- Always speak quietly and behave calmly.
- Step over—not on—the threshold when entering a holy place.
- Stay in the back of a room in which people are kneeling in prayer.
- Never walk in front of someone praying or someone on a prayer rug.
- Never smoke or drink alcoholic beverages on the grounds of holy places.
- Ask permission before photographing holy places, objects, and images.
- Some shrines have separate worship areas for men and women. Never wander into an area you shouldn't be.
- Never touch statues or paintings.
- Before planning an event, ask your guests whether they have any dietary requirements. Always have at least one vegetarian dish available.

The information provided in this section is only a starting point. Take the time to learn more about the religions and philosophies of the area you'll be visiting. Most Asians enjoy talking about their beliefs with informed, non-judgmental people.

Confucianism, Taoism, and Buddhism

These three philosophies helped shape China and other countries in East and Southeast Asia. In general, they're more eclectic than dogmatic, humanistic than theological, and communal than individual. In theory and practice, there's significant overlap among them. It's not unusual for someone to practice elements of all three.

Confucianism

Strictly speaking, Confucianism isn't a religion; it has no clergy, doesn't worship a god or gods, and doesn't teach the existence of an afterlife. Rather, it's a way of life based on the ideas of Chinese philosopher Confucius (551–479 BC).

Confucianism focuses on solving the practical problems of everyday life and helping people become ideal citizens. It's a guide to personal morality, interpersonal relations, social responsibility, and good government.

Over the centuries, Confucianism absorbed ideas from Taoism and other philosophies and religions. Along the way, Confucians began to practice certain rites or rituals for their fate in *this* world (long life, children, wealth), not for the next.

Because Confucian philosophy emphasizes allegiance to the group—be it family, work team, company, or nation—many believe Confucianism is a major factor in modern Asia's success.

Because Confucianism focuses on interpersonal relationships, Confucian ethics don't have a code for dealing with outsiders. Followers traditionally consider foreigners "nonpersons"—that is, they're not socially definable. Once foreigners become business colleagues or friends, Confucians can define the relationship and know how to treat them.

Confucianism doesn't dictate a specific diet, and there are no gifts to avoid giving Confucians.

Taoism

Chinese philosopher Lao-tzu was a contemporary of Confucius, and his teachings became the basis of Taoism (pronounced "DOW-ism"), which became an organized religion about second century AD.

Taoism differs from Confucianism in two main ways: its mysticism and its emphasis on harmony with nature (rather than social harmony).

As a philosophy, Taoism has had a profound impact in East and Southeast Asia. For example, Taoist philosophy heavily influenced classical Chinese art and literature.

The book *Tao-te Ching* (*Classic of the Way of Power*) contains the Taoist philosophy. The *tao* (or "way") means understanding what makes each thing what it is. It promotes the idea that experiencing divinity comes from avoiding all worldly interests and desires and following intuitive or mystical methods, including magic, meditation, special attention to diet, breath control, and scripture recitation.

Achieving balance and harmony is Taoism's objective. A Taoist strives to avoid conventional social obligations and lead a simple, spontaneous, meditative life close to nature. The ultimate goal of Taoism is immortal life.

Taoism doesn't dictate a specific diet, and there are no gifts to avoid giving Taoists.

Buddhism

Indian teacher and philosopher Gautama Siddhartha (or Buddha Gautama) founded Buddhism around 500 BC. At various times, Buddhism heavily influenced the cultures of China, Japan, Korea, Thailand, Vietnam, and Tibet. In all these areas, Buddhism has combined with elements of other religions, like Hinduism. Today, Buddhism's nearly half-billion adherents are primarily in Asia.

Buddhists have faith in Buddha (both the original and those who achieve a certain level of enlightenment), his teachings (dharma), and the religious community he founded (*sangha*). Unlike Confucianism and Taoism, Buddhism focuses on human suffering, escaping that suffering, the existence of an afterlife, and achieving nirvana (state of perfect peace and happiness). Also central to Buddhist teaching are the ideas of karma (the influence of one's past actions upon his or her future lives) and *samsara* ("The Wheel of Life," the continuous cycle of death and rebirth).

Buddhism has four major branches or schools: Theravada, Mahayana, Mantrayana, and Zen.

Theravada

Theravada Buddhism is the dominant religion of Thailand and other countries of Southeast Asia. It emphasizes the importance of Buddha as a historical figure, the virtues of the monastic life, and the authority of the *Tipitaka* (teachings of Buddha). In Theravada, the ideal Buddhist is an arhat (a saint who has achieved enlightenment).

Mahayana

Most followers of Mahayana Buddhism live in Japan and East Asia. The Mahayanists emphasize the existence of many Buddhas—those in heaven as well as those yet to become Buddhas. They believe Buddhas can save people through grace and compassion. The Mahayanist ideal is the bodhisattva, a person who forgoes nirvana and vows to become a Buddha in order to save others.

Mantrayana

People in the Himalayas, Mongolia, and Japan practice Mantrayana (also known as Vajrayana and as Shingon in Japan).

Mantrayana Buddhism accepts most Mahayana doctrines, but it also emphasizes a close relationship between a guru (spiritual leader) and a small group of disciples who spend much of their time reciting mantras (prayers or hymns), performing sacred dances and gestures, and meditating.

Zen

Zen originated in China, but it's practiced chiefly in Japan. It's probably the form of Buddhism best known in the West.

Zen accepts Mahayana doctrines, but like Mantrayana, it also emphasizes a close relationship between master and disciples. Zen has developed distinctive practices designed to lead to satori (state of spiritual enlightenment). Many followers of Zen believe that satori comes in a sudden flash of insight; others believe one achieves it only gradually through self-discipline, meditation, and instruction.

Some Buddhists are vegetarian; ask about dietary restrictions when entertaining Buddhist guests. In case Buddhist colleagues practice vegetarianism or veganism, avoid giving leather gifts.

When Visiting a Buddhist Temple

- Remove hats, scarves, and sunglasses and extinguish cigarettes before entering a temple.
- Enter the temple through the right door, and exit through the left door.
- Place incense sticks upright in the urn at the temple's entrance.
- Kneel before the altar on one of the red pillows, and bow your head with each beat of the monk's drum.
- Walk clockwise around Buddhist structures—inside and outside.
- Buddhists expect visitors' heads to be lower than the monks when sitting or speaking with them.
- Be careful of where you sit. Worshipers reserve some seats for the gods.
- Ask sincere questions about the different postures of the Buddha images—each signifies a different stage in his life and teaching.
- Your host may invite you to have an astrologer read your fortune. Accept this gift graciously. Your host will probably pay the fee.
- Women shouldn't touch or offer to shake hands with a Buddhist monk and should maintain a distance of two feet from a monk. They shouldn't sit next to a monk on public transportation.
- To receive an object from a woman, a monk may extend part of his robe on a table or floor. The woman then places the object on the robe.

When Visiting a Wat (Thai Buddhist Temple)

- Be careful to step over thresholds when walking through the wat. Tradition holds that souls reside in thresholds.
- The *bot* (ordination hall) is the temple's most sacred area. Remove your shoes before entering, and don't remain standing once inside.
- In the *bot*, don't sit on the floor with legs crossed in front of you. Instead, sit in a kneeling position with legs tucked under you to one side (women) or with one leg tucked under and one in front (men). If you're uncertain how to sit, follow how others (but not monks) are sitting.
- Never climb on statues of the Buddha (to pose for a photo, for example). Always remember that they're revered objects.
- *Wai* (keeping fingers together and pointed up, press palms together close to the chest, then bow slightly) before the Buddha and make your wishes. You may get them!
- If you want to make an offering, Buddhists will give you a candle, a flower, a piece of gold leaf, and three incense sticks. Light the candle and place it with others. Put the flower in the water vessel. Light the incense with the candle. Place the incense sticks in the urn and press the leaf onto the Buddha image.

Shinto

Shinto is Japan's oldest surviving religion. No one knows exactly when or how Shinto began, but Japan's aboriginal people likely created it before the massive immigration from mainland Asia. Today, up to fifty million Japanese practice some form of Shinto and worship at public and private shrines.

Influenced by both Buddhism and Confucianism, Shinto developed such moral standards as honesty, kindness, and respect for one's elders and superiors. Shintoists worship many kami (gods), ancestral spirits, and spiritual forces in mountains, rivers, rocks, trees, and other natural forms. Kami are also the fundamental forces behind creativity, growth, healing, and other processes.

Shinto's main concern is obtaining the gods' blessing for daily events. Shintoists hold ceremonies to bless new life and new beginnings. Even large corporations enlist a Shinto priest for ceremonies involving openings, anniversaries, and other special occasions. Other ceremonies are for long life, peace, abundant harvests, and good health.

Even though Shinto focuses on the present and Buddhism on the afterlife, many Shintoists follow Buddhist beliefs without apparent conflict. In Japan, it's common for marriages to be Shinto ceremonies and funerals to be Buddhist ones.

Because many Shintoists follow some Buddhist practices, some may be vegetarian. Ask about dietary restrictions when entertaining Shintoist guests. In case Shintoist colleagues practice vegetarianism or veganism, avoid giving leather gifts.

Before entering a Shinto shrine, remove hats, scarves, and sunglasses and extinguish cigarettes. Gently splash your hands and mouth with water from the container near the entrance. Don't splash water in or out of the container, and don't drink the water.

Hinduism

Hinduism is one of the world's oldest religions, and it's India's major religion, with roughly eight hundred million followers.

Unlike Asia's other major religions, one individual didn't inspire Hinduism. Instead, diverse religious, philosophical, and cultural influences let the religion evolve organically. It focuses on divinities, life after death, and how its followers should conduct their lives.

Like Buddhism, central to Hindu doctrine are the concepts of transmigration and karma. Transmigration describes what happens after death, when the soul passes to a new body. How people act in one life—their karma—determines what kind of body they'll have (human or animal) and how happy or miserable they'll be in the next life. When a person achieves spiritual perfection, upon death the soul enters *moksha*, the final level of existence.

Unlike Buddhists, Hindus worship many gods. The four most important divinities are Brahma, the creator of the universe; Vishnu, its preserver; Shiva, its destroyer; and Shiva's wife, who has many names and is goddess of motherhood and of destruction. Hindus also believe animals have souls and worship many animals as gods. Cows are the most sacred, but monkeys, snakes, and other animals are also revered.

Here are other important facts about Hinduism and tips when interacting with Hindus:

- Hindus worship as individuals rather than as a congregation.
- Most Hindu temples have a principal shrine devoted to an important god or goddess and several other shrines devoted to lesser divinities.
- Wash your feet before entering a temple.
- Some Hindu temples don't allow non-Hindus to enter the inner sanctum or even the temple itself.
- Be careful of where you sit. Worshipers reserve some seats for the gods.

- Many Hindu observances and ceremonies take place in the home. Most homes have a shrine devoted to a divinity chosen by the family, and the husband or wife conducts daily worship.
- If offered to you as a blessing, never refuse saffron powder, holy water, or food.
- Brahman priests may touch your forehead with sandalwood paste and vermillion then give a blessing. They'll expect you to donate a few rupees to the temple.
- Many Hindu temples don't allow leather. In a Hindu temple, don't wear leather shoes or belts, and don't carry leather purses, camera cases, and so on.
- Don't touch a Hindu statue or painting.
- If attending a Hindu funeral, wear white, not black.

The Hindu principle of karma is the basis for India's millennia-old caste system, which dictates the way of life for many Hindus. Karma dictates that someone's behavior in previous lives determines his or her status or caste in this life.

There are four main castes (*varnas*):
- Brahmans (priests)
- Kshatriyas (princes and warriors)
- Vaisyas (merchants and landowners)
- Sudras (farmers, laborers, and servants)

The caste system includes thousands of subcastes, each with its own rules of behavior. In addition, one large group—the Untouchables or Dalits—existed for centuries outside the caste system and ranked below the lowest caste. Hindu belief asserts karma is presumably punishing these people for past misdeeds. Some Dalits have converted to Christianity or Buddhism to repudiate a religion that considers them subhuman.

Dietary Notes

Hindu dietary restrictions vary according to region, local custom, caste, and acceptance of outside practices.
- Orthodox Hindus prefer food that people outside their caste or religion haven't touched.
- Because the cow is sacred, beef is taboo.
- Because of Hindu doctrines of nonviolence, karma, and rebirth, orthodox Hindus shun all animal and fish products—except milk and honey, which orthodox Hindus consider pure because of their nonviolent connections to the cow and bee.
- Some Hindus eat eggs.

- While westernized Hindus may drink alcohol, most Hindus don't. Always offer fruit juices or soft drinks as alternatives, especially to women.
- When in doubt, ask for preferences. The question won't offend Hindus.

Gifts
- Present gifts with both hands. Never present a gift with only your left hand.
- Fruit and candy are good gifts.
- Don't use black or white gift-wrap; use yellow, red, or green gift-wrap.
- Don't give leather products, especially cowhide.

Islam

In sixth century Mecca, Muhammad believed he was sent to guide his people and call them to worship Allah (God). His doctrine became the Islam faith. Today, as one of the world's largest religions, Islam has more than a billion followers (Muslims).

The Islam holy book, the Koran (Qur'an), contains Muhammad's teachings and revelations. One of its main teachings is that Allah is just and merciful and wishes people to repent and purify themselves so they can attain paradise after death.

To Muslims, life on earth is a period of testing and preparation for the life to come. One can attain salvation through The Five Acts of Worship or The Pillars of Islam:
- Profession of faith (*shahadah*)
- Prayer or worship (*salat*)
- Giving alms (*zakat*)
- Fasting from dawn to sunset during the holy month of Ramadan (*sawm*— Muslims joyfully celebrate the end of the long fast in a three-day festival called Eid al-Fitr.)
- Pilgrimage to Mecca, or the hajj (All able Muslims must make the pilgrimage at least once.)

Muslims pray five times daily: at dawn, at noon, in the afternoon, in the evening, and at nightfall. Friday is the day of worship, during which Muslims attend noon prayers at a mosque. At worship, Muslims ceremonially wash their faces, hands, and feet immediately before prayer. The prayer leader faces Mecca. The men stand in rows behind the prayer leader, and the women stand behind the men.

Although Islam doesn't have an organized priesthood, an imam (person chosen for piety or scholarship) usually leads prayer services and gives sermons. Any virtuous Muslim, however, may lead prayers in most mosques.

Here are other important facts about Islam and tips when interacting with Muslims:

- Mosques are for undistracted, uninterrupted prayer. A mosque's interior lacks icons or statues because Muslims believe it's blasphemous to imitate the work of Allah.
- Always pronounce *Muslim* "MUHZ-lim," never "MAHZ-lim." Don't use the spelling *Moslem*.
- Never call Islam "Muhammadanism" and its followers "Muhammadans." Muslims don't worship Muhammad.
- Orthodoxy among Muslims varies just as it does among Hindus and Buddhists. Not all Muslim women wear hijabs, not all Muslims abstain from drinking alcohol, and so on.
- When entertaining or hosting Muslims, discreetly ask whether they'd like time to pray. Prepare a quiet place for them to do so, and politely indicate which way is Mecca.

Body Language

- Many observant Muslims don't touch members of the opposite sex outside the family. If you're a woman, don't take offense if a Muslim man doesn't shake your hand.
- As a display of humility, devout Muslims may avoid looking into your eyes.
- Don't touch anyone, especially a child, on the head.
- To Muslims, the left hand is unclean. Don't eat, pass things, or gesture with your left hand, even if you're left-handed. You can use both hands when it's absolutely necessary (lifting something heavy, for instance).
- Be careful with your feet. The foot is the lowest part of the body and thus is unclean. Don't touch or move objects with your feet. Don't point or gesture at anything with your foot. Don't cross your legs or stretch your legs straight out in front of you. Keep your feet on the floor; never prop them on a desk or chair.

Dietary Notes

- Food that Muslims may eat is *halal*, meaning lawful. For meat to be *halal*, the animal must have been slaughtered in a certain way.
- Pork is not *halal*; avoid serving ham, bacon, pâté, hotdogs, or sausage. Avoid food prepared with lard—this can include piecrusts and other pastries.
- If hosting a banquet that includes Muslim guests, it's a good idea to avoid offering any pork dishes, because the other dishes might become contaminated in preparation or serving.

- Don't serve crab or lobster. Shellfish and fish without fins aren't *halal*. Fish is an acceptable alternative.
- Observant Muslims don't consume alcoholic beverages.
- Avoid food cooked in alcohol, even if it has evaporated in cooking.
- For toasts, serve fruit juices to Muslims who can't consume alcoholic beverages.

A business acquaintance once told me about his trip to Malaysia for which he should have better prepared. He had scheduled to arrive on Thursday afternoon and depart on Sunday. Upon arrival, he phoned several companies, asking if he could make a courtesy call the following day.

To his dismay, he couldn't get a single appointment. The companies he wished to visit were Muslim run and were closed from noon Friday until noon Saturday. He left Sunday morning without having made a single contact.

Gifts
- Give and receive gifts with your right hand or with both hands.
- A high-quality compass makes an excellent gift for Muslims, who must face Mecca for prayers.
- Don't give alcoholic beverages or perfumes that contain alcohol.
- Don't give pigskin products or anything that contains pork.
- Don't give toy dogs or pictures of dogs. To Muslims, the dog is unclean.
- Don't give artwork depicting the human body, especially nude or partially nude females.

When Visiting a Mosque
Mosques strictly enforce the rules, and few are open to nonbelievers. When entering a mosque, follow these guidelines:
- Greet the person at the door with a salaam (a low bow while touching the right hand to the forehead).
- If you haven't been invited to the mosque, ask the greeter's permission before entering.
- Take off your shoes at the entrance and put them in the shoe rack (if provided).
- Wash your hands and face in the adjacent tiled washing area.
- If provided a robe, put it on.
- Kneel on prayer rugs facing Mecca.
- Women must cover their heads in a mosque.

- A woman should never touch a man in a mosque. If she does, he must rewash his hands and face.

Christianity

Although to many Asians Christianity has the stigma of being a Western belief, the number of Christian converts in Asia has steadily increased over the last few decades. Today, Christian Asians number over a quarter billion.

Many Christian Asians have adapted liturgical elements to suit their cultures. For example, some use drums and dance during services, and some Asian artists have combined Christian themes with Asian images.

Here are other important facts about Christianity and tips when interacting with Christians is Asia:

- Most Christians celebrate the Sabbath on Sunday.
- Most Christian churches welcome nonmember participation in their services. Ask before you take Communion. Some churches invite all participants to partake in Communion, and some allow only members of the faith to partake.
- Few Christian groups have dress restrictions or requirements for members.
- Most Christians don't have dietary restrictions except during Lent. Some Christian groups forbid consumption of alcohol or caffeine.
- Unless you know someone very well, it's best to avoid giving a Christian a religious gift.

Catholicism

Over 90 percent of the Philippines' population is Christian, and nearly of all of them are Catholic.

- Non-Catholics are invited to participate in every part of Mass except Communion. Only Catholics are allowed to receive Communion.
- If non-Catholics wish a priest's blessing, they should cross their arms across their chests and approach the altar with the communicants. A priest or deacon can administer a blessing, but a layperson distributing Communion can't.
- Catholics are required to abstain from eating meat only on Ash Wednesday and on Fridays during Lent. Ash Wednesday and Good Friday are also fast days, on which adults eat two small meals and one regular meal, and no food between meals. Some Catholics choose to abstain from eating meat on Fridays throughout the year.

Ancestor Worship

Confucians, Shintoists, and others venerate ancestors, but not to the level of those who practice ancestor worship.

Common in China and Vietnam as well as other places, this practice believes in an afterlife and a spirit world. It holds that the living can communicate with the dead. If a family worships its ancestors' spirits, it'll be rewarded with prosperity and good fortune. Most ancestor worship takes place at shrines in the home and at ancestors' graves.

Many followers of ancestor worship also follow another religion, like Buddhism. Never imply that ancestor worship is a backward or silly custom.

Ancestor worship doesn't dictate a specific diet, and there are no gifts to avoid giving those who practice it.

Animism and Feng Shui

Animism is a belief system that gives inanimate objects and natural phenomena conscious life and souls. These spirits can influence others positively or negatively.

People in many parts of Asia practice some form of animism, often in combination with another religion. Among its best-known adherents are the Chinese of Hong Kong, who use feng shui (pronounced "fung shway")—a practice that governs the positioning of buildings, doors, and windows as well as objects like desks, beds, chairs, and even people. The goal of feng shui is to harmonize with spiritual forces that inhabit the objects and create positive chi (pronounced "chee") or energy.

Although you may not believe in feng shui, if you want to do business in Hong Kong and some parts of China, respect this tradition. Many Westerners have ignored or dismissed it with disastrous results: Followers simply won't do business without feng shui approval. Even recruiting employees is difficult if a workplace violates feng shui principles.

> In 2005, the Walt Disney Company consulted a feng shui master when constructing Hong Kong Disneyland. Using the practitioner's advice, the company redesigned and added several features to insure the flow of positive chi.

Before opening a factory, office, or other facility in areas that practice feng shui, first consult a feng shui practitioner for advice on facility and entrance locations as well as moving and opening dates. The practitioner will position furniture and equipment to harmonize with cosmic forces and bring blessings and good luck to the business. Ask a local businessperson for the contact information of a reliable feng shui practitioner.

Animism and feng shui don't dictate a specific diet. Before purchasing a gift for someone who practices feng shui, consult a reputable feng shui practitioner. This person will likely ask you detailed questions about the recipient and the nature of the gift, then guide you to a lovely gift.

An American executive with years of international experience was sent to Hong Kong to open a branch of his bank. After he furnished an elegant office suite, his Chinese employees expressed concern about the position of his furniture, especially his desk. It faced the door, a direction that invited evil spirits to cause trouble.

After much discussion, he agreed to place a plant between his desk and the door to appease his employees—and, he hoped, to end all talk of evil spirits.

He soon left on vacation, and on his return he found the office in turmoil: The once-healthy plant was dead. He immediately rearranged his furniture per feng shui principles and now advises others to consult a feng shui practitioner before decorating their offices.

Tradition and Superstition

Tradition and superstition play integral parts in Asian society. For business success in Asia, you'll need to respect both.

Astrology

The Chinese zodiac has a twelve-year cycle. Each year is named after a different animal (like tiger, rat, or monkey) that imparts distinct characteristics.

Advocates of Chinese astrology believe a person's birth year best determines his or her personality traits, physical and mental attributes, and degree of success and happiness. Many won't enter into a marriage without knowing whether the proposed partner has a compatible sign.

Numbers and Colors

Many numbers and colors have special meanings that vary among Asian countries. These superstitions are important to many people—and not observing them could offend your Asian colleagues. To learn what colors and numbers bring good or bad luck in a certain country, check the gift section of that country's chapter in this book.

Here are a few examples of numbers and colors with special meanings:

> The Beijing Olympics are scheduled to begin at 8:00 PM on August 8, 2008—a very lucky number indeed.

Numbers

- The Cantonese (spoken in Hong Kong and southern China) word for "one" sounds like the word for "assured." It's especially lucky when combined with the number eight, which means "prosperity."
- Three is a lucky number in Thailand and Hong Kong. In these countries, give gifts in threes.
- Four is bad luck in Japan, Korea, China, and Hong Kong, where the word for "four" sounds like the word for "death." Many buildings (including the hotels at Hong Kong Disneyland) give another number to fourth floors (for example, "upper three") and never number rooms "four."
- The Cantonese word for "six" is a homonym for the word for "deer," a symbol of longevity.
- Nine is a lucky number in Hong Kong. The Cantonese word for "nine" sounds like the word for "eternity."
- Give odd numbers of items for gifts, if possible.

> Although during his reign Mao Zedong tried to stamp out numerology as a backward tradition, the practice grew.
>
> Having "lucky" numbers isn't only a nod to Chinese tradition; it's also a status symbol. For example, in Guangzhou, China, the government auctions off license plate numbers. The highest winning bid at a 2006 auction was 2,932,000 yuan—that's US $366,500—for the plate AC6688. The Chinese believe the number four, associated with death, is a very unlucky number to have on one's license plate, especially as the last number (in which case the "final thought" is "death").
>
> Chinese cell phone companies sell "lucky" phone numbers, and one regional airline reportedly paid over two million yuan (US $300,000) for the telephone number 8888 8888.

Colors

- Don't wear white to an Asian wedding or any celebration. Although white may symbolize purity, throughout much of Asia it's the color of mourning and sorrow.
- Don't wear purple to a wedding in Japan. The Japanese believe the color fades and might make the couple's happiness fade.
- Green represents Islam, but in Malaysia (which has a substantial Muslim population), it's associated with disease. In China, however, green represents health and harmony.
- Red means anger in Indonesia, and South Koreans may associate the color with Communism. Although red indicates happiness and joy to the Chinese and Japanese, never write a person's name in red ink; doing so represents a wish for the person to die. Also, because brides in China wear red, women shouldn't wear red to Chinese weddings.
- Black symbolizes violence in Indonesia. In China, black and white are the colors used in funerals.
- In China, yellow is the imperial color. It means happiness in Indonesia.

During Christmas week in Tokyo, everything seemed wonderful for the investment community. The share market appeared to have boundless energy, and the Nikkei Stock Average had soared to a spectacular all-time high.

Then investors took a closer look at the numbers. Uh-oh.

The overnight close had been 38,915.87. In Japanese numerology, the number 389 bears a phonetic resemblance to the word *sa ba ku* ("desert"). The number 15 suggests the word *i ko*, meaning "to go," and number 87 suggests the word *wa na*, meaning "a trap." Some mystical force warned, "You are heading into a trap and will be left in the desert."

That day was December 29, 1989. From its peak, the market would plummet some 63 percent, trapping hundreds of thousands of investors in a financial wasteland from which they have yet to escape.

Part II

COUNTRY INFORMATION

BANGLADESH
PEOPLE'S REPUBLIC OF BANGLADESH

Greetings from Bangladesh

Greetings from the land of fantastic natural beauty and exotic wildlife. Elephants still roam free in the east, and the endangered Royal Bengal Tigers (our most famous native animal) wander in the southwest.

Although an independent Bangladeshi state has existed for only the last few decades, our culture is millennia old. Small Buddhist and Hindu kingdoms controlled the land until Muslim conquests began in the early thirteenth century. In 1757, the British East India Company took control; a century later, they ceded power to the British government.

The United Kingdom ruled the area until 1947, when the independent nations of India and Pakistan were formed. The rest of the area was divided into two regions, separated by Indian territory: the largely Muslim East Bengal (later renamed East Pakistan) and the largely Hindu West Bengal (West Pakistan). These regions differed markedly in language, ethnicity, and culture.

Since the creation of the regions, the people of East Pakistan (the Bengalis) desired independence from West Bengal. They got their wish. After a nine-month civil war in 1971, Bangladesh finally became an independent nation.

Although we Bangladeshis formed our nation as a secular state, we have one of the world's largest Muslim populations. More than 80 percent of our population is Muslim. Our attachment to folk traditions enriches our devotion to Islam. We frequently consult *Ojha* (shamans) and *fakirs* (Muslim holy men who perform exorcisms and faith healings). And despite becoming increasingly rare and discouraged, polygamy is still officially legal.

Many Westerners think Bangladesh is an overcrowded, poor country. It is true that almost half of Bangladeshis live in poverty. But steady economic growth has encouraged us, and Chittagong has been an important trading port for centuries.

We know our population is growing too quickly for young people to find good local jobs. Many must leave to work in places like Saudi Arabia and Malaysia. But they still keep strong family ties. In fact, money sent home from expatriate Bangladeshis accounted for 6 percent of our gross domestic product in 2004. We believe these funds will help give us the means to continue to grow and improve.

Although 80 percent of us live in rural areas, urbanization rates are rising and pollution has become a problem in our cities. We are working hard to solve the problem with programs for reducing emissions and other methods.

We know that education is the key to our future. We have embraced literacy programs and have seen first hand how education can improve lives. Our government is working toward attaining 100 percent literacy in the next decade.

While we obviously want the comforts and advantages that more developed countries enjoy, we do not want to lose our culture. Bangladeshis respect age, position, and hierarchy, and believe the group is more important than the individual. Although its influence is diminishing, social class is still very important to us. We highly value friendship and do not extend our friendship casually.

We are fatalistic. When things go wrong, we will not panic or get angry. More commonly, we will shrug and say, "As Allah wills." But we are also hardworking and friendly. Please come to our beautiful, ancient land and find out for yourself.

Vital Statistics

Population	147,365,352
Capital	Dhaka
Area	55,599 square miles, slightly smaller than Iowa
Government	Parliamentary democracy
Living Standard	GDP = US $2,100 per capita
Natural Resources	Natural gas, arable land, timber, coal
Agriculture	Rice, jute, tea, wheat, sugarcane, potatoes, tobacco, pulses, oilseeds, spices, fruit, beef, milk, poultry
Industries	Cotton textiles, jute, garments, tea processing, paper newsprint, cement, chemical fertilizer, light engineering, sugar
Climate	Tropical; cool, mild winter; hot, humid summer. The monsoon season runs from June through October and brings most of the annual rainfall. Floods and frequent cyclones are severe enough to dampen development and the economy.
Currency	Taka (BDT)

The People	
Correct Name	noun: Bangladeshi(s)
	adjective: Bangladeshi
Ethnic Makeup	Bengali 98%, tribal groups, non-Bengali Muslims, 2%
Languages	Bangla (official—also known as Bengali), English
Religions	Muslim 80%, Hindu 13%, other 1%

Meeting and Greeting

Bangladeshis are hospitable and enjoy meeting new people, especially foreigners.

- As a greeting, men and women commonly salaam (a low bow while touching the right hand to the forehead) to one another and among themselves.
- Men may also lightly shake hands with other men. They rarely shake hands with (or otherwise touch) women, especially in public.
- Western women may extend a hand to Bangladeshi women in urban areas or to those used to interacting with Westerners. (In villages, however, the women may be too shy to shake hands and would prefer a nod instead.)

   Western men should wait for Bangladeshi women to extend a hand (which is unlikely). If a woman doesn't extend her hand, simply nod to her.
- Western women shouldn't extend a hand to Bangladeshi men. Some traditions forbid touching between sexes, especially in public. If a Bangladeshi man extends his hand to a foreign woman, she may shake it.
- If possible, have a respected third party introduce you.

Names and Titles

- Bangladeshi name order is first name (given name) + last name (surname). Some women, however, have only first names.
- Bangladeshis address one another by courtesy title + last name. Either Bangla titles or English titles (Mr., Mrs., or Miss) are acceptable.
- It's acceptable to address someone by courtesy title only, especially when you don't know a person's last name.
- People of the same age and class generally use first names. Don't use first names until your Bangladeshi colleagues do so.
- When addressing older people or people with authority, Bangladeshis add honorary suffixes to first names to show esteem and the level of closeness. Bangladeshis don't expect foreigners to use these suffixes, but they'll appreciate the show of respect if visitors use them.

English	Bangla	Pronunciation
Mr.	*Bahadur*	(bah-ha-DUR)
Mrs. or Madam (less common)	*Begum*	(BEH-gum)

Suffix	Meaning	Pronunciation	Situations When Used
-b'ai	"brother"	(bye)	Addressing an older man or a man with authority
-bhabi	"wife of older brother"	(BAH-bih)	Addressing a friend's wife
-apa	"older sister"	(UP-uh)	Addressing an older woman or a woman with authority

Language

Bangladesh's official language is Bangla (Bengali), which descended from Sanskrit and was influenced by the Persian, Arabic, Turkish, and English languages. The Bengali alphabet is derived from the Brahmi alphabet, the ancestor of modern Indian alphabets.

A number of Bangla dialects are spoken across the country, and small ethnic groups speak their own languages.

In the mid–twentieth century, language become a point of contention between East and West Pakistan. When the West Pakistan–dominated government excluded Bangla as an official language, the Bengalis used the slight to rally for an independent state (now Bangladesh).

- Bangladeshis with a university education usually speak English. When doing business with Westerners, most speak English.
- Many young Bangladeshis understand Hindi (because of the language's prevalence in media).
- Written Bangla is read just like written English (that is, left to right, top to bottom).

> In 1913, Rabindranath Tagore was the first Asian to win the Nobel Prize in Literature. He wrote poetry in his native tongue.

Conversation

- Bangladeshis consider indirect language polite and sophisticated. For example, they say, "That will be difficult" instead of "no."

- Bangladeshis appreciate flowery, expressive speech, but they don't appreciate jokes or sarcasm.
- Use a soft, modulated tone when speaking. Bangladeshis consider loudness impolite.

Acceptable topics
- Sports, especially football (soccer) and cricket
- Hindi movies (very popular in Bangladesh)
- Travel
- Your home country (but never compare your country to Bangladesh)

Unacceptable topics
- Someone's profession or family (although you may discuss them after establishing a personal relationship): It's particularly rude to ask a man about his wife.
- Any criticisms of elders or people of high status

Topics that require sensitivity
- Bangladesh's history and current relationships with Pakistan and India
- Interfaith relationships

Body Language
- Don't expect Bangladeshis to return a smile. Although friendly, they don't smile as often as Americans do. They often consider smiling a sign of immaturity.
- Bangladeshis generally don't touch one another while speaking. When talking with a peer of the same sex, they stand closely to one another. When talking with someone of a different status, they stand farther apart. When talking with someone of the opposite sex, they never stand close together.
- Never touch someone of the opposite sex in public.
- When speaking with peers, maintain eye contact. Bangladeshis believe eye contact shows sincerity. When addressing older people or senior colleagues, however, look down to show respect.
- Rural women may not make eye contact with men at a first meeting.
- Don't cross your legs or show your soles. Doing either is disrespectful.
- Don't touch anything with your foot. Bangladeshis consider it disrespectful to touch anything with the lowest part of the body, especially books or other written materials (which may contain sacred references).
- Point with your chin rather than with your hand or finger.

- Never pass or move anything with your left hand. Bangladeshis consider the left hand unclean.
- Don't gesture to beckon adults; Bangladeshis believe doing so is rude. If you must beckon a child, motion with your hand (palm face-down and fingers together).
- To Bangladeshis, the "okay" sign is crude, and the thumbs-up gesture indicates rejection.
- Don't blink at people; Bangladeshis think blinking is rude.

Phrases

Bangla uses the Bengali alphabet and there's no standard transliteration into English. Below are the phonetic equivalents.

English	Bangla	Pronunciation
Hello (literally, "peace be upon you")	*Assalam walaikum*	(uss-UH-luhm wuh-LIE-koom)
And peace be upon you (response to "peace be upon you")	*Walaikum assalam*	(wuh-LIE-koom uss-UH-luhm)
Please	*Onugraha kore*	(oh-new-gruh-HUH kor-eh)
Thank you	*Dhanyabad*	(DOH-nah bad)
You're welcome	*Apnakeo dhanyabad*	(uhp-NAH-kay DOH-nah bad)
Yes	*Zee ha'a*	(jee HAH)
No	*Na*	(nah)
Excuse me	*Kichu mone korben na*	(KEE-chew MOH-nay KOR-ben nah)
Goodbye (literally, "may God be with you")	*Khoda hafez*	(koh-DAH ha-fez)
Nice to meet you	*Porichito hoye valo laglo*	(pohr-EE-chee-toh HOH-yeh VAH-loh lah-GLO)
How are you?	*Kemon achen?*	(kah-MOHN AH-chen)

Note: For Hindi phrases, see page 156.

Dining

Bangladeshi cuisine is known for its tantalizing blend of wonderful, fragrant spices, as well as its numerous sweets made from milk.

- Bangladeshis serve many foods from a communal plate.
- Many Bangladeshis eat with their right hands (left hands are unclean because they're used for personal hygiene). They may eat sweets with a spoon.
- Visitors may ask to use utensils.
- There may be a separate plate to place bones and other food refuse.
- During meals, men and women may be segregated (common at formal occasions).
- Be prepared for little to no conversation. Bangladeshis are usually silent while eating.

Drinking

Bangladeshis commonly drink soft drinks, fruit juices, lassi (a yogurt-based drink), and tea—especially chai (spiced tea with milk). Bangladesh produces only 2 percent of the world's tea supply, but tea is a vital part of the country's economy.

Although most Bangladeshis are Muslim, many drink alcohol. In fact, most hotels have bars. Nonetheless, don't order or request an alcoholic beverage unless your Bangladeshi colleagues do so first or offer you one.

Toasting

Toasting isn't a common custom in Bangladesh. If dining with traditional Bangladeshis, don't propose a toast.

If dining with Bangladeshis who are familiar with Western toasting etiquette and will receive toasts well, men or women may propose a short toast to friendship or other appropriate subjects.

Tipping

- Restaurants: The bill usually doesn't include a service charge. Bangladeshis rarely tip servers, but servers may expect Westerners to tip 5 percent of the bill.
- Taxis: Tip BDT5 to BDT10.
- Bellhops: Tip BDT20 to BDT50.
- Porters, doormen, hair stylists, and barbers: Tip BDT50 to BDT100.

Manners

Bangladeshis expect calm, serious behavior. Make sure your comportment falls in line.

- Never refuse an invitation directly. If you must decline an invitation, say, "That will be difficult, but I will try" or "I will have to see."
- Remove your shoes before entering a home, mosque, or temple.
- Always wash your hands before eating. If a home or restaurant doesn't provide an obvious hand-washing area, ask where you should wash your hands.
- No one eats until the oldest person at the table begins eating.
- If eating with your hands, never eat or pass food with the left hand. Also, don't let your fingers touch the sauces when dipping food. See pages 39–40 for more information on eating with your hands.

> Although the caste system in Bangladesh isn't as established as it is in India, some Bangladeshis won't accept items that someone of a lower caste hands to them.

- Hosts will urge guests to eat. To decline additional helpings, politely praise the food and say, "I'm full."
- Some Bangladeshis eat meals in their homes sitting on the floor. In this case, men sit with legs crossed in front, and women sit with legs to one side. Be careful not to direct your soles at anyone while in this position.
- Don't smoke in the presence of an older person or senior colleague, whether or not he or she smokes.
- Don't eat, drink, or smoke on the street during Ramadan (the ninth month of the Islamic year). Doing so is offensive.
- When dining in a restaurant with friends or family, the bill may be split or the person who extended the invitation may pay. If the latter, the others will protest but out of courtesy only. The person, in turn, should insist on paying.

  In business situations, however, the person who extended the invitation pays the bill.
- It's rude to give an end time on an invitation for a social event.
- It's very rude to refuse an offer of tea.

Punctuality

Bangladeshis believe promptness shows respect. Arrive on time for business appointments to prove your dedication to creating or maintaining a business relationship.

Arrive on time for social events as well. Although hosts may serve dinner several hours after the given "start time," they may have scheduled entertainment before the meal.

Dress

Bangladeshi men in urban areas often wear Western fashions. Some rural men wear a *lungi* (a circular piece of cloth knotted at the waist) with a *genji* (sleeveless vest). Some men wear special white clothing for prayer and religious rituals.

Most Bangladeshi women wear traditional dress. Many never wear slacks. For daily wear, they often don an outfit called *shalwar kameez* (long blouse, pajama-like pants, and shawl). For formal occasions, they usually wear a sari (long piece of printed cloth wrapped around the waist and over the head or shoulder). Many wear jewelry as accessories and as a sign of wealth. Many Muslim women don't wear veils, especially in the cities.

Western women should dress conservatively. They should never wear tight clothing and should make sure their shoulders are covered and skirt hemlines fall below the knee. Open-toed shoes aren't acceptable. While Bangladeshis may expect native women to cover their heads, they don't expect Western women to do so.

- For business, men wear slacks with short-sleeved shirts, although they wear lightweight suits to initial meetings and important occasions. Women wear tailored suits (fitted not too tightly and skirt hemline falling below the knee).
- For casual occasions and at restaurants, men wear trousers with dressy shirts. Women wear dresses or skirts with blouses. Many wear *shalwar kameez*.
- For men and women, wearing shorts or dressing shabbily is never acceptable when in public.

Gifts

- Bangladeshis believe the thought behind giving a gift matters more than the gift itself. Nonetheless, they expect recipients to reciprocate with a tangible gift or an invitation to a meal or event.
- People generally don't open gifts in the giver's presence. Recipients thank the giver sincerely and put gifts aside to open later.
- Bangladeshis in urban areas give birthday gifts, but people in rural areas may not.
- Make sure gifts are nicely wrapped, and always present gifts with both hands.
- Never give Muslims alcoholic beverages or items that aren't *halal* (lawful to the Islamic faith). Never give Hindus items containing beef or cow leather.

Hostess Gifts

Along with giving a gift, invite the hostess to an occasion if possible.

Consider giving
- Pastries
- High-quality chocolates or other sweets
- Travel books
- Gifts from your home region
- Flowers, except frangipani or any white flowers (for funerals only)

Don't give
- Obviously expensive items (difficult to reciprocate)
- Tobacco

Business Gifts

- Giving a small, inexpensive gift to a Bangladeshi colleague is a token of goodwill.
- Gifts that feature your company logo are acceptable.
- Although not compulsory, business colleagues may give gifts on religious holidays, especially after Ramadan and hajj.

Consider giving
- Office supplies
- Sweets to share

Don't give

- Obviously expensive items (difficult to reciprocate and may be considered bribes)

Health and Safety

- Be aware that medical facilities in Bangladesh are below U.S. standards. There is no emergency medical care system in the nation, and emergency cases may have to be transported to Singapore or Bangkok.
- Prescription medicines purchased in Bangladesh may be unavailable or untrustworthy. Make sure to pack an ample supply of your medications.
- See page 373 to obtain updated information on recommended vaccines and medical preparations for visiting Bangladesh.
- Especially in urban areas, don't carry large sums of money, wear expensive jewelry, or walk alone after dark (streetlights are rare). Pickpocketing and snatch-and-grab crime is common.
- Always store valuables in your hotel's safe.
- Don't drive in Bangladesh. Roads are narrow, poorly maintained, and extremely crowded. If you get into a traffic accident, a crowd will quickly gather and

Although Bangladesh is a beautiful country with many wonderful, peaceful people, violence is overshadowing the nation.

For example, the radical Islamist group Jama'atul Mujahideen Bangladesh (JMB) has claimed responsibility for a number of bomb attacks over the past few years. On August 17, 2005, JMB coordinated 459 bomb blasts in a single hour across most of Bangladesh, killing two people and injuring several dozen. JMB calls for Bangladesh to institute strict Islamic law and names the United States and the United Kingdom as enemies of Bangladesh.

In addition, Reporters Without Borders reported in 2004 that more journalists were attacked or threatened in Bangladesh than in any other country. Human rights activists have also been attacked.

These and other security concerns have prompted the U.S. Embassy in Bangladesh to advise Americans to avoid travel to certain districts in the country. Before your trip, check with the embassy or the U.S. Department of State to receive updated information and warnings.

judge the more affluent party to be at fault—a potentially dangerous situation for you.

- Don't hire rickshaws or "baby taxis" (small three-wheel taxis). Neither is safe.
- Avoid using ferries; their safety record isn't good. Many people die every year from capsized ferries.

Corporate Culture

Bangladesh is working to modernize, and there's been steady 5 percent growth over the last several years. But inefficient state-owned enterprises, inadequate port facilities, delays in exploiting natural gas reserves, and a corrupt government at all levels make modernization a struggle.

Small and medium-size businesses employ about 25 percent of the total labor force in Bangladesh (80 percent of industrial jobs) and constitute 25 percent of the gross domestic product (GDP).

The service sector generates half of the GDP, but the agriculture sector employs nearly two-thirds of Bangladeshis.

Structure
- Bangladeshis expect leaders to be parent figures, whose subordinates expect and appreciate strong leadership.
- The most senior executive makes the decisions that are best for the entire group. Foreigners who hope to decentralize the decision-making process must be patient and persistent.

Meetings
- Initial meetings are for getting acquainted, not for doing business. Have a respected third party introduce you to meeting participants.
- Subsequent meetings are for presenting decisions. The most senior person sets the agenda, content, and pace.
- Small talk over tea usually precedes meetings. Let your Bangladeshi colleagues initiate business discussions.
- Bangladeshis believe taking notes expresses respect and acceptance, but they may consider written agendas just guidelines.
- Meetings end when all relevant business is completed, which may be well after the stated end time.
- With that said, meetings may end without obvious resolution of problems. Don't show impatience or frustration.

Appointments

- Regular office hours are 9:00 AM to 5:00 PM, Saturday through Thursday. Some offices close at noon on Saturdays. Offices are closed on Fridays.
- You can't do business during a *hartal* (nationwide strike to show political protest). During a *hartal*, industries and offices close and public transportation stops. Fortunately, political parties usually announce *hartals* ahead of time. When in Bangladesh, check local English-language media for the dates of upcoming *hartals*, and plan meetings accordingly.
- When scheduling initial meetings, it's extremely important to give your title and credentials. Some Bangladeshis refuse to meet with someone of lower rank or status. Likewise, you may lose face if you meet with a Bangladeshi of considerably lower rank or status.

Communication

- Always defer to the most senior person.
- Keep your feelings in check. Showing emotion causes you to lose face (and thus respect), especially when talking with someone older or more senior than yourself.
- While Bangladeshis respect age and status, never bully or talk down to people. They'll especially resent condescending foreigners.
- Communication must follow the appropriate hierarchy. Don't try to skip levels, which will make everyone involved lose face.
- You won't get direct answers to questions, so ask them in several different ways to make sure you understand the real answer. Bangladeshis believe direct communication is rude and direct disagreement causes loss of face.
- It's essential to always be courteous to the receptionist and other office staff. They control appointments and communication with high-level employees.

Business Cards

- Bangladeshis exchange business cards upon first meeting.
- Make sure your card includes your academic degree(s) and formal title.
- Present your business card with your right hand only.
- Accept someone's card respectfully with your right hand only. Read it carefully, then place it in your briefcase or business card case.
- Be sure to present your business card to the receptionist upon arrival.

Be Aware

- Whom you know is as important as what you know. To make connections, you must interact one-on-one. This means you need to understand at least the basics of Bangladeshi culture and a few words of the local language.
- Confidence and trust motivate Bangladeshis. Always let people save face.
- Bangladeshis expect formal behavior; they consider casual behavior disrespectful.
- Bangladeshis may not take deadlines seriously. If deadlines are important, closely monitor a project's progress.
- Government officials expect great deference and respect.
- Corruption, including extortion and bribery, is a serious problem in Bangladesh.

Socializing

- Bangladeshis do business entertaining both at home and in restaurants.
- They sometimes include spouses in business functions.
- It's good manners to host a meal at a restaurant for your Bangladeshi colleagues. Hotel restaurants are usually appropriate.

Especially for Women

Many more women than men in Bangladesh live in poverty, suffer abuse, and are in poor health. Women don't have the same educational and economic opportunities as men have. As a result, the literacy rate for women is roughly half that for men. Workplaces are highly patriarchal, and many women are unemployed.

Middle-class women are leading the fight for gender equality, and the Bangladeshi government has taken steps toward that goal. The constitution guarantees men *and* women equal rights (although women's rights aren't always enforced). The number of girls enrolling in school has been rising, at least on the primary level.

Of the women who do work, a large number of them work in export-oriented industries (garments, for example), which compose 70 percent of

Rokeya Sakhawat Hussain was an author and activist who, in the early twentieth century, worked for gender equality in Bengal (now Bangladesh). She established the first school for Muslim girls, and among her several works was *Sultana's Dream*, a story about gender role reversal.

the nation's foreign exchange. Thus, women are undeniably an important part of the Bangladeshi economy. Grandparents or older siblings traditionally provide childcare when a mother works.

- Western women may have some difficulty doing business in Bangladesh, but Bangladeshis generally accept them.
- It's acceptable for a Western woman to invite a Bangladeshi man to a business dinner at a restaurant. She should arrange payment with the wait staff beforehand.
- Women should avoid making eye contact with people while walking on streets. They'll attract unwanted attention if they do.

Holidays and Festivals

January	New Year's Day (1)
February	Shaheed Day (21)
March	Independence and National Day (26)
April	Bengali Solar New Year (13, 14, or 15)
May	Labor Day (1)
July	Bank Holiday (first Monday)
August	National Mourning Day (15)*
November	National Revolution Day (7)*
December	Victory Day (16)
	Christmas Day (25)
	Boxing Day (26)
	New Year's Eve (31)

* Actual date depends upon the party in power.

Notes: Islamic and Hindu holidays vary with the Islamic and Hindu calendars. Check when they're observed for the year you're traveling to Bangladesh.

   Hindis generally participate in Islamic festivals in their community, and Muslims participate in Hindu festivals.

CHINA
PEOPLE'S REPUBLIC OF CHINA

Greetings from China

Greetings from one of the world's oldest living civilizations. With one-fifth of the world's population, ours is also the most populous country. We are urbanizing rapidly, and the number of large cities is growing.

We are not a single monolithic country with a single market, but a collection of provinces, regions, and municipalities. We are proud of our regional differences. Each area's language, cuisine, and culture are unique.

Our reliance on pace, energy, and change have led to staggering accomplishments in the last half-century. During the 1960s, life expectancy in China doubled to seventy years. Since 1978, more than two hundred million Chinese have risen out of poverty—a feat we believe no other nation has accomplished. We joined the World Trade Organization in 2001, and now we are getting ready to host the 2008 Olympics.

We revere age, rank, and belonging to a group. Our focus is the family. While our government officially discourages its practice, religion—especially Buddhism, Taoism, and Confucianism—still strongly influences traditional Chinese life.

To the dismay of the older generation, our youth are finding more interest in the present than in our history and traditions. They are becoming increasingly success oriented. More young people are wearing blue jeans and sunglasses, drinking Coca-Cola, and driving motorbikes. Big cities especially are westernized. People spend their evenings in discos, dancing and singing karaoke. Many are studying English, and it is easy to find someone who speaks English in large cities.

Our society is growing more affluent. The large American investment bank Morgan Stanley estimates that by 2020, three hundred million Chinese (about 40 percent of the population) will be middle class. As our middle class grows, the individual is becoming more important than the group. Some of us worry our increasing prosperity is creating elitism. Those wealthy enough are flocking to gated communities. They often use material items like clothes, cars and drivers, and servants as symbols to demonstrate rank.

Many Westerners believe our human rights record is abysmal—and many of us agree. Our constitution is more an aspiration than an accomplishment, and our government does not follow it.

The Chinese were once world leaders in both art and science. Chinese inventions and innovations include silk cloth, gunpowder, paper making, moveable type, the compass, and the seismoscope.

Repression of personal freedoms, regional income inequalities, reproductive restrictions, gender inequalities, an aging population, and epidemics of deadly diseases (namely, HIV/AIDS) are just a few societal problems we face.

We also know our environmental problems are gargantuan. Our decisions have contributed to air pollution, acid rain, soil erosion, water shortages, water pollution, and deforestation. As the world has learned, borders do not restrict one country's environmental problems. Our difficulties affect the entire world, and we are working to solve the problem.

Westerners, especially Americans, do not think as we do. Millennia-old ideas shape our way of life. Unlike the United States, our nation has had dynastic rule, foreign invasion and occupation, and civil war—just in the last century. We adapted to all these situations, and we have adapted to our present government.

We admit we need more interaction with foreigners. But we dislike dealing with strangers, and we never want to appear to rely on outside help, especially from Americans. If you wish to do business in China, you must do things our way. There are no shortcuts. You must take the time to get to know our people. You will need to have ample patience and a long-term view. It may take months to reach an agreement.

We are a proud people. We do not like to lose face as individuals or as a nation. We do not expect visitors to learn our language, but we do expect them to learn about our culture. Show us the respect we deserve and always keep an open mind. When we get to know you, we generally like you very much and are eager to do business.

Population	1,313,973,713
Capital	Beijing
Area	3,705,407 square miles, slightly smaller than the United States
Government	Communist state, consisting of 23 provinces, 5 autonomous regions, and 4 municipalities
Living Standard	GDP = US $2,280 per capita
Natural Resources	Coal, iron ore, petroleum, natural gas, mercury, tin, tungsten, antimony, manganese, molybdenum, vanadium, magnetite, aluminum, lead, zinc, uranium, hydropower potential (world's largest)
Agriculture	Rice, wheat, potatoes, corn, peanuts, tea, millet, barley, apples, cotton, oilseed, pork, fish
Industries	Mining and ore processing, iron, steel, aluminum, other metals, coal, machine building, armaments, textiles and apparel, petroleum, cement, chemicals, fertilizers, consumer products (including footwear, toys, and electronics), food processing, transportation equipment (including automobiles, rail cars and locomotives, ships, and aircraft), telecommunications equipment, commercial space launch vehicles, satellites
Climate	Tropical in south and subarctic in north
Currency	Yuan (CNY); also referred to as the Renminbi (RMB)

The People

Correct Name	noun: Chinese
	adjective: Chinese
Ethnic Makeup	Han 91.9%, Zhuang, Uygur, Hui, Yi, Tibetan, Miao, Manchu, Mongol, Buyi, Korean, and other nationalities 8.1%
Languages	Standard Chinese or Mandarin (Putonghua, based on the Beijing dialect), Yue (Cantonese), Wu (Shanghaiese), Minbei (Fuzhou), Minnan (Hokkien-Taiwanese), Xiang, Gan, Hakka dialects, other minority languages
Religions	Taoist, Buddhist, Christian (3–4%), Muslim (1–2%); *note*: China is officially an atheist country.

Meeting and Greeting

- Chinese introductions can be very formal, even austere. The Chinese generally introduce guests by full title and company name. Do the same when introducing yourself.
- The Chinese may not smile when introduced (they're taught to not show emotion openly).
- Senior people initiate greetings. When meeting another party, they greet the oldest, most senior person before all others.
- In group introductions, the Chinese line up according to seniority, with the most senior person at the head of the line.
- Although handshakes have become increasingly popular, the Chinese may nod or bow instead. Unlike the Japanese, who bow from the waist, the Chinese bow by nodding their heads and hunching their shoulders slightly. Foreigners may initiate a handshake upon meeting.
- A group of Chinese may greet foreigners with applause. Foreigners should join in.

Names and Titles

English	Chinese	Pronunciation
Mr.	*Xiansheng*	(shee-ehn-SHUNG)
Mrs.	*Taitai*	(TIE-tie)
	Furen	(FOO-ren)
Miss	*Xiaojie* (also used to politely address a waitress, female cashier, or female elevator attendant)	(shee-OW-jyeh)
Ms.	*Nushi*	(noo-SHEE)

- Traditionally, Chinese name order is last name (surname) + first name (given name). Some may print their names in "Western" order (first name + last name) on business cards. Listen carefully to how others address the person to make sure which is the first name and which is the last. (As a reminder, you may want to note this information on the person's business card at a later time.)

- The Chinese address one another by last name + courtesy title or government or professional title, if applicable. Never address a Chinese person by only his or her last name.
- Be aware: In China, it's difficult to distinguish women's first names from men's. Also, Chinese women keep their maiden names after marrying. They use Mrs. (*Taitai* or *Furen*) to indicate marital status. For example, Mrs. Wang may be married to Mr. Li.

  In addition, most Chinese women don't wear wedding rings. Don't assume someone is single because she lacks a wedding ring.

> Among themselves, the Chinese may call you *quai loh* or *lao wai* ("foreign devil" or "barbarian"), or perhaps *mei guo lao* ("Yankee"). Although the terms are condescending, the Chinese apply them to foreigners in general, perhaps as a reflection of the traditional view of China's exalted position as the Middle Kingdom (the center of the world).

- If you don't know someone's name and title, address him or her simply as *Xiansheng* or *Nushi*.
- Chinese may address foreign women by Miss + first name.
- Use a shortened version of your name if possible ("Jon" instead of "Jonathan"), and don't use initials. If you have a hyphenated first or last name, consider shortening it to one name.
- The Chinese may use first names with close friends and family. Don't use first names until your Chinese colleagues specifically invite you to do so.
- Some Chinese people take common Western first names to use in business.
- Never call anyone "comrade."

Language

Known to Westerners as Mandarin, the national language is *Putonghua* (a version of the Beijing dialect). A 2001 national law mandates all mass media, government offices, and schools must primarily use *Putonghua*. The law also prohibits the overuse of dialects in films and broadcasting.

Chinese officials estimate that only about half its people speak *Putonghua*; 95 percent speak Chinese dialects. Different dialects of Chinese (up to fifteen hundred, including Cantonese, Hakka, and Wu) may be mutually incomprehensible because of lexical differences. Some dialects are more distinct from one another than European languages are (English and French, for example).

Because all dialects use the same written characters, however, speakers of different dialects can read the same language.

Written Chinese includes over fifty thousand characters (ideograms), but only thirty-five hundred are required for basic literacy. In 1956, the Chinese government began implementing a plan to simplify written Chinese. Those outside of China (in Hong Kong and Taiwan, for example) didn't follow these reforms. Consequently, some schools in these areas teach traditional or classical Chinese.

All Chinese dialects are tonal—that is, a word's meaning changes when pronounced with a high, level tone; a rising tone; a drawling tone; or a sharply falling tone. Because English isn't a tonal language, Westerners often have trouble

The transliteration of Chinese characters into English is purely phonetic, and there are three main systems: Wade-Giles (developed by two British scholars in the nineteenth century), Yale (developed by the American university in the 1940s), and Pinyin (declared the official system of the People's Republic of China in 1958).

Western news media and scholars largely use Pinyin, but the other systems are still in use. As a result, you'll see multiple English spellings of Chinese words like Lao Tzu, Lao-tsu, and Lao-tse; Peking and Beijing; and Mao Tse-tung and Mao Zedong. In general, try to use the Pinyin system.

In many Chinese dialects, the Chinese word for the number eight is a homonym for the word that means "prosperity." Chinese businesses like to have the number eight in their phone numbers and addresses. They'll often pay enormous sums to get the desirable numbers.

learning Chinese. (Most Chinese speakers, however, will likely understand foreigners who speak the language in a flat tone.)

Conversation

Above all else, Chinese society values reputation and honor. When conversing with the Chinese, never embarrass, criticize, or contradict them publicly. Doing so may make them lose face, thus risking an end to the relationship.

You'll also risk ending a relationship if you force a Chinese person to say no. To save face, the Chinese prefer to say "maybe" or "we'll see" instead of "no." Avoid asking yes-or-no questions. For example, ask, "When will you have this proposal ready?" instead of "Will this proposal be ready by Friday?"

As a way to make small talk with new people, the Chinese ask personal questions such as, "How much money do you make?" "How many children do you have?" or "Are you married?" If you're uncomfortable answering these questions, answer discreetly (especially money questions) or change the subject.

When meeting a Chinese colleague, you may ask about his or her family, especially children and elderly relatives. But don't ask direct questions like "Are you married?" or "How many children do you have?" Instead, ask "Do you have family in this city?" Once you've developed a relationship, always inquire about your colleague's family.

Here are other conversation tips:

- Always call the nation "China" or the "People's Republic of China," never "Red China," "Communist China," or "Mainland China."

- Always call Taiwan "Province of Taiwan" or just "Taiwan," never "China," "Republic of China," or "Free China." (Although Taiwan calls itself "Republic of China," the Chinese don't because doing so would concede that Taiwan is an independent republic and not a province.)

> When Chinese President Hu Jintao visited Washington in April 2006, the White House committed a major faux pas. It introduced the Chinese national anthem as that of the Republic of China—the official name of Taiwan. The official name of China is the People's Republic of China.
>
> Dozens of foreign policy officials and diplomats assembled on the lawn must have silenced a collective groan.

- The Chinese appreciate humor; however, be aware that jokes seldom cross cultural lines. Wait until you've established a secure relationship before attempting humor.

- Never talk (or behave) loudly, boisterously, or flamboyantly.

- Never interrupt conversations or periods of silence.

Acceptable topics

- The weather
- Chinese history, culture, and cuisine
- Sports, especially table tennis, swimming, and football (soccer)
- The 2008 Olympics
- A person's hometown or home region: Many Chinese live far from where they grew up.

Unacceptable topics

- Divorce
- Suggestions that Taiwan isn't part of China
- Sex, including family planning
- China's human rights record
- Mental health problems
- Comparisons among Chinese regions and cultures
- China's relationships with other Asian nations

Many Chinese people view America as very dangerous. A Chinese friend of mine once told me that before he left to visit the United States for the first time, his mother had warned him, "Don't go out at night in America. Everyone carries guns."

Topics that require sensitivity

- Politics
- Religion
- China's economic progress over the last few decades (The advances have come with serious human, cultural, and environmental costs.)
- Events surrounding World War II, the Chinese civil war, and the Cultural Revolution

Body Language

- The Chinese dislike strangers touching them. Don't hug, link arms, back-slap, or otherwise touch a Chinese person.
- Close friends of the same sex may hold hands when walking.
- The Chinese don't queue. They don't mind being crowded, and they'll push one another to enter trains, buses, and so on.
- The Chinese consider snapping fingers or whistling rude behavior.
- Watch your feet. Never put your feet on furniture, gesture with your feet, point your foot at someone, or use your foot to move an object.
- To beckon someone, extend your hand (palm down), then curl and flex your fingers together. Never use your index finger to beckon anyone.
- The Chinese point with an open hand. Never point with your index finger.
- To express distress or surprise at a proposed request, the Chinese will suck air in quickly and loudly between their lips and teeth. If you encounter this reaction, try to change your request. Doing so lets the Chinese person avoid confrontation and save face.
- The Chinese often stare. Expect others to stare at you, especially in small villages.

Chinese is a tonal language. That is, a word's meaning depends not only on pronunciation, but also on pitch. Mandarin has four tones; Cantonese has six to nine.

The following phrases are only approximations. (The complexities of Chinese pronunciation are beyond the scope of this book.) Your Chinese colleagues will appreciate any attempt you make to speak a few words of the language. You'll pick up the nuances of common words' pronunciations by listening carefully and practicing at every opportunity. If you want to learn how to speak Chinese more accurately, use audio language sources or a comprehensive phrase book.

English	Chinese	Pronunciation
Hello (also "good afternoon" and "good evening")	*Ni hao*	(NEE-how)
(when answering a phone)	*Wei*	(way)
Good morning	*Zao an*	(zhow AN)
How are you? (a common greeting)	*Ni hao ma*	(NEE how mah)
Please	*Qing*	(cheen)
Thank you	*Xie xie*	(see-EH see-EH)
You're welcome	*bu yong xie*	(boo yohn see-EH)
Yes	*Shi*	(shih)
No	*Bu shi*	(boo SHIH)
Excuse me	*Qing rang*	(shing ree-AH)
Goodbye	*Zaijian*	(dzeye zhee-EHN)

Dining

The food served in many Chinese restaurants in the United States bears little or no resemblance to authentic Chinese food. Familiar dishes like chow mein and chop suey may be more American than Chinese in origin. (That is, they may possibly be the creations of Chinese immigrants to the United States in the nineteenth century.)

Westerners may be surprised to learn that white rice isn't common in some parts of China. For example, in northern China wheat, millet, and soybeans are staples.

Authentic Chinese cuisine may test some Westerners' palates. While some areas of China do serve cat and dog, hosts are far more likely to offer guests snails or duck feet or heads.

Although most Chinese people prefer their own cuisine over Western fare, Western fast-food chains are appearing across the country and are popular. In addition, restaurants in major hotels that cater to foreigners usually serve Western food.

Here are a few additional comments on Chinese dining:

- The Chinese are superb hosts. Twelve-course banquets with frequent toasts are a Chinese trademark.
- The Chinese generally eat dinner earlier than Westerners do.
- Most meals have a soup course.
- People use chopsticks for all Chinese-style meals. (See pages 41–42 for information on chopsticks etiquette.)
- Carry your own chopsticks to use when eating in rural areas or small urban restaurants serving local clientele. If you don't have your own chopsticks, try to discreetly pour boiling water or tea over those provided to clean them.
- China has eight major cuisines: Shandong, Sichuan (Szechuan), Guangdong (Cantonese), Fujian, Jiangsu, Zhejiang, Hunan, and Anhui. There are also many more minor and ethnic variations. Each region's history, geography, climate, resources, and lifestyles contributed to the development of its unique foods. Before traveling to China, learn about the cuisine of the region you'll be visiting.

When Dining in Restaurants

- If you extend the invitation, let your Chinese colleagues choose the restaurant. Most Chinese people prefer Chinese food, but may be too polite to say so.
- The person who extended the invitation pays the bill, without exception.
- Hotel restaurants are always busy. Reserve a table early in the day, and be prompt. Restaurants will give your table away if you arrive late.
- Seat yourself in less formal restaurants. If a restaurant is crowded, strangers will share tables. (If strangers sit at your table, you don't need to talk to them.)
- Most restaurant tables are round and have a revolving tray with several different dishes for people to sample. Try each dish at a meal or banquet.
- If you're the host, order one dish for every guest plus one extra. Also order rice, noodles, and buns. The host should invite guests to begin eating a new dish.

- Government-owned or -managed restaurants have poor service and food, and they usually close by 8:00 PM. They often seat foreigners in an area separate from locals. Never object to where you're seated.

When Dining in Homes

- The Chinese rarely invite guests to their homes. If you receive such an invitation, always remember it's an honor. Be on time or a little early, and bring a small gift.
- Bedrooms and kitchens are private areas. Never enter these rooms without an invitation.
- The host always seats the guest of honor at the head of the table, facing the door. The host sits opposite him or her.
- In homes, the Chinese serve all dishes at once. The host places servings of each dish on guests' plates. Be sure to sample each one.
- After the meal, hosts walk guests to their cars and wave goodbye until guests are out of sight.

Drinking

- Tea is part of the Chinese lifestyle and culture. The Chinese believe tea has health benefits, which the rest of the world is just beginning to discover. In 2004, China produced nearly a million metric tons of over five hundred types of tea and exported over a quarter-million metric tons (about 20 percent of global tea exports).
- Coffee is becoming popular among stylish urbanites. Coffee sales in China increased more than 90 percent between 1998 and 2003 and are expected to grow another 70 percent before 2008.
- Most Chinese choose to drink beer over other alcoholic beverages.
- Chinese liquors may have a very high alcohol content. Drink with caution.
- When a Chinese colleague offers you a drink, try not to refuse it. If you must, sip or pretend to drink it.
- In social situations, drunkenness is perfectly acceptable for men. The Chinese consider intoxication a way to relax and have a good time. Women, however, should drink sparingly and never become intoxicated.
- At each place at banquets, the Chinese set three glasses: a large one for beer, soda, or mineral water; a small wineglass; and a stemmed shot glass used for toasting (usually with mao-tai, a very strong sorghum liquor).

Toasting

- The Chinese toast often. Be prepared to make a small toast at any occasion.
- The host normally gives the first toast during or after the first course, not before. After the next course, the guest of honor should reciprocate.
- Don't drink until you toast others at the table. The Chinese consider drinking alone rude. You may simply raise your glass and make eye contact. If you're the recipient, sip your drink in reply.
- You may offer a toast to your table and surrounding tables. Sometimes a host may move among the tables, offering a toast at each one, but usually only at large banquets.
- The standard toast *gambei* (GAHM-bay) means "bottoms up." The Chinese may drain their glasses, but you don't have to. Try to follow your host's example.
- The Chinese may accompany toasts with long speeches, or they may merely raise their glasses.
- People often make a toast upon the arrival of a new dish (especially shark fin soup).
- A toast to friendship among companies will help cement a business relationship.
- A foreign woman may make a toast if she's the delegation's leader. Otherwise, it's uncommon for women to propose toasts.

Tipping

The Chinese once considered tipping a degrading custom—people only offered a tip to someone they believed was clearly inferior. Today, while the Chinese don't expect tips from fellow Chinese, they frequently expect them from foreigners. They also appreciate modest souvenirs from foreigners' home countries, like pins and magazines.

Officially, tipping with a foreign currency is illegal. Nonetheless, people tip with foreign currency in areas or at establishments that foreigners patronize.

- Restaurants: Tip extra change; however, the bill in some expensive bars and restaurants may include a service charge. Also, if you host a banquet at a restaurant, consider offering a gratuity for exceptional service. Between 10 and 15 percent is common, but the appropriate amount varies according to the city and the venue. When arranging the banquet, ask a knowledgeable colleague for advice.

- Taxis: Tip extra change. Drivers will appreciate larger tips for extra service, like helping with bags.
- Bellhops, porters, restroom attendants, coat-check attendants: Tip small change.
- Hair stylists and barbers: Tip small change if especially happy with the service.
- Personal drivers and maids: Tip small change.
- Ushers: No tip necessary.
- Guides and translators: Tip an amount appropriate to the amount of time and level of service. Ask a knowledgeable colleague or the hotel concierge for advice.

Manners

Officially, the Chinese still view foreigners as intruders and discourage interacting with them. In practice, however, the Chinese are usually friendly and polite to foreign guests.
- Never act as through you're starving, and never ask to have your leftovers boxed to take with you.
- Let the host begin eating before joining in yourself.
- Don't discuss business at dinner unless your host initiates the discussion.
- Chinese hosts will keep refilling guests' plates or teacups. When you've had your fill, leave a small amount of tea in your teacup or a small amount of food on your plate at the end of each course. Doing so demonstrates appreciation for your host's generosity.
- Slurping soup and belching are acceptable at the table.
- Cover your mouth with your hand when using a toothpick.
- Put bones, seeds, and other food refuse on the table—never in your rice bowl. Hosts sometimes provide a dish for this purpose.
- Never tap your chopsticks on the table. Doing so is very rude.
- When finished eating, place your chopsticks neatly on the table or on the chopstick rest.
- Banquets have their own etiquette. See pages 38–39 to learn the manners for banquets.
- No one leaves before the guest of honor. If you're the guest of honor, leave shortly after the meal is finished.
- People commonly spit or blow their noses directly onto a street or sidewalk. They believe it's disgusting to blow a nose into a handkerchief then

tuck it into pocket. Use a tissue to blow your nose, then throw it away immediately.

- Always show respect to older people. Offer your seat to older people, open doors for them, and so on.
- The Chinese culture isn't chivalrous toward women.
- Always ask permission before photographing anyone.
- If someone applauds you, always join in.
- Smoking in China is ubiquitous. It's acceptable to smoke nearly everywhere. Some restaurants and hotels may have smoke-free areas, but enforcement is lax.
- Chinese women rarely smoke or drink in public; however, Western women may do so in moderation.

China is the world's largest producer of cigarettes, and the Chinese are the world's most enthusiastic smokers. A 2001 study published in the *British Medical Journal* found that two-thirds of Chinese men smoke and predicted that one in three men will die of a smoking-related illness.

A far smaller percentage of women smoke, but women die in large numbers of diseases caused by secondhand smoke.

The Chinese government is working toward reducing smoking-related deaths. It's set on strictly controlling smoking in public spaces and strengthening regulation of tobacco production and business activities.

Punctuality

The Chinese expect foreigners to be punctual. Always arrive exactly on time for a meeting, dinner, or banquet. (But never arrive early to a meal or banquet. Doing so says you're hungry, and you'll lose face.)

Dress

Western fashions are becoming increasingly popular in China, but plain and simple attire is the rule. While some Chinese (usually young people) wear bright colors and jeans, foreigners should wear conservative, simple clothing.

Laundry facilities are often inadequate, so try to pack clothing made of wash-and-wear fabrics. Also, keep in mind that many restrooms in China have only squat toilets; you'll need to dress accordingly.

If visiting northern China, you'll need to pack warm clothing, hats, and shoes with thick soles.

- For business, men wear sport coats and ties. For summer business meetings, slacks and open-necked shirts are generally suitable, but follow the local custom. Women usually wear dresses or pantsuits in subtle colors and styles. Avoid wearing heavy makeup and dangling, gaudy jewelry.
- For formal occasions, including banquets and meals at restaurants, men wear jackets and ties (you may remove both in the summer, but follow the local custom). Women wear simple, floor-length dresses or slacks, blouses, and fitted jackets. (Slacks are acceptable for even the most formal occasions.)

    Be aware that the Chinese wear white at funerals (it's the color of mourning). Traditional wedding dresses are red, although today some Chinese brides are wearing white.
- For casual occasions, men wear pants with open-necked shirts with short or long sleeves. Women wear dress pants and blouses. They never wear shorts or styles that expose their backs.

Gifts

Once illegal, gift giving is now a generally accepted custom. The Chinese love giving gifts, and many give them on Christmas, Valentine's Day, Father's Day, and Mother's Day.

- The Chinese generally don't open gifts upon receipt. Recipients thank the giver sincerely and put aside the gift to open later.
- Wrap a gift simply (no ribbon or bows), preferably in red gift-wrap (red symbolizes prosperity). Don't use white or black gift-wrap (symbolizes death or tragedy). Don't use red ink on cards or notes (the Chinese use red ink only for the dead).
- Always present a gift with both hands.
- Older Chinese people usually refuse a gift initially. Offer it a second time; they'll likely accept it.
- Don't give gifts in sets of four (the Chinese word for "four" is a homonym for the word for "death") or thirteen (connotes bad luck, just as it does in the West).
- Never give an obviously expensive gift. Unless you're very close friends, doing so will embarrass the recipient.
- The Chinese don't routinely give flowers; they consider them too funereal.
- "Red envelopes" are common gifts. (See page 58.)

- Upon arrival in China, be aware that Chinese customs officials may curiously scrutinize gifts that look unusual to them. If asked "What is this?" or "How does this work?" respond with a friendly explanation. You'll likely not have a problem keeping the items.

Hostess Gifts

When invited to someone's home, always bring a small gift.

Consider giving
- Brandy
- Chocolates
- Cakes
- Gifts from your home region

Don't give
- White items (color associated with death)
- Handkerchiefs (connote grief)
- Personal items
- Clocks (associated with death)
- Knives or other sharp objects (connotes a severing of the relationship)
- Fruit or basic foods (implies poverty): These items, however, may be acceptable for close friends.
- Wild rice (The Chinese consider the color unattractive.)

Business Gifts

The Chinese expect to exchange gifts at initial meetings. Be prepared to give a small gift to your Chinese colleagues.

Always give a gift to each member of the Chinese delegation that meets you—in order of introduction. A group gift is an acceptable alternative to individual gifts. Present a group gift to the group leader.

Consider giving
- Cognac or other French brandy
- Whiskey
- Small items like cigarette lighters, pens, or other desk items
- Books or framed paintings
- Gifts from your home region
- Western-grown ginseng
- Brand-name calculators or watches (for younger colleagues—some popular watch brands include Citizen, Swatch, SEIKO, Enicar, Casio, Rossini,

Tissot, and Longines) or slightly more expensive brand-name electronics (for older or more senior colleagues)

Don't give
- White items (color associated with death)
- Foreign currency, including commemorative coins
- Handkerchiefs (connote grief)
- Clocks, especially to an older person (associated with death)
- Green headwear (signifies that somebody in the recipient's family is an adulterer)
- Umbrellas (A homonym for the Chinese word for "umbrella" means the recipient's family is going to disperse.)
- Obviously expensive items: It's appropriate, however, to give an expensive gift after the successful completion of a business deal.

Helpful Hints

- Ask a Chinese friend to purchase items from a Chinese shop for you. Some shopkeepers may charge Westerners prices that are two to three times greater than those they'd charge Chinese people.
- Bargaining is acceptable at street booths and in privately owned stores. Don't bargain at department stores.
- Always bargain with a taxi driver before taking the trip.
- When phoning a Western colleague staying in a hotel, ask for the room number, not the guest's name. Western names are often difficult for operators to understand.

Health and Safety

- Terrorism isn't a problem in China, and the crime rate is low (although increasing). Be alert for petty crimes like pickpocketing.
- Carry currency in small denominations. You may receive counterfeit currency if you pay in large denominations (especially for taxi rides).
- It's legal to exchange currency only at hotels, banks, and official exchange offices.
- Never photograph anything even remotely related to the military—this includes airports, railroads, bridges, and so on.
- Don't drive in China. Traffic is chaotic, and gridlock and traffic fatalities are common.

- Health facilities in large Chinese cities are good, but rural clinics may have only rudimentary equipment and supplies. Major hospitals may have VIP wards for foreigners, but even then, cultural and language differences may cause problems. For peace of mind, obtain medical insurance that will transport you to Hong Kong for emergency medical care.
- Always call your embassy if a medical problem arises.
- Pack ample supplies of any medications. Western prescriptions and over-the-counter medications aren't widely available in China.
- Never drink tap water, use ice cubes, or eat raw or unpeeled fruits and vegetables. Although some major hotels have water purification systems, it's safest to drink only bottled or boiled water.
- Avoid eating dairy products or foods that must be refrigerated (refrigeration is often poor).

Corporate Culture

The Chinese are practical in business matters; they realize they'll need Western investment for business success. The nation must create fifteen million jobs per year to sustain its economic growth.

Putting practicality aside, however, the Chinese dislike having to depend on foreign investment. Many believe foreigners are culturally and economically corrupt, and they fear foreigners will cheat or bully them. Thus, for business success in China, it's vital to establish trust with your Chinese colleagues.

In 2003, the Chinese published over four hundred daily newspapers—despite vigorous government censorship. Always remember that China doesn't have a free press. Be skeptical of what you read in Chinese newspapers and on official Chinese websites. Read any websites with a ".cn" suffix (indicates the site is registered and governed in China) with skepticism.

The Chinese have become major Internet users (more than 111 million at the end of 2005), even though the government blocks unapproved websites (like the sites for *The New York Times* or the BBC). Many Chinese people are outraged with the censorship, but others believe it's necessary for national security and don't find the restrictions as oppressive as Westerners may believe.

Structure

The Chinese organizational structure is vertical, with strong emphasis on seniority, rank, and title. They expect lifetime loyalty to superiors in return for lifetime employment.

Bureaucracy sets the tone and pace and determines the feasibility of any business venture. A project must win the support of government officials, who control the approval process.

The Chinese defer personal interests to those of the group. They discourage independent expression; people express themselves through the group, and the group is accountable, not the individual. Conformity requires consensus, which often results in indecision. Foreigners must be patient.

Meetings

- Meetings always begin on time.
- The Chinese prefer to negotiate with a group of two to seven people. Make sure your negotiating team is technically competent, and begin negotiations with middle managers and technical experts. The level of management the Chinese sends will match that of your team.

KFC (Kentucky Fried Chicken) is a success story in China. Although it stumbled at first (the "finger-lickin' good" catchphrase was mistranslated to "eat your fingers off"), the American company did a great job of analyzing Chinese tastes and adapting to the market.

For example, when KFC began offering dark meat in its chicken burgers (a cultural preference to white meat), sales of the sandwiches doubled. It also offered seasonal vegetables and congee (rice porridge) instead of mashed potatoes and coleslaw.

Such decisions have paid off. In 2003, 15 percent of KFC's parent company's operating profits came from China.

Guanxi (GWONG-she) is the web of relationships and obligations that ties people and businesses together. It's vital to any successful business arrangement in China.

If negotiations with your Chinese colleagues break down, don't formally end them. Instead, to save face you (or your Chinese colleagues) should say, "Let's temporarily cease negotiations." If the deal ultimately falls through, never speak ill of your Chinese colleagues. Doing so may poison your guanxi.

- Meetings begin with a certain procedure. To designate the leader, the highest-ranking person for each party enters the room first. The rest of the foreign team enters the room together, then shakes hands with the Chinese team before formal introductions. The Chinese leader welcomes everyone. The foreign leader introduces his or her team, then the members distribute their business cards to the Chinese team members. The leader invites the Chinese leader to introduce his or her team, then the Chinese members distribute their business cards to the foreign team members. If Chinese members don't have business cards, the foreign leader provides a sheet of paper and asks each to write down his or her name, position, and organization's name on it.

  For very small groups, a member of the foreign team may distribute his or her business card before the leader introduces the next person. This way, the Chinese leader can see the importance of each team member.
- The most important guest sits to the host's right.
- The Chinese make small talk before beginning business discussions, which the foreign team initiates.
- Foreigners should set the meeting agenda and obtain agreement on its major points at the beginning of negotiations. Present your proposals in detail, and support them with technical and factual data.
- Take notes during meetings. The Chinese rarely (if ever) will let you audio- or video-record meetings.
- Negotiations usually start slowly and stiffly, but eventually become informal. Send as much information as possible beforehand; the Chinese don't like surprises in meetings or negotiations.
- Be prepared for long monologues and seemingly endless cups of tea. Once comfortable, the Chinese like to speak at length on topics and listen to your opinions on them.
- Making decisions (and implementing decisions) is extremely slow and cumbersome. The Chinese call numerous meetings until a decision reaches consensus. Be prepared for long meetings (often over successive days) and protracted negotiations with many delays. You'll likely need to make multiple visits.
- Try to have meetings in rooms that are larger than necessary. Many Chinese people smoke, and long meetings in a small, smoke-filled room can test even the toughest negotiators.

- Either party may end a meeting by politely requesting the scheduling of the next meeting.
- Always send the same team to continue negotiations. Continuity in relationships is important to the Chinese.

Appointments

- Appointments are absolutely necessary in China.
- Schedule appointments for a time between 10:00 AM and 3:00 PM, Monday through Thursday.
- Most businesses are open Monday through Saturday, 8:00 AM to 11:30 AM and 1:30 PM to 6:00 PM.
- Many people leave their offices by 4:00 PM, and some aren't in their offices on Fridays.
- Avoid scheduling appointments for the weeks before and after Chinese New Year.

Communication

- The Chinese don't speak English in business meetings (although some may understand it without letting you know). Hire a reputable translator, request one from the host company, or use someone from your company to translate (but make sure that person fully understands the subject matter).
- Use simple words and short sentences. Also, speak in lay terms as much as possible. The Chinese delegation will include both technical and managerial people, so be sure to clearly define managerial terms for technical people and technical terms for managerial people.
- Communicate in writing whenever possible. Verbal communication, especially on the telephone, tends to lose important information in the translation.
- There may be periods of silence in conversations. Never speak to fill these gaps; let your Chinese colleagues break the silence.

Business Cards

- Have your information printed in English on one side of your business card and in Chinese (simplified characters) on the other side. If planning to visit Hong Kong or Taiwan, which uses classical characters, mark the boxes of business cards in some way to avoid using cards with classical characters in China and simplified characters in Hong Kong or Taiwan.
- The Chinese exchange business cards upon meeting. See page 69 to learn more information about exchanging business cards.

Be Aware

- Brand loyalty is very strong in China.
- The Chinese behave formally in business meetings, but are more relaxed in private situations.
- The Chinese are slow to divulge information; be

> Although Chinese culture discourages personal friendships with foreigners, the working relationship you develop with your Chinese colleagues will determine the success of your business venture—even more so than the products or services you're offering.

patient but persistent. It may take years to successfully enter the Chinese market or show a return on your investment.

- The Chinese consider contracts drafts subject to change, not binding documents. To them, cooperation is more important than contracts.
- The Chinese believe a person's status or qualifications should match the job at hand. Don't insult the Chinese by sending a junior colleague to make initial contact or by sending your CEO to haggle over arcane details.
- Make sure your Chinese colleagues are fully authorized to take necessary action. It may be hard to determine who's the ultimate authority.
- If your Chinese colleagues want to abandon a deal, they may not tell you. To save face, they may instead become increasingly inflexible, forcing you to break off negotiations. Thus, they'll avoid blame for the failure.

> In 2004, China consumed over 50 percent of the concrete and nearly 40 percent of the steel produced in the world. Since 1990, nearly seven thousand buildings taller than eleven stories have been built in Shanghai. (New York City has only fifty-five hundred such buildings.)

- Chinese negotiating teams may have women members, whom they may use to deflect criticism or respond negatively to proposals.
- Be prepared to make sizeable concessions, especially at the end of negotiations. Also, beware the phrase "Based on the principles of equality and mutual benefit…": It usually means your Chinese colleagues have an additional request or condition.

> The Chinese are shopping mall fans. The South China Mall in Dongguan is nearly three times larger than Minnesota's Mall of America. The Golden Resources Mall in Beijing employs twenty thousand people. A mall in the southern city Guangzhou sees over half a billion shoppers on a busy day. Some experts predict that by 2010, seven of the world's ten largest malls will be in China.

- The Chinese often treat foreign companies as if they've unlimited resources. They may also use manipulation to make foreigners agree to concessions. For example, they may try to make you feel guilty about any negotiation setbacks, then use your guilt to obtain concessions. Other tactics to achieve this goal include staging temper tantrums and feigning a sense of urgency (when none exists).
- Even if you have a time constraint, never act as though you do. If the Chinese know that you're under pressure to obtain a signed agreement, they'll extract concessions. To speed up approvals or break an impasse, have senior executives apply pressure.

Socializing

- A formal banquet is the most popular form of business entertainment.
- The Chinese generally don't directly discuss business at meals, but they may try to learn another's position through indirect conversation.
- The hosting Chinese organization generally gives a welcome banquet. Foreign guests should reciprocate with a comparable banquet toward the end of the visit, inviting everyone with whom they've dealt.
- The Chinese usually don't include spouses at business functions, although businesspeople may bring their secretaries.
- Business breakfasts aren't customary, but you may request one.

Especially for Women

China is a male-dominated society, but it's a difficult place for foreigners of either sex to do business.

China does have many women in business, some in high-ranking positions and important managerial jobs. (Asians consider Chinese women to be the most assertive in Asia.) But gaining acceptance was difficult and took time. One of the principles of the Chinese Communist system is to work toward equality between the sexes.

People in rural areas still arrange marriages, but those in major cities marry upon mutual attraction. Regardless of how people choose a spouse, many Chinese still consider it a disgrace to marry a woman who's not a virgin.

Socially, men dominate, but women hold the power in the family. They allow men to save face by letting them appear to hold the power.

- It's acceptable for a Western woman to invite a Chinese man to a business dinner. She should arrange payment with the wait staff beforehand.
- China is relatively safe for women, but use common sense. Avoid unknown areas, especially at night.

Holidays and Festivals	
January	New Year's Day (1)
March	International Women's Day (8)
May	Labor Day (1)
	Youth Day (4)
June	Children's Day (1)
July	The (Communist) Party Day (1)
August	Army's Day (1)
October	National Day (1)

Notes: China also celebrates traditional Chinese holidays like Chinese New Year, the Lantern Festival, and the Duan Wu (Dragon Boat) Festival. These festivities follow the lunar calendar; check when they're celebrated for the year you're visiting China.

Many Chinese also celebrate American holidays, like Mother's Day, Father's Day, Thanksgiving, and Christmas.

HONG KONG
HONG KONG SPECIAL
ADMINISTRATIVE REGION

Greetings from Hong Kong

Greetings from one of the world's most dynamic and fascinating regions. There is no other place on earth like Hong Kong.

Eastern and Western cultures fuse together on the "Pearl of the Orient," creating dazzling contrasts. Spectacular ocean liners command the harbor amid junks and old wooden boats. Rolls-Royces park in front of luxury hotels and drive down squalid alleys. Market vendors sell shoes and chicken feet while chatting on cell phones.

For years, Hong Kong has been the economic and cultural bridge between the East and West, between Communism and capitalism. We incorporate ancient Chinese traditions with westernized business practices. In fact, our pace is as fast and modern as that of any Western city.

Until the nineteenth century, Hong Kong was part of China. In 1842 China ceded Hong Kong Island to the United Kingdom (UK) as part of the agreements to end the first Opium War. Roughly twenty years later, China ceded Kowloon Peninsula to the UK, essentially giving the British complete control of the harbor. In 1898, China leased the entire region to the UK for ninety-nine years. The lease expired in 1997, and China again resumed control, which made some of us worry about the future of our civil liberties. Today, however, we optimistically await the fate of democracy and free market under "one country, two systems."

Hong Kongers are a complex mix of people from all over China (95 percent of us are Chinese). But much of our culture is distinctly British—just look at our school system, free market economy, double-decker buses, afternoon teas, and English pubs. We even queue (stand in line), unlike most other Asians.

Although British culture influences us, always remember that we are *not* British. Following Confucian philosophy, we believe everyone has a position in the family and society. One's actions, education, wealth, and reputation positively or negatively reflect his or her entire family. We highly value loyalty, obedience, and respect for elders.

We have the world's highest population density. Our islands are steep and living area is limited; 90 percent of us inhabit only 15 percent of available land. Many of the world's tallest buildings are in Hong Kong.

> Hong Kong is the "Wall Street of Asia." It's one of the world's largest offshore banking and financial centers and is the world's largest foreign exchange center.

Wealth distribution is unequal, but overall we enjoy a higher standard of living than our neighbors in China. We are unafraid to flaunt our wealth and social status with cars, clothes, and cell phones. We enjoy one of the world's highest life expectancies and lowest infant mortality rates.

We value family and tradition, but we especially appreciate making money. Hong Kong has become the place to trade and conduct business, and we do both aggressively and successfully.

Although in the last decade we weathered two major Asian economic crises and an outbreak of a deadly disease (severe acute respiratory system or SARS), today our gross domestic product (GDP) compares to the more prosperous European nations, and we look forward to continued growth. We are proud that our tax system is one of the world's simplest and our tax rates are among the world's lowest.

Over the last several decades, as manufacturers moved operations to China for its cheaper labor and land costs, our economy began relying increasingly on the service sector, especially tourism and financial services. Nearly our entire GDP comes from service industries.

We have the world's third-largest film industry. In fact, walking our streets you may feel as though you have wandered onto a film set. You will see Chinese medicine shops, street vendors, dim sum shops, and old men with caged birds walking in the park. Take our tiny Star Ferry between Hong Kong Island and Kowloon to shop for goods from around the globe, dine on cuisine from all over the world, then sleep in first-class hotels.

Hong Kong is a wonderful place to visit, do business, and make money. Visit us soon and see for yourself!

Note: To further understand Hong Kong culture, read the chapter on China in this book (pages 109–132) as well as the chapter on the UK in my book *European Business Customs & Manners* (Meadowbrook Press).

Vital Statistics	
Population	6,940,432
Capital	None
Area	422 square miles, about half the size of Rhode Island
Government	Limited democracy as a special administrative region of China
Living Standard	GDP = US $29,350 per capita
Natural Resources	Outstanding deepwater harbor, feldspar
Agriculture	Fresh vegetables, poultry, pork, fish
Industries	Textiles, clothing, tourism, banking, shipping, electronics, plastics, toys, watches, clocks
Climate	Cool and humid in winter, hot and rainy from spring through summer, warm and sunny in fall
Currency	Hong Kong dollar (HKD)

The People	
Correct Name	nouns: Hong Konger, Hong Kong resident, Chinese adjectives: Hong Kong, Hong Kong Chinese, Chinese
Ethnic Makeup	Chinese 95%, other 5%
Languages	Chinese (Cantonese) and English (both are official)
Religions	Mix of Buddhism, Taoism, Confucianism, and Animism 90%, Christian 10%

Meeting and Greeting

- Hong Kongers shake hands with everyone—men, women, and children—upon meeting and departure. They may shake hands less firmly than Westerners do.
- People introduce higher-ranking people before those of lower rank, older people before younger ones, and women before men. They greet family members from oldest to youngest.
- Hong Kongers bow or nod slightly during a handshake.
- When greeting people, it's polite to ask about their health or activities.
- Hong Kongers may ask, *"Nay sik jo fan mei ah?"* (nay sick JO fan may ah), which means "have you eaten?" This question is similar to "how are you?" and requires a simple "yes" as an answer.
- At social functions, people may introduce themselves.

Names and Titles

- Name order in Hong Kong is last name (surname) + first name (given name). Young people, however, may use "Western" name order (first name + last name).
- Address Hong Kongers by last name + professional or courtesy title.
- Hong Kongers use first names only with family members and close friends. Don't use first names until your colleagues specifically invite you to do so.
- Some Hong Kongers take Western first names.
- In written correspondence, salutation is Dear + courtesy or professional title + last name. If unsure of a person's title or marital status, use his or her full name.

English	Chinese (Cantonese)	Pronunciation
Mr.	*Sinsaang*	(SEEN-sahng)
Mrs./Ms.	*Taaitaai*	(TIE-tie)
Miss	*Siuje*	(see-oo-JEH-eh)

Language

One of Hong Kong's national languages is Cantonese, a Chinese dialect. All Chinese dialects are tonal—that is, a word's meaning changes when pronounced with a high, level tone; a rising tone; a drawling tone; or a sharply falling tone. Because English isn't a tonal language, Westerners often have trouble learning Chinese. (Most Chinese speakers, however, will likely understand foreigners who speak the language in a flat tone.)

Unlike China, which uses simplified characters in writing, Hong Kong uses classical characters.

The nation's other official language is English. Hong Kongers speak British English and understand American English. All Hong Kong schools teach English. Employees of most major hotels and restaurants speak English. Signage and documents are often in both Chinese and English.

Conversation

- Hong Kongers ask personal questions. If you're uncomfortable answering them, give vague answers or say, "In my country, that would be a strange question."

- With that said, never say or do anything that makes someone lose face. Doing so will surely end a relationship.
- Don't take it personally if someone refers to you as a *guei lou* ("foreign devil"). The term reflects the millennia-old belief in Chinese culture's superiority.
- Hong Kongers often use stories and anecdotes to express ideas. They're famous for communicating by "saying it without saying it."
- When Hong Kongers say "okay," they mean "I understand," not "I agree."
- Many Hong Kongers speak quickly and loudly, but you should speak quietly.
- Speak in simple, short sentences. Never assume Hong Kongers understand you just because many speak English.
- Try to speak a few words of Chinese. Hong Kongers greatly appreciate any attempts to speak their language.

Acceptable topics
- Family (yours or theirs): Keep in mind, however, that today's families in Hong Kong are smaller and the clash between traditional and modern values often puts stress on family life.
- Sports, especially table tennis, football (soccer), cricket, squash, basketball, boating, and horseracing
- Money (yours or theirs): Unlike other Asians, many Hong Kongers are eager to talk about money and business.
- Hong Kong's natural beauty: About 40 percent of the land is conserved parkland, one of the highest rates in the world.

> The countryside is beautiful and easily accessed. Take the famous Peak Tram to the top of Victoria Peak for breathtaking views.

Unacceptable topics
- Any failure
- Poverty
- Death
- Criticisms of Hong Kong or China

Topics that require sensitivity
- Compliments: Hong Kongers give compliments, but they may receive them with embarrassment. When someone compliments you, politely decline to show humility. Never say "thank you."
- Hong Kong's role as special administrative region of China

- Chinese politics
- Taiwan
- Macao
- Human rights

> Hong Kongers are proud of their free press, and they're ready to challenge any limitations to it.

Body Language

- Hong Kongers are often uncomfortable with body contact. Don't hug, kiss, or pat people on the back.
- With that said, people may stand closely to one another when talking.
- Hong Kongers don't smile as often as Americans do.
- People of the same sex may hold hands while walking as a sign of friendship.
- Don't wink at anyone. Hong Kongers consider winking rude behavior.
- When sitting, don't swing your legs. Fidgeting shows disrespect or a lack of interest.
- To beckon someone, extend your arm (palm down) then curl and extend your fingers together.
- Hong Kongers never point at people with an index finger. Instead, they gesture with an open hand.

Phrases

English	Chinese (Cantonese)	Pronunciation
Hello	*Nei ho*	(NEE-how)
(on the telephone)	*Wai*	(why)
Good morning	*Jou san*	(DJOH-sun)
Good afternoon	*Ngh on*	(NNG ohn)
Please	*My goi*	(mm-GOY)
Thank you	*Dojeh*	(doh DZEH)
You're welcome	*M'sai m'goi*	(MM-sigh mm-goy)
Yes	*Haih*	(high)
No	*Mh-haih*	(mm-HIGH)
Excuse me	*Deui mh jyuh*	(der-MM-dyoo)
Goodbye	*Joigin*	(djoy-GEEN)
How are you?	*Neih hou ma*	(nay HOH ma)

Dining

Though more subtle than other Chinese cuisines, Cantonese is known for its freshness and emphasis on natural flavor. Many consider it one of the best in the world.

One can find every cuisine in the world in Hong Kong's over twenty thousand restaurants. Many restaurants and most hotels serve Western fare, and some restaurants are as elegant and Western as establishments in Paris or New York City.

- Hong Kongers seat the guest of honor facing the entrance, with the host seated opposite him or her. They seat high-ranking guests next to the guest of honor, and seat the rest of the guests in descending order of importance, with the least important people at the ends of the table.
- People use Western utensils or chopsticks according to the meal. (See page 41 for information on chopstick etiquette.)
- Eight- to fourteen-course banquets aren't unusual in Hong Kong. (See pages 38–39 for information on banquet etiquette.)
- At some formal banquets, wait staff serves courses to each guest, including the hosts.
- Hong Kongers serve oranges or other fruits to signal the end of the meal.

> Hong Kongers consider it disgusting to eat food held with bare hands. Many use plastic gloves to eat food like French fries, or else they'll eat all of a fry except the end held with a bare hand.

Drinking

- Tea is the customary beverage for all occasions, and Hong Kongers drink it straight. They consider adding sugar and cream to tea a strange Western habit.
- If you want more tea in restaurants, place the teapot lid upside down on the pot (or leave it up, if attached to the teapot).
- Beer—especially San Miguel, the only locally brewed beer—is popular in Hong Kong.
- Because of high taxes, imported wine is expensive in Hong Kong. Prohibitive prices likely discourage wider consumption.
- Other popular liquors include *zhian jing* (rice wine served warm, like sake) or *liang hua pei* (plum brandy).

- Hong Kong women generally don't drink alcohol in public, usually opting for tea or orange juice instead. Western women, however, may drink alcohol in public.

Toasting

- Toasting is an important part of Hong Kong dinners. Typical toasts include:
  * *Yum boui* (yum BOO-oy), which means "cheers."
  * *Yum sing* (yum sing), which is a challenge to drain your glass. (You may drain your glass just the first time; you may sip subsequent drinks.)
  * *Gambei* (GAHM-bay), which means "bottoms up." (This toast is in Mandarin, not Cantonese. Use only if others in your group use it.)
- If toasted as the guest of honor, follow this procedure: smile, raise your glass, make eye contact with the person offering the toast, drink, raise your glass, then thank the host and guests.
- At the end of the dinner, the guest of honor rises and thanks the host on behalf of everyone present with a polite, short toast to friendship, success, and cooperation.
- At banquets, the host makes a toast at each table. He or she often makes a toast when a new dish is served, especially shark fin soup. (Hong Kongers offer this very expensive delicacy only to special guests. Be sure to show appreciation if your host offers the dish.)

Tipping

Tipping is mandatory in Hong Kong. Tip everyone for everything.
- Restaurants: The bill generally includes a 10 percent service charge, but leave an additional tip—usually extra change. If the bill doesn't include a service charge, tip 10 percent. For excellent service, leave an additional 5 percent.
- Taxis: Tip small change for short rides and 10 percent of the fare for longer rides or if the driver helps with your luggage.
- Restroom attendants: Tip HKD5.
- Coat-check attendants: Tip HKD10.
- Bellhops and porters: Tip HKD10 per bag but no less than HKD20 total.
- Hair stylists and barbers: Tip 10 percent of the bill.
- Maids: Tip small change.

- Guides: Tip an amount appropriate to the amount of time and service rendered. Ask the hotel concierge or a knowledgeable colleague for advice.

Manners

- Show older people great respect.
- If store staff is rude, ignore their behavior and walk away.
- Don't remove your shoes when entering a home.
- When dining with British people living in Hong Kong, use your best Western manners.
- Never refuse an invitation to lunch or dinner. If you can't make the date, suggest another one.
- Hosts may not provide napkins. Instead, they may offer hot towels to cleanse hands and faces before and after the meal.
- Hong Kongers generally place food in the center of the table, and everyone helps themselves.
- The host may place unusual delicacies on your plate. At least taste them.
- To place food in your bowl, use the serving spoon, your porcelain spoon, or the wide ends of your chopsticks (that is, don't use the ends you put in your mouth).
- When serving yourself, don't take the last serving of any dish.
- Don't fill your own glass. Your dining partners will fill it when empty, and you should fill theirs.
- Hosts may serve a whole fish, with the head pointing toward the guest of honor. The guest of honor uses chopsticks to divide the fish, then the guests help themselves. Never turn the fish over—doing so is bad luck (signifies the fisherman's boat has capsized).
- Hong Kongers serve rice as a filler; don't eat large amounts of it. Doing so implies the host hasn't served enough food.
- Place bones, shells, and other food refuse directly on the table—never in your rice bowl. Hosts may provide a dish for this purpose.
- Hong Kongers consider belching, slurping, clanging utensils, and making loud noises at the dinner table acceptable, even complimentary, behavior.
- Always leave some food on your plate when you're finished with a course. If you don't, your host will give you another serving. Likewise, leave tea in your teacup if you're finished.
- When finished eating, always set your chopsticks on your chopstick rest or neatly on the table. Never stick them in your rice bowl.

- In restaurants, wait to be seated. If the restaurant is full, you may be seated with strangers. You don't need to talk with them.
- To obtain your bill, make a writing gesture on your palm.
- It's polite manners to leave soon after the meal ends.
- If you're the guest of honor at a banquet, be sure to reciprocate with a comparable banquet. Your hotel can help with arrangements.

Punctuality

Hong Kongers expect punctuality. Make sure you're on time for all appointments and events, especially banquets. (You may, however, be up to fifteen minutes late for other social events.) If you'll be late, always call, explain, and apologize.

Allow plenty of time to get anywhere; traffic in Hong Kong is terrible. If someone is late for an appointment with you, allow thirty minutes of "courtesy time." Heavy traffic may be the reason for the lateness.

Dress

Hong Kongers dress ostentatiously in styles more popular in Japan than in the United Kingdom or the United States. They wear all kinds of designer fashions with lots of jewelry, especially high-quality watches. To fit in, visitors should make sure to dress as well as Hong Kongers do.
- For business, men wear lightweight, Western-style suits and ties. (Bankers, however, usually wear pinstripe suits.) Private clubs are popular places to do business, and most clubs require men to wear coats and ties.

    Women wear dresses, tailored suits, or skirts and blouses in conservative styles and colors.
- At restaurants, men wear suits and ties. (Most European-style hotel restaurants require them, especially in the evening.) Women wear cocktail dresses or elegant pantsuits.
- People tend to dress up for evening events, whether for business or pleasure. (Hong Kong has a vibrant nightlife.) Ask your host, colleagues, or the hotel concierge for the expected attire.
- For casual occasions, men wear open-neck shirts with cotton trousers. Women wear dresses, skirts or slacks, and blouses; they never wear shorts in the city.

Gifts

Gift-giving is a tradition in Hong Kong that communicates respect and friendship. They appreciate (perhaps expect) expensive, brand-name, high-quality—even ostentatious—gifts.

- Hong Kongers generally don't open gifts in front of the giver. Recipients thank the giver sincerely and put aside the gift to open later. Never ask to open a gift or insist a recipient open your gift.
- Wrap gifts elegantly (professionally, if possible) in red (considered lucky) or gold (symbolizes wealth) gift-wrap, never in white or black gift-wrap (colors symbolize death or tragedy).
- Present and receive a gift with both hands.
- The Chinese word for "three" is a homonym for the word for "life," the word for "eight" is a homonym for the word for "prosperity," and the word for "nine" is a homonym for the word for "eternity." Give gifts in these numbers, if possible.
- Don't give gifts in sets of four. The Chinese word for "four" is a homonym for the word for "death."
- "Red envelopes" are common gifts. (See page 58.)

Hostess Gifts

Never visit a Hong Kong home without bringing a gift.

Consider giving
- Fruit
- Candy
- Cookies
- Gifts from your home country or region

Don't give
- White flowers (symbolize mourning)

Business Gifts

- Be prepared to present a group gift or a small gift for each person at the first meeting, perhaps after the meeting or at a dinner to celebrate the first meeting. Let your hosts initiate the gift giving.
- A Hong Konger with extensive experience in Western business customs may ask you to open a gift; if this is the case, open the gift. Also, if a group gives an individual a gift, they may insist the person open the gift.
- It's illegal to give a civil servant a gift.

Consider giving
- High-quality cognac or brandy
- Candy
- Pen sets

Don't give
- Clocks (associated with death): High-quality watches, however, make good gifts.
- Knives (connotes the severing of a relationship)

Helpful Hints

- Bargain in all shops, except department stores and high-fashion boutiques. But bargain only if you intend to buy an item.
- Avoid using triangles (in your company logo, for example). Hong Kongers associate the triangle with negativity.
- It's a good idea to make restaurant reservations, especially for lunch.
- Be careful of shoddy knockoffs when purchasing merchandise from street vendors or stalls.

Health and Safety

- Some, but not all, taxi drivers speak English. Ask your hotel concierge to write down your destination for your taxi driver. Carry your hotel's business card (in Chinese) to give return directions to the hotel.
- Police with a red patch on the shoulder of their uniforms speak English.
- Hong Kong's medical care is excellent, but clinics and hospitals may require immediate cash payment for services.
- Tap water in Hong Kong is safe to drink.
- In 1998, avian influenza (bird flu) sickened hundreds of people in Hong Kong. Authorities reacted quickly, containing the infection. But to be safe, avoid contact with live poultry and don't eat undercooked poultry or eggs.
- Hong Kong has a low crime rate and one of the world's highest police-to-population ratios. Nevertheless, be alert for crimes of opportunity, including pickpocketing and purse snatching.
- Traffic in Hong Kong is crowded and chaotic. About 90 percent of Hong Kongers rely on public transportation, and so should visitors. The region has a superb public transportation system and an excellent infrastructure. Its airport, subway system, taxis, buses, and trains are generally safe.

- Hong Kong's air quality is terrible, and Hong Kongers are realizing it's beginning to hurt business. A 2006 survey of members of the American Chamber of Commerce in Hong Kong discovered that many members left (or were thinking of leaving) the region because of its air pollution.

  People with respiratory ailments should talk to their physicians before traveling to Hong Kong.

Corporate Culture

Hong Kong's business climate is wide open, with a free market and limited government involvement. The Cato Institute (a nonprofit public policy research foundation) has named the Hong Kong economy the world's freest economy every year since 1970. And in 2004 the Milken Institute (a publicly supported independent economic think tank) ranked Hong Kong as the world's second-best market for entrepreneurial finance.

> Hong Kongers have a three-step plan for launching a successful business:
> 1. Morning of day one: Register business.
> 2. Later in the morning of day one: Rent premises.
> 3. Afternoon of day one: Make money.

Structure

Hong Kong companies make decisions from the top down. The senior executive has absolute authority to make decisions and implement them.

Hong Kong's business leaders are well educated (often in Western schools and universities), well traveled, highly motivated, and bicultural. The labor force is flexible, hardworking, and quick to learn.

Meetings
- Meetings generally begin on time.
- Foreigners should send senior people with technical and commercial expertise. Make sure they're prepared to function as a team and make decisions on the spot.
- Hong Kongers serve tea at meetings. Don't drink your tea until your Hong Kong host takes the first sip.
- Negotiations may be slow and detailed, but very efficient.
- Be prepared to compromise.
- Hong Kongers may seal business deals with just a handshake, showing trust.

- Never bring your company's lawyer to the initial meetings. Hong Kongers don't include lawyers in negotiations until both parties have signed contracts.

Appointments
- Banking contacts are important. Always use a bank to set up your meetings.
- Make appointments for crucial business meetings a month before arrival. It's often possible to schedule a meeting on short notice by phone, but don't count on it.
- Normal business hours are 9:00 AM to 5:00 PM, Monday through Friday, and 9:00 AM to 1:00 PM on Saturday. Some businesses work six-day, forty-eight–hour weeks. Foreign companies and government officials usually work five-day, forty-hour weeks.
- October through November and March through June are the best times for business meetings. Avoid scheduling appointments for the weeks before and after Christmas, Chinese New Year, or Easter.

Communication

- Hong Kongers conduct business discussions in English.

- Hong Kongers are polite, modest, and quiet, but they're also direct and results oriented. They get

> Hong Kong has a modern communications system that includes the world's first fully digitized telephone network. Commuters can even use the free Internet service offered at several of Hong Kong's subway stations.

down to business quickly. Unlike other Asians, they don't care as much about etiquette and protocol. To them, making money is what counts.
- Be aware: "Yes" means "I hear you" rather than "I agree." "No" often means "I will have to wait" or "This may be very difficult."

Business Cards
- Have your information printed in English on one side and in Chinese (classical characters) on the other side. If planning to visit both Hong Kong and China (which uses simplified characters), mark your boxes of business cards in some way to avoid mix-ups.
- Upon introduction, present your business card with both hands and with the Chinese side up.
- Be sure to look carefully at a person's business card upon receiving it. Never write on a business card in front of the person who gave it to you.

Be Aware

- Never try to open an office or factory without first consulting a feng shui master. (See pages 86–87.)
- Always take time to build relationships. It may take several meetings to accomplish goals.
- Do business in person whenever possible. Courtesy calls are vital to success.

Socializing

Hong Kongers, young and old, work hard and play hard.

- Hong Kong companies may throw foreign guests an elaborate banquet.
- Hong Kongers often do business entertaining in restaurants, on boats, or in clubs. Business lunches are common, but businesspeople make many deals over dinner.
- Be prepared: Hong Kongers frequently work and entertain late into the evening. The pace can be exhausting and expensive.
- Business breakfasts are popular in Hong Kong.
- Hong Kongers usually don't include spouses in business occasions. If spouses are present, business isn't discussed.

Especially for Women

Women in Hong Kong are still underrepresented in business and politics. With that said, more women are entering the government and business workplaces. A small number hold top corporate jobs.

Hong Kong businesswomen are modern and westernized. Professional families today no longer depend on relatives, neighbors, and public agencies for childcare. Nearly 9 percent of Hong Kong households employ domestic workers from other nations, mainly the Philippines. (Unfortunately, accusations of abuse of domestic workers have also arisen in recent years.)

- Foreign businesswomen should have little trouble doing business in Hong Kong.
- A foreign woman may invite a Hong Kong man to a business dinner and will have no trouble paying the bill.

Holidays and Festivals

January	New Year's Day (1)
March/April	Easter (Friday–Monday)
April	Ching Ming Festival (5)
May	Labor Day (1)
July	Hong Kong Special Administrative Region Establishment Day (1)
October	National Day (1)
December	Christmas (25–26)

Note: Hong Kongers also celebrate Chinese traditional public holidays based on the lunar calendar, including Chinese New Year, Buddha's Birthday, Dragon Boat Festival, Mid-Autumn Festival, and Chung Yeung Festival.

INDIA
REPUBLIC OF INDIA

Greetings from India

Greetings from a land of staggering contradictions. We are both modern and primitive, industrial and agrarian, fabulously wealthy and hopelessly impoverished. Our scale and diversity are overwhelming.

We are one of the world's most ethnically diverse countries. With one billion people, we are home to nearly a fifth of the world's population. Only China's population is larger, but we are set to overtake China as the world's most populous country by the middle of this century. Because more than half of our population is younger than age twenty-five, we think our country has an economic advantage over an aging China.

We are positioning ourselves to emerge as one of the world's largest economies. In the 1980s and '90s, we embraced market reforms in response to economic crises. Today, all the world's powers are courting us. Our ties to the United States and China (two of our top trading partners) are growing strong.

From Mumbai to Bangalore to Chennai, we are becoming an economic success story. We are wizards in software and business process outsourcing. Indian companies hold about two-thirds of the world's offshore information technology (IT) services (between one-half and two-thirds of Fortune 500 companies have outsourced jobs to India). Since 1994, our economy has grown by an average of more than 7 percent a year, and our poverty rate has dropped by ten percentage points.

We are proud of our economy, but we believe our greatest achievement has been our almost uninterrupted preservation of democratic rule since our independence in 1947—even when our leaders were assassinated.

We are a religious and philosophical people. India is the birthplace of Hinduism, Buddhism, Jainism, and Sikhism. Our faith is the basis for our humility, self-denial, tolerance, purity, refinement, and social harmony. Families take precedence over individuals, and extended families generally live together or near one another.

Many people consider us a Hindu nation, and 80 percent of us are Hindus. But we have the world's fourth-largest Muslim population. In fact, our president is a Muslim, our prime minister is a Sikh, and the leader of the Congress party is a woman who was raised in a Roman Catholic family.

With such diversity, it is not easy for us to find a common value system. Conflict exists between traditional and modern values, and there is tension among people of different religions and castes, especially Dalits or Untouchables (see page 81). In 1950, our constitution legally abolished the discrimination of Dalits. But enforcement has been lax—sometimes nonexistent, especially in rural areas. We continue to repudiate the caste system as unfair and economically harmful.

> In his *New York Times* column in March 2006, Thomas Friedman described India as a "beacon of tolerance and stability." He said, "Call me biased, but I have a soft spot for countries of one billion people, speaking a hundred different languages and practicing a variety of religions, whose people hold regular free and fair elections...."

We know we have other challenges to overcome. Decades of poverty and illiteracy have blighted us. We believe we suffer from the world's most bureaucratic bureaucracy; high tariffs and limits on foreign investment have hampered growth. We export only about 1 percent of the world's goods. Our labor laws and banking systems need updating. We also have a terrible infrastructure.

Our huge middle class numbers over three hundred million, but there is also a glaring disparity between the very wealthy and desperately poor. A quarter of all Indians live below the poverty line. Especially among the poor and undereducated, a traditional fatalism makes us accept our lot. Even in hardship, we accept our course in life as God's will or fate.

> Although the caste system is still a strong influence in Indian life, there are signs that it's weakening in urban areas. Today many educated Hindus of different castes mix freely with one another. In fact, former Indian President K. R. Narayanan (1997–2002) was an Untouchable.

As members of the world's largest democracy, we continue to work to find balance as our society continues to change. Come meet us, but be prepared to accept us on our own terms.

Vital Statistics

Population	1,095,351,995
Capital	New Delhi
Area	1,269,345 square miles, slightly more than one-third the size of the United States
Government	Federal republic (28 states and 7 union territories)
Living Standard	GDP = $830 per capita
Natural Resources	Coal (fourth-largest reserves in the world), iron ore, manganese, mica, bauxite, titanium ore, chromite, natural gas, diamonds, petroleum, limestone, arable land
Agriculture	Rice, wheat, oilseed, cotton, jute, tea, sugarcane, potatoes, cattle, water buffalo, sheep, goats, poultry, fish
Industries	Textiles, chemicals, food processing, steel, transportation equipment, cement, mining, petroleum, machinery, software
Climate	Tropical monsoon in south, temperate in north
Currency	Indian rupee (INR)

The People

Correct Name	noun: Indian(s) adjective: Indian
Ethnic Makeup	Indo-Aryan 72%, Dravidian 25%, Mongoloid and other 3%
Languages	15 official languages: Bengali, Telugu, Marathi, Tamil, Urdu, Gujarati, Malayalam, Kannada, Oriya, Punjabi, Assamese, Kashmiri, Sindhi, Sanskrit, and most prominently Hindi (spoken by 30% of Indians); English is an associate official language, used mostly for political and business communication.
Religions	Hindu 80.5%, Muslim 13.4%, Christian 2.3%, Sikh 1.9%, other 1.8%, unspecified 0.1%

Meeting and Greeting

- Because it may be difficult to determine a person's religion, Westerners may greet Indians by saying (in English) "Pleased to meet you" or "How do you do?" Most Indian businesspeople are fluent in English.
- Men shake hands with men when meeting and leaving, but not with women.
- Traditionally, Indian women shake hands with foreign women but not with men (although educated and more modern Indian women may). Western women may shake hands with Indian women or westernized Indian men, but not with traditional Indian men.
- When shaking hands with Muslims, use only your right hand.
- If you meet Indians around noon, they may ask if you've eaten. This is usually a straightforward inquiry, not a polite remark. If you haven't eaten, they may invite you to join them for a meal.

Greetings

Phrase	Recipients	Accompanying gestures
Namaste (nah-mahss-TAY)	Hindus	Slight bow with palms together and fingers pointed up
Namaskara (nah-mahss-CAR)	Southern Hindus	Slight bow with palms together and fingers pointed up
Salam alaikum (sah-LAAM ah-LIE-come)	Muslims	Low bow while touching right hand to the forehead
Sat sri akal (saht SREE ah-KAAL)	Sikhs	Palms together and fingers pointed up

Names and Titles

- Never address any Indian by his or her first name.
- Unless you're thoroughly familiar with Hindu, Muslim, or Sikh titles, use the following information to address Indians.

Hindus

Hindu naming conventions vary according to region and ethnicity. Here's some general information.

In the North
- Name order is first name (given name) + last name (surname).
- Upon marriage, women often take their husbands' last names.

In the South
- Name order is father's first name (or first initial of father's first name) + first name.
- Upon marriage, women may replace their fathers' first initial of first name with their husbands' initial.

Across India
- Address Hindus by English courtesy title (Mr., Mrs., or Miss) or professional title (like Doctor or Professor) + last name (in the north) or first name (in the south).
- After establishing a relationship, Hindus may give you a familial nickname like "uncle" or "mother." Never refuse this offer of friendship.
- Common Hindu last names include Gopal, Krishna, Ram, Lal, and Prakash.

Muslims
- Traditional name order is first name + bin (used for men) or binti (used for women) + father's first name.
    Examples: Ali bin Isa is the son of Isa bin Osman.
               Zaitun binti Isa is the daughter of Isa bin Osman.
- Some Muslims may eliminate bin or binti in their names (name order is simply first name + father's first name).
- Some Muslims add a family or tribal name that begins with the prefix "al-" to the end of their names.
    Example: Ali bin Isa al-Nizami is the son of Isa and belongs to the family or tribe of Nizami.
- Address Muslims by English courtesy title or professional title + first name.
    Example: Address Ali bin Isa al-Nizami as Mr. Ali. Address Zaitun binti Osman as Mrs. Zaitun.
- Upon marriage, women don't usually take their husbands' names.
- Common Muslim names include Khan, Ali, Muhammad, and Hussein.

Sikhs
- Sikh names have three parts: first name, middle name, and last name.
- Traditionally, Sikhs don't use last names. Last names indicate caste, and Sikhs don't honor the caste system. Middle names (Singh or Kaur) serve as

last names. As they interact more with people outside India, however, some Sikhs are using their last names or using Singh as the last name for their entire family.

- Keep in mind that not all people with the last name Singh are Sikhs.
- Most Sikh first names can be used for either men or women. Middle names traditionally denote sex. All Sikh men have the middle name Singh (pronounced "sing"), which means "lion" in Sanskrit. All Sikh women have the middle name Kaur (pronounced "core"), which means "princess" in Sanskrit.
- Upon marriage, women traditionally don't take their husbands' names.
- Address Sikhs by English courtesy title (Mr., Mrs., or Miss) or professional title (like Doctor or Professor) + last name.

Language

More than three hundred languages are spoken in India, including fifteen official languages and one associate language (English). The majority of Indians don't share one language—not even Hindi, one of the world's most spoken languages.

English may be the most useful language throughout India. It's the language of national communication and a primary language used in business and government. There are more English speakers in India than in the United States and the United Kingdom combined.

While many Indians understand English, only some people (mainly businesspeople) actually speak it. Roughly one in three Indians can converse in English.

Conversation
- Indians often converse indirectly. When someone says, "I will try," he or she generally means "no."
- Never express anger when conversing with Indians.
- Indians may ask personal questions as a way to get to know you. Don't take offense. If you don't want to answer a question, give a vague answer or smile and say, "In my country, that would be a strange question."

Acceptable topics
- Sports, including field hockey, football (soccer), tennis, badminton, and especially cricket (India has produced many world-class cricket players. Learn enough about the game to ask intelligent questions.)

- Family
- Local cuisine
- Someone's home region
- Indian cinema
- Indian culture and pre-Colonial history

India is one of the world's largest motion picture industries. Although its share of global cinema revenue is just 1 percent, the nation produces more films than any other country.

Unacceptable topics
- Criticisms of Indian customs
- Criticisms of Mahatma Gandhi: Indians revere the founder of modern independent India.
- Relations with Pakistan
- Violence among adherents of different religions
- Caste issues (including asking about a person's caste)
- Praise of Indian children (praise may attract the attention of the "evil eye")

The province of Kashmir has been the source of festering tensions between India and Pakistan. In 2004, however, the Indian government agreed to a cease-fire with Pakistan, and each nation resumed commercial flights to the other country for the first time since 2001. Later that year, the Indian cricket team played against Pakistan for the first time in fifteen years.

Topics that require sensitivity
- Disparity between the rich and poor
- Economic reforms of the 1980s and '90s
- India's history as a British colony
- Feminism

Body Language
- Indians consider public displays of affection improper behavior.
- Don't stand closely to Indians; they value personal space. They generally allow an arm's length of distance between themselves and others.
- Men don't touch women in public as a sign of respect.
- Indian men may pat one another's back as a sign of friendship. Women may hug one another when they meet.
- When Indians smile and jerk their heads backward or move their heads in a figure eight motion, they're saying "yes."

- Indians often interpret a hand waving from side to side as "no" or "go away," not "hello."
- Use only your right hand to touch someone, eat, pass money, or pick up merchandise. Indians consider the left hand unclean.
- Never touch anyone—especially a child—on the head. Tradition holds that the soul resides there.
- To beckon anyone politely, extend your arm (palm down), then curl and flex your fingers together.
- Grasping your earlobe expresses remorse, repentance, or sincerity.
- Never point your feet at anyone or show the soles of your shoes. Doing so is an insult. Apologize immediately if your feet or shoes touch another person.
- Point with your chin (but not at superiors), whole hand, or thumb—never with one or two fingers. Indians use one or two fingers only to point at inferiors.

Phrases

Hindi is written in the Devanāgarī alphabet. Below are the phonetic equivalents.

English	Hindi	Pronunciation
Hello	*Namaste*	(nah-mahss-TAY)
Please	*Kripa ya*	(krip-ah-YAH)
Thank you	*Dhanyavaad*	(doohn yah-VAHD)
You're welcome	*Aapakaa svaagat hai*	(AHP-kah SWAHG-aht HAY)
Yes	*Ha*	(ha)
No	*Nahi*	(nah-HEE)
Excuse me	*Shamma kare*	(shah-MAH kar-EH)
Goodbye	*Namaste*	(nah-mahss-TAY)
Pleased to meet you	*Aap se milkar*	(AHP say MILL-kur)
How are you?	*Aap kaise hai*	(AHP kay-seh HAY)

Dining

India's diverse cultures and geography contribute greatly to the country's cuisine. One uniting element of Indian fare is the use of spices to create distinct flavors and aromas.

- For religious reasons, Hindus and Sikhs don't eat beef; many are vegetarians. Strict dietary rules restrict Muslims from eating pork.
- Orthodox Hindus prefer that people outside their caste or religion don't touch their food.
- In traditional homes, guests generally eat with men, the elderly, and children. Women eat alone later.
- Many Indians eat with their hands. See pages 39–40 for more information on eating with your hands.
- Better hotels and some restaurants serve Western food.
- Westernized homes, hotels, and restaurants offer Western eating utensils.
- Meals may end with *paan*, a betel nut mixture believed to aid digestion.

Drinking

- India produces about a quarter of the world's tea. On average, Indians drink tea more than twice a day.
- In 2005, India was the world's sixth-largest producer of coffee. Coffee has been traditionally popular in southern India, but consumption is rising across the nation.
- When first offered tea or coffee (or any food, for that matter), it's polite to refuse once before accepting—unless you're already sitting at a restaurant table, a banquet table, or your host's dining table. Then you may accept the initial offer.
- Some Indian states prohibit alcohol consumption. Foreigners, however, may obtain a permit that allows them to legally purchase and consume alcohol throughout the country.
- Beer is widely available, but it isn't as popular as in Western countries. Whiskey, gin, rum, and other spirits also are available.
- Strict Muslims don't drink any alcohol; neither do most devout Hindus or Sikhs (especially women).
- In India, not all spirits labeled "liquor" are equal.
  * "Foreign liquor" or "Indian-Made Foreign Liquor" (IMFL) = high-quality and inexpensive spirits of foreign origin (whiskey, brandy, gin, and so on) produced in India
  * "Country liquor" = traditional Indian spirits, like *feni* (a coconut or cashew apple juice), served in places called "country bars"
  * "Indian liquor" = often refers to illegally produced spirits that can be dangerous—even deadly—to consume

Toasting

Except at ceremonial banquets or other formal occasions, Indians generally don't offer toasts.

- If the host proposes a toast, reciprocate with one.
- When hosting, you may propose a toast, but your guests may or may not reciprocate.
- The following are acceptable (English) toasts:
    * "To your health"
    * "To your country"
    * "To your prosperity"
- Women may propose toasts at business or government functions.

Tipping

The necessity of tipping varies in India. Some people may offer to help you, then expect a tip after completing a service; others will require a tip in order to get something done.

Don't be surprised if someone throws a tip on the ground in apparent disgust. He or she will eventually pick it up; you needn't give more.

- Restaurants: In some major hotels and restaurants, the bill includes a 10 percent service charge. If the bill doesn't include a service charge, tip 10 percent of the bill in urban areas and 5 percent in other areas.

    Check your bill's accuracy. If it's incorrect or unclear, question your server.
- Taxis: Tip 5 to 10 percent of the fare.
- Hired driver: Tip INR10 for a half-day and INR20 to INR25 plus meals for a full day.
- Bellhops and porters: Tip INR5 per bag handled.
- Tour guides: Tip INR5 to INR10 per hour.
- Shoe guardian (at a temple or mosque): Tip INR2.
- Room waiter: Tip INR5 per night.
- Doormen: Tip INR5.
- Hair stylists and barbers: Tip 5 to 10 percent of the bill.

Manners

- Ask permission before smoking, and don't smoke in the presence of elders or seniors.
- Don't offer cigarettes to Indian women or Sikhs.
- Show great respect for elders.
- Don't stare at anyone, especially the poor. Doing so humiliates them.
- Never wink at a woman, and women should never wink. Indians consider winking a demeaning gesture.
- Don't whistle in public. Doing so is disrespectful and uncouth behavior.
- Many Indians don't wear shoes in their homes. Follow your host's example. Make sure to wear clean socks without holes in case you need to remove your shoes.
- When finished conversing with someone, ask for his or her permission before leaving.
- At social gatherings, hosts often place flower garlands around guests' necks. Guests may remove them after a few minutes, then carry them in hand to show humility.
- Let your host seat you. Hosts seat the guest of honor first.
- Be sure to wash hands before and after meals. (Indians may provide a bowl of hot water with a slice of lemon at the table.) Use your own handkerchief to dry them.
- Don't serve yourself; let your host serve you. When hosting an event, serve your guests.
- Wait for the host to start eating and invite you to do so before you begin eating.
- If hosts eat with their hands, assure them you enjoy doing the same. (See pages 39–40 for information on eating with your hands.) Take food from a communal dish with a spoon, never your fingers.
- Tear *chappati* or *poori* (bread) into small chunks, then wrap them around pieces of meat or use them to scoop up vegetables and sauces from your plate.
- Never let the serving spoon touch your plate.
- Never refuse food, but you don't have to clean your plate. Hindu hosts, in particular, won't let their guests have empty plates.
- Saying *namaste* (nah-mahss-TAY) politely indicates you've had enough food.
- If using utensils to eat, place your spoon and fork together on your plate when finished eating. If you don't, hosts will offer you more food.

- To show you're finished eating when using a banana leaf, fold the leaf in half with the fold toward you. (See also page 40.)
- If you can't finish your food, don't offer it to anyone or return it to the serving dish. Once you've touched food, Indians consider it tainted.
- Never take food out of the eating area.
- After meals, expect to stay for approximately an hour of conversation.
- Never beckon wait staff with your index finger, and never snap your fingers or hiss as Indians sometimes do. Instead, extend your arm (palm down), then curl and flex your fingers together.
- In restaurants, the person who extended the invitation pays the bill.
- When reciprocating a dinner, never make it more lavish than the one hosted for you—doing so could embarrass your host.
- Sikh temples don't allow leather inside (shoes, belts, purses, camera cases, and so on). See pages 75–85 for additional etiquette information when visiting temples, mosques, and other holy places.

Punctuality

Indians expect punctuality in business, but be aware: they may not show up for scheduled meetings. Be prepared to reschedule.

Indians don't expect punctuality in social situations. You may arrive fifteen to thirty minutes late.

Dress

- In most parts of India, light, loose-fitting clothing is best. Northern India, however, is cold in the winter; you'll need warm clothing during those months.
- In major cities, many Indian women are beautifully, expensively dressed. They often wear saris (long lightweight cloths wrapped about the waist and over the head or shoulders).

  If a foreign woman wants to wear a sari, she should ask an Indian woman to help choose an appropriate one and demonstrate how to wear it correctly. (Indians drape the fabric according to socioeconomic status and/or religious affiliation.)
- In general, foreign women should wear modest clothing, especially in Muslim areas. Revealing clothing may prompt unflattering remarks and unwanted staring.

- For business and formal occasions, men wear suits and ties. In very warm weather, they may omit the jacket. Women wear conservative pantsuits or dresses, although they may wear simple, floor-length dresses or saris for formal occasions.
- For casual occasions, men wear cotton shirts and pants. Women wear dresses or blouses with skirts or slacks. Most restaurants don't have dress codes. Neat, casual attire is appropriate.
- When visiting a temple or mosque, men must wear long pants, but short-sleeved shirts are acceptable. Women wear skirts, dresses, or long dress pants; their arms must be covered. Remove shoes before entering a temple or mosque.

> In the past, a *bindi* (red dot on the center of the forehead) symbolized femininity and indicated the wearer was married. Widows didn't wear a *bindi*.
>
> Today, the *bindi* has become a beauty accessory, and women often wear one in a color that matches their outfit.

- Men and women cover their heads when entering sacred buildings. Always carry a large clean handkerchief with you for this purpose.
- Avoid wearing leather. If you do, you risk offending strict adherents of some Indian religions that revere cows or forbid the killing of any animal.
- Wear shorts only at beaches or for athletic activities. Women may wear bikinis only at pools and beaches, but conservative one-piece swimsuits are more appropriate.

Gifts

- Indians normally don't open gifts in the giver's presence. If, however, your Indian colleague urges you to open a gift, you may open it.
- Wrap gifts in yellow, red, or green gift-wrap (the colors symbolize happiness or luck), never white or black gift-wrap (the colors symbolize misfortune).
- Always give and receive gifts with both hands.

Hostess Gifts

- Guests should also give small gifts to any children in the home.
- After visiting someone's home, guests should reciprocate with a dinner of comparable value.

Consider giving
- Fruit
- Flowers (Ask a florist for an appropriate choice for the occasion.)
- Candy
- Wine or Scotch (if the recipient drinks alcohol)
- Books about your home country
- Gifts from your home country (for example, perfume, chocolates, small china pieces, or crystal objects)

Don't give
- Religious items
- Beef or leather items

Business Gifts

Indians don't normally exchange gifts at the first meeting. They may give them once a relationship develops; be prepared to exchange gifts when that occurs.

Consider giving
- Whiskey (if the recipient drinks)
- Pens
- Ties

Don't give
- Alcohol, if the recipient is Muslim
- Large or very expensive gifts (may cause embarrassment)
- Beef or leather items

Helpful Hints

- Never bargain in government emporia or large department stores. Bargain freely with street vendors or in small shops and stalls. To bargain, make an initial offer of one-half the asking price. If it's refused, then bargain to 70 or 75 percent of the price.
- Always refuse "touts" (people paid by merchants to aggressively bring in customers) and tour guides who offer to take you to a shop. They'll add a commission to the price of your purchase. Just thank them, decline, then walk away.
- In crowded restaurants, you may share a table with strangers. You needn't speak with them.

Health and Safety

- Check your medical insurance coverage before traveling to India. Medical care is adequate in major cities but limited in rural areas.
- Many doctors in India speak English, and some have been trained in the West.
- Be aware: Dental care in India isn't up to Western standards.
- If possible, drink only bottled water or other bottled drinks with tamper-proof seals intact. If bottled water isn't available, drink only water that has been boiled and filtered.
- Always carry water purification tablets and a plastic glass with you to use if you're uncertain of water's purity.
- If you must drink water from a communal container (a common practice in villages), do so without your lips touching the container.
- Don't put ice in your drinks—even in good hotels.
- Eat only thoroughly cooked meats, and eat only fruits or vegetables you know have been washed in diluted permanganate solution or have been cooked and peeled.
- Avoid swimming in fresh water. Many freshwater sources in India are polluted or contaminated with water-borne diseases.
- Wear shoes to avoid contracting hookworm or other parasites. Always wear footwear with rubber soles in showers, bathrooms, and kitchens. Wiring and plumbing problems could cause an electrical shock.
- Many international brand-name pharmaceuticals are available over the counter.
- Petty crime is common, especially personal property theft. Watch your belongings when on public transportation, in crowds, and around airports and train or bus terminals. Keep valuables in a money belt inside your clothing.
- Don't give money to beggars. Instead, act indifferently and walk away. The Indian government considers begging a racket and is trying to wipe it out. If you give money, you'll become an immediate target for other beggars.
- Street people may approach you as if to shake your hand. Don't let them. If you do, they'll fasten a religious bracelet on your arm and demand money.

Corporate Culture

Structure

Either one person or a small group at or near the top of an organization makes all decisions. Foreigners often find Indian bureaucracy very cumbersome. Indians consider all decisions major, and they make them slowly. Middle managers value job security and will check every decision with many people at various levels.

Attempt to deal initially with the highest-level person possible, even if middle managers will work out the details.

Meetings

- To obtain a goal or reach a decision, many meetings are necessary to get through multiple layers of management.
- At the start of meetings, never begin business discussions immediately. Instead, first ask about attendants' families, interests, and hobbies. You also may ask for opinions on current economic and political issues, but never offer your comments—especially if they're negative.
- During meetings or negotiations, Indians may offer you sugary or milky tea, coffee, or soft drinks. Never refuse this offer. Your hosts may refill your glass or cup when empty.
- Make presentations in a reserved, controlled manner.
- In negotiations, Indians generally stick close to original proposals; however, never make your best offer at the outset.

Appointments

- Always request an appointment in advance. You may stop at someone's office and request an appointment.
- The normal hours for meetings are 10:00 AM to 5:00 PM.
- Avoid scheduling your business trip for May through June (very warm) or July through August (monsoon rains). October through March are the best months for business trips.
- Try to do any business in banks or government offices early in the day. Lunch hours can extend well into the afternoon, especially in government offices.

Communication

- In business, Indians commonly speak English. They write contracts in a local language and English.

- Never get angry if told something can't be done. Instead, restate your request firmly but with a smile. Emphasize the urgency and importance of your task and your appreciation for any assistance and support. Politely ask for suggestions on how to get the job done, how to get around restrictions, and so on.

Business Cards
- Indians always exchange business cards upon introduction. Make sure to bring plenty of your cards.
- Business cards in English are appropriate.

Be Aware
- Knowing the right people is vital to success. To help you make necessary contacts, hire an agent (a person or company knowledgeable in local customs who can negotiate contracts, apply for necessary permits, research and visit local plant sites, and so on) to represent you and your interests.
- Indian businessmen touch and backslap a great deal as a sign of friendship.

Socializing
- Indians usually do initial business entertaining in restaurants of prestigious hotels.
- Business lunches are acceptable, but Indians usually do business over dinner.
- Never flatly refuse an invitation to someone's home or dinner in a restaurant. Make a plausible excuse instead.
- When hosting an event, always invite your Indian colleagues' spouses. Muslims probably won't bring them, but non-Muslim spouses will likely attend.
- Indians discuss business during meals; however, let your host initiate the conversation.
- At social functions, men usually talk to men and women talk to women. Don't be surprised if women go to a corner to talk.

Especially for Women

Technically, the Indian constitution enshrines the principle of gender equality, but the enforcement of this principle is debatable. India is a male-dominated society, especially in rural areas. In fact, traditional Muslim women never interact with strangers, especially men.

Traditionally, parents still arrange marriages. Although officially illegal, dowries are a common practice. The bride's family must provide a dowry to the husband, and some brides still endure abuse if their husbands' families believe the dowries are insufficient.

Because dowries can be very costly, many families prefer sons to daughters. Selective abortion by sex is officially illegal but rarely prosecuted. The practice occurs among all socioeconomic classes—perhaps most prevalently among educated women (likely because they have access to the technology and can afford ultrasounds). Some experts estimate that as many as ten million female fetuses have been aborted since 1985.

Furthermore, boys generally get better food, education, and medical care than girls get—especially in rural India.

Women's conditions in India are improving. In 1990, Parliament formed the National Commission for Women to guard women's rights and legal entitlements. Amendments to the constitution in 1993 reserve one third of seats in local governments to women. The Ministry of Women & Child Development works to ensure the economic and social empowerment of Indian women. Between 1991 and 2001, female literacy rates rose 14 percent; in 2001 over half the women in India could read and write.

Although relatively few Indian women work outside the home, women are advancing in the fields of medicine, science, commerce, and politics. Furthermore, official statistics don't measure women's economic contributions completely. For example, statistics don't count the work women do farming or selling homemade handicrafts.

- India is a difficult place to do business, particularly for women. To gain acceptance, a Western woman must establish her position and credentials immediately.

"Eve-teasing" is sexual harassment of women in public places, ranging from verbal teasing and offensive jokes to physical contact like pinching, grabbing, and rubbing. Some instances have led to rape and murder.

To avoid attracting unwanted attention, dress modestly, avoid making eye contact with strangers, travel with a group (especially after dark), and be aware of your surroundings.

If you become a victim of eve-teasing, shout or scream to alert others of your predicament, then leave the area. Report the harassment to the nearest police station.

- Although increasingly rare, some older or rural Indian men may not include women in social events or conversation. But a Western woman likely won't have a problem striking up a conversation with men, especially in cities.
- If a Western woman telephones or enters a government office or bank, employees may serve her but won't consider her important. Be firmly persistent that they should take you seriously.
- Women may eat alone in restaurants without harassment.
- A Western woman may invite an Indian man to a business lunch or dinner and have no trouble paying the bill.

Holidays and Festivals

January	Republic Day (26)
March/April	Good Friday
April/May	Buddha Purnima
August	Independence Day (15)
October	Mahatma Gandhi's Birthday (2)

Notes: Observed Islamic and Hindu holidays vary with the Islamic and Hindu calendars. Check to see when they're observed for the year you're traveling to India.

There are also numerous festivals and fairs that are observed in some states as holidays, the dates of which change from year to year. Check to see when they're observed for the year you're traveling.

INDONESIA
REPUBLIC OF INDONESIA

Greetings from Indonesia

Greetings from the world's largest archipelagic nation. More than thirteen thousand islands compose Indonesia, and we Indonesians call our country *Tanah Air Kita* ("Our Land and Water").

Our people and cultures are as numerous as our islands. Indonesia is the world's fourth most populous nation, and our residents come from more than three hundred different ethnic groups and speak more than seven hundred languages. Many Westerners are surprised to learn that ours is the world's largest Muslim nation.

Hinduism, Buddhism, and paganism have also influenced our religious practices. Most of us, however, consider ourselves only moderately religious. We believe karma (fate) determines all outcomes, good or bad.

Unity, honor, and respect for social rules as well as for the individual are the basis of our culture. We are extremely loyal to family and friends. Traditionally, several generations live together. The extended family offer alliances, friendships, and support for children and the elderly. In fact, we view all of Indonesia as an extended family, with our president its "father."

As part of the Pacific Ring of Fire, our nation has more active volcanoes than any other country. We also have 10 percent of the world's tropical rainforests (second only to Brazil) and are home to monkeys, tigers, crocodiles, pythons, the Komodo dragon, and the dazzling bird of paradise.

We fervently work to protect our unique ecosystem, but we are encountering problems. Illegal logging, for example, is devastating our rainforests, which shrunk to half the size in the last half-century. Two-thirds of all logging is illegal.

In 1998, after huge numbers of our young people protested against a corrupt, authoritarian presidency, we enthusiastically embraced democracy. In 1997 our Asian neighbors experienced an economic crisis; shortly afterward, we suffered our own dramatic economic collapse. Thankfully, a few years later our economy stabilized, a condition we hope is permanent.

Nonetheless, today our society faces numerous challenges. Millions live in extreme poverty. A crippling debt burden and corruption continue to plague us. Ethnic tensions have led to violence, and separatist movements aren't uncommon, given our diverse population spread across more than three thousand miles. Lastly, our tourist industry is still hoping to recover from the horrific December 2004 tsunami and the October 2005 Islamic extremist bombings in Bali.

With shopping malls common in our cities and more and more young people (especially women) wearing Western fashions, we worry that consumerism and material possessions are replacing traditional values. But despite a small number of religious radicals, the majority of us are tolerant, inclusive, and unafraid of modernity or change.

We are quick to smile and welcome strangers. We believe offering hospitality is an honor.

Indonesia's natural disasters are legendary. In 1883, Mount Krakatau erupted, generating tsunamis more than 130 feet high that killed nearly forty thousand people (the most killed in any volcanic eruption in history) and destroyed hundreds of coastal towns. The blast's atmospheric effects were visible for several years.

On December 26, 2004, the fourth-largest earthquake since 1900 shook the west coast of Sumatra. The resulting tsunami killed people as far away as Somalia, but Indonesians suffered the most: More than 110,000 were killed, and damage topped four billion US dollars.

To us, Western businesspeople often seem cold and impersonal; if you want to do business in Indonesia, we insist you invest enough time to build a solid relationship. The "time is money" attitude will not succeed in our lovely nation.

If you are patient and relaxed, you will enjoy working with us. Come discover all that we have to offer!

Vital Statistics

Population	245,452,739
Capital	Jakarta
Area	741,100 square miles, slightly less than three times the size of Texas
Government	Republic
Living Standard	GDP = US $1,590 per capita
Natural Resources	Petroleum, tin, natural gas, nickel, timber, bauxite, copper, fertile soils, coal, gold, silver

Vital Statistics (*cont.*)

Agriculture	Rice, cassava (tapioca), peanuts, rubber, cocoa, coffee, palm oil, copra, poultry, beef, pork, eggs
Industries	Petroleum and natural gas, textiles, apparel, footwear, mining, cement, chemical fertilizers, plywood, rubber, food, tourism
Climate	Tropical but more moderate in highlands
Currency	Indonesian rupiah (IDR)

The People

Correct Name	noun: Indonesian(s) adjective: Indonesian
Ethnic Makeup	Javanese 45%, Sundanese 14%, Madurese 7.5%, coastal Malays 7.5%, other 26%
Languages	Bahasa Indonesia (official), English, Dutch, local dialects (Javanese most widely spoken)
Religions	Muslim 88%, Protestant 5%, Roman Catholic 3%, Hindu 2%, Buddhist 1%, other 1%

Meeting and Greeting

- Customarily, Indonesians shake hands only upon introduction and when someone leaves for or returns from a long journey. When meeting Indonesians for the first time, shake hands and nod slightly. At subsequent meeting, simply bow or nod slightly.
- When parties of different ranks meet, those of lower rank bow lower than those of higher rank.
- To show respect, always bow slightly when meeting elders.
- After shaking hands, Indonesians may cover their hearts with their right hands, especially when meeting officials or other high-ranking people. If they do, cover your heart with your right hand, too.
- Foreign men and women should shake an Indonesian woman's hand only if she offers it.
- To get someone's attention, Indonesians generally say *halo* (pronounced "HUH-low"), a word derived from *hello*. They greet people with *selamat* (suh-LAH-maht), which means "peace."
- It's polite to introduce yourself to strangers.

Names and Titles

- Indonesian name order is first name (given name) + last name (surname).
- Indonesian courtesy titles are *Bapak* (BAH-pahk) and *Ibu* (EE-boo), which mean "sir" and "madam," respectively.
- Indonesians customarily use titles (professional, political, military, and so on). Listen carefully for one's title when meeting a person for the first time.
- When introducing someone, use *Bapak* or *Ibu* + title + first name + last name. Then give his or her business or social position.
- Because last names are often long and complicated, most Indonesians address one another by *Bapak* or *Ibu* + first name. If you don't know people's names, address them by courtesy titles alone.
- After marrying, middle-class urban women usually take their husbands' last names. Rural women often keep their maiden names.
- In written correspondence, use only *Bapak* or *Ibu* + first name in the salutation; never use last names

    Examples: To the most respected *Bapak* Ismail:

    Dear *Bapak* Ismail:

Language

Bahasa Indonesian ("Indonesian language"), a dialect of the Malay language, is Indonesia's official language. More than seven hundred other languages are spoken in the nation, most prominently Javanese.

When Indonesia was a colony of the Netherlands, the Dutch introduced the Latin (Roman) alphabet, which Bahasa Indonesian adopted. Many older adults still speak Dutch, but English is the leading international language.

Because Bahasa Indonesian uses the Latin alphabet and each letter represents only one sound, Westerners may find the language relatively easy to learn.

Conversation

- When conversing with Indonesians, speak slowly and clearly. Don't use slang or strong, rude language. Repeat yourself often. Don't assume people understand what you're saying, even if they nod and say they do.
- To avoid conflict, Indonesians prefer to use indirect language. "Yes" means "I understand" or "I hear you," not "I agree." Don't force anyone to admit error or say "no." In fact, don't expect "no" for an answer; instead, Indonesians usually say *belum* (BUH-luhm), which means "not yet."

- Indonesians may ask personal questions. If you're uncomfortable answering them, give a vague answer or say, "In my country, that would be a strange question."
- Never use the term "Indo." Indonesians consider it an insulting way to refer to a person of mixed race.

> Indonesians are among the world's best badminton players. In 1992, when badminton became an Olympic sport, Indonesia won its first gold medals—in women's and men's badminton singles. It also won the silver and bronze medals for the latter category.

- Never correct, criticize, shame, or disagree with anyone in public or cause them to lose face. Never laugh at someone's mistakes or mock someone's behavior—even someone you know well.
- *Tomorrow* may mean anytime in the future. Don't assume *tomorrow* means "the day following today."

Acceptable topics

- Family: Indonesians love to talk about their families. Ask about children and spouses.
- Sports, especially golf, football (soccer), basketball, and badminton
- The local region, including culture and cuisine: Indonesians are proud of their regions.
- Indonesia's beauty and splendid ecosystems
- Kiting: Kite festivals are popular.

> Be prepared to hear open discussions about birth control. If uncomfortable discussing the subject, you may give humorous, lighthearted answers. Or say, "In my country, many consider this topic very personal." Indonesians will pick up on your discomfort and drop the subject.

Unacceptable topics

- Corruption
- Bureaucracy
- Ethnic tensions
- Comparisons among Indonesian regions
- Indonesia's environmental problems

> Java is home to more than half of Indonesians. Government plans to relocate people from Java to less populated areas failed miserably. While millions moved, few found success in their new homes.

Topics that require sensitivity

- Religion
- Politics
- Travel: Many Indonesians travel only for tragic reasons, like illness or a death in the family.

Body Language

- Indonesians disapprove of public displays of affection.
- People in good relationships touch one another a lot. Always let Indonesians initiate pats on shoulders (never backslaps) and other physical gestures of friendship. They dislike being touched before they've established a relationship.
- Except to shake hands, men and women don't touch one another in public.
- Indonesians consider the head sacred. Never touch anyone, including children, on the head.
- When sitting, don't cross your legs, and never rest your ankle on a knee. Sitting up straight with both feet on the floor is a sign of respect. Never let the soles of your shoes face or point at another person.
- Never use your left hand to shake hands, touch others, point, eat, or give or receive objects. Indonesians consider the left hand unclean.
- Point with your thumb, not your index finger.
- Never beckon someone with your index finger. Instead, extend your arm (palm down), then curl and extend your fingers together.
- The thumbs-up gesture made with the right hand means "please go first."
- Standing with hands on hips or in pockets or with arms crossed on chest is a sign of defiance or arrogance. Indonesians find the gesture insulting.

Phrases

English	Indonesian	Pronunciation
Hello/Goodbye	*Selamat*	(suh-LAH-maht)
Good morning	*Selamat pagi*	(suh-LAH-maht PAH-ghee)
Good afternoon	*Selamat siang*	(suh-LAH-maht see-AHNG)
Good night	*Selamat malam*	(suh-LAH-maht MAH-lam)
Please	*Silahkan*	(see-LAHK-ahn)
Thank you	*Terima kasih*	(terr-EE-mah KAHS-ee)
You're welcome	*Sama*	(SAH-mah)

English	Indonesian	Pronunciation
Yes	*Ya*	(ee-YAH)
No	*Tidak*	(TEE-dahk)
Excuse me	*Permisi*	(pare-MEE-see)
Goodbye	*Sampai jumpa*	(SAHM-pie JOOM-pah)
How are you?	*Apa kabar*	(ah-PAH KAH-bar)

Dining

Rice and hot, spicy mixtures of vegetables, chicken, seafood, and other meat are staples of the Indonesian diet. Because of Islamic doctrine, Muslims don't eat pork.

- Many Indonesians use forks and spoons to eat. They use the fork (held in left hand) to push food onto the spoon (held in right hand). They put only the spoon in their mouths.
- When finished eating, place the fork (tines down) on your plate with the spoon (rim of bowl down) crossed over the fork.
- Some Indonesians eat with their hands. When eating with your hands, use only the right hand, and keep both hands above the table. (See pages 39–40 for more information on eating with your hands.)
- Indonesians in Java who eat with their hands use finger bowls and napkins throughout the meal.
- Always pass and accept food and drinks with your right hand only.
- Indonesians seat the male guest of honor next to the host and the female guest of honor next to the hostess.
- There is minimal conversation during meals.

Drinking

- Don't drink until your host invites you to do so.
- Hosts will always refill empty glasses. Leave a little liquid in your glass if you don't care for more.
- In 2005, Indonesia was sixth in global tea production. Indonesians drink hot tea and iced tea, both liberally sweetened.
- Indonesia was also third in global coffee production in 2005. Most Indonesians drink their coffee sweetened.

- Although many Indonesians drink alcohol, practicing Muslims don't. Never offer a Muslim an alcoholic beverage.

Toasting

- Toasts aren't common in Indonesia, but if you wish, you may make a general toast to friendship in English.
- Women may propose toasts.

Tipping

- Restaurants: At better restaurants, the bill usually includes a 10 percent service charge; if the bill doesn't include a service charge, leave a 10 percent tip. You may leave small change as an additional gratuity for excellent service.
- Taxis: Although optional, a tip of IDR500 is common.
- Bellhops, porters, hair stylists, barbers, and restroom attendants: Tip the equivalent of US $1.

> Have your hotel or your hosts call you a cab from a reputable company; never hail cabs. Always agree on the fare before getting in the cab.

Manners

As they try to determine your status, Indonesians may behave formally. As they get to know you, they'll probably loosen up and behave less formally.

- Never refuse an offer of food, drink, or other gesture of hospitality. To Indonesians, refusing their hospitality means personally rejecting them.
- Make sure you offer refreshments (including coffee and tea) when hosting someone. Indonesians believe offering refreshments is a sign of politeness and respect.
- If your host isn't wearing shoes, remove yours at the door. Never wear shoes on carpeted floors in someone's home.
- Don't eat until your hosts begin eating. Compliment the food sincerely and often.
- Try not to request salt, pepper, soy sauce, or spices. Doing so will insult the cook.
- Never talk with your mouth full.

- On public transportation, be courteous whenever you can. Always give your seat to the elderly. Men should offer their seats to women. Offer to hold packages for anyone standing. (If standing yourself, feel free to ask someone seated to hold your packages.)
- Avoid using a toothpick in public. If you must use one, cover your mouth. Indonesians believe only animals show their teeth.
- Don't chew gum or yawn in public. If you can't avoid yawning, cover your mouth.
- Never sit on a table or desk.
- In restaurants, the person who extended the invitation pays the bill. Make a scribbling gesture on your palm to request the bill.
- Don't eat while standing or walking on streets.
- To beckon wait staff, raise your hand. Address a waiter as *mas* (pronounced "mahs"), an older waitress as *bu* (pronounced "boo"), and a younger waitress as *mbak* (pronounced "mm-BAHK").
- See pages 75–85 for etiquette information when visiting a mosque or other place of worship.

Punctuality

Although Indonesians consider punctuality less important than establishing personal relationships, they expect Westerners to arrive on time for business appointments (but don't be surprised if Indonesians arrive late). Always call if you're delayed. When you do arrive, don't rush or fret over lost time. Indonesians consider haste more rude than lateness.

For social events, Indonesians usually arrive thirty minutes late. For events at someone's home, guests should arrive ten to twenty minutes late.

Dress

Indonesian climate is hot and humid, so lightweight, breathable fabrics are best. If traveling to mountain areas, however, sweaters and jackets are necessary.
- Batik (a cotton fabric dyed in patterns) is one of Indonesia's most famous exports. In Java, batik clothing is traditional attire for both men and women. The Javanese appreciate foreigners wearing batik (but not at business meetings).
- A sarong (length of printed cloth wrapped around the waist) is also traditional attire, especially for women.

- In Indonesia, Muslim women don't usually wear veils.
- For business, men wear coats and ties with dress trousers. Except for formal occasions or meetings with senior government officials, Indonesians generally don't wear suits, although foreigners should wear them for first meetings. Women wear conservative dresses or skirts and blouses. Foreign women should avoid wearing bright colors and flamboyant fashions. They should never wear sleeveless tops.
- For casual occasions, men wear batik or Western-style shirts (long- or short-sleeved) with dress pants or stylish jeans. Women wear cotton dresses or skirts or slacks with blouses.
- For formal occasions and at better restaurants, men wear coats, ties, and dress trousers, perhaps with long-sleeved batik shirts. Women wear dresses or skirts and cotton or batik blouses (never sleeveless).
- Shorts, halter tops, and tank tops are appropriate only at the beach or at sporting events. Bikinis are acceptable only at beaches and pools.

Gifts

Indonesians generally don't expect gifts, but they welcome compliments and notes of appreciation.
- If given a gift, always receive it appreciatively; never refuse it.
- Always give or receive gifts with your right hand.
- Except at ceremonies, Indonesians don't open gifts in front of the giver.
- See page 58 for information on giving "red envelopes" to Chinese colleagues.

Hostess Gifts
Always bring a small gift when invited to someone's home. If the family has children, consider giving them pens and notebooks.

Consider giving
- Flowers
- Cakes or candy
- Stationery
- Heavyweight cotton towels
- Scarves

Don't give
- Alcoholic beverages
- Any item featuring dogs or pigs

Business Gifts
- Indonesians generally don't exchange business gifts. If they do, they exchange them after most business has been concluded.
- Bosses may give secretaries small gifts as tokens of appreciation.

Consider giving
- Fruit
- Candy
- Lighters
- Tie pins
- Items that feature your company logo discreetly

Don't give
- Alcoholic beverages
- Any item featuring dogs or pigs

Helpful Hints

- Treat elders, superiors, and civil servants with great respect. Indonesians honor them highly.
- Most Indonesian Muslims are tolerant of all religions. They don't adhere to the rigorous codes of conduct that exist in some Muslim nations.
- If someone asks to photograph you, don't refuse. To Indonesians, photographing someone is a way to honor the person.
- Except in large stores (where prices are fixed), barter when purchasing goods.
- In crowded restaurants, strangers may share your table. You needn't speak with them.

Health and Safety

- Tuberculosis, malaria, and cholera are widespread in Indonesia. Proper vaccination is necessary before traveling to the country (see page 373).
- In general, tap water isn't safe for consumption. Drink only boiled or bottled water, even to brush your teeth. Avoid using ice cubes, unless you know the water was boiled before freezing.

- Much of Indonesia has an excessively warm climate. Always carry a bottle of water with you to help prevent dehydration.
- Eat only thoroughly cooked food. Eating salads and unpeeled fruit may cause illnesses like dysentery. Avoid drinking milk and eating ice cream or other dairy products (pasteurization isn't common). Eating fish may make you sick if the fish isn't fresh (and it's usually hard to confirm when a fish was caught).
- Industrial pollution and volcanic ash clouds make air quality poor. People with respiratory ailments should talk to their physicians before traveling to Indonesia.
- For medical treatment, Catholic or missionary hospitals are usually good and many have English-speaking staff. If you're seriously ill, your embassy or consulate will refer you to a good medical facility.
- Most hospitals require at least partial payment for services in advance. They don't care to bill for treatment.
- Indonesian clinics may reuse needles without first properly sterilizing them. If you need regular injections or must give blood samples, bring your own needles and syringes.
- Be aware: In recent years, Islamic extremists have targeted Western tourists, often in nightclubs.
- Avoid driving in Indonesia. Traffic is a huge problem, and traffic jams are common as are traffic accidents.
- Pickpocketing is common, most often on crowded buses and trains—especially during busy holiday periods. Always store valuables in a money belt underneath your clothing.
- Credit card fraud and ATM fraud in Indonesia are increasing. Before traveling to Indonesia, let your credit card company know you'll be using your card in the country. Also be aware of others around you when using your card. Don't leave the card on display (on a store counter, for example); thieves may try to memorize the number. Carry your card in a secure money belt if you must take it with you; otherwise, lock it in your hotel safe.
- Some young people will try to irritate foreigners. They may make jokes or obscene gestures, or try to pinch you. Don't confront them—just leave.

Corporate Culture

Structure

Many major industries are state owned and operated. Army generals directly or indirectly control some companies.

Indonesian firms make decisions at the top. It's best to initiate negotiations at the top level, then move to the operating level to discuss technical matters. The top level concludes discussions. Only senior executives of foreign companies can access Indonesian executives.

Indonesians call the boss *bapek* (pronounced "bah-PAHK"), which means "father." Employers look after employees and expect (and get) obedience and deference in return. The boss is always right, and employees want to keep him happy at all costs. Good ideas come from the boss (even if subordinates came up with them).

Meetings

- For business success in Indonesia, patience is absolutely essential. Meetings are formal and proper, and negotiations are slow and calculated.
- Participants enter a room by rank and don't sit until the senior-ranking host invites them to do so.
- Initial meetings may last forty-five minutes to one hour—without any substantial accomplishment. Visitors should set the next meeting before departing.
- Initial conversation at meetings tends to be casual, friendly, and unrelated to business. Indonesians initiate business discussions slowly and gently.
- Make sure presentations are authoritative, detailed, and backed by charts, graphs, and other exhibits. Know that Indonesian companies evaluate a foreign offer on the company's reputation, experience, and service (especially in the local market), as well as on price, product quality, delivery time, and reliability. Promote these points clearly.
- Summarize and clarify main points at every stage of negotiations. If you disagree with a point, be diplomatic and avoid argument.
- Don't grant concessions too quickly. Indonesians love to bargain, and they view quick concessions as naiveté or weakness.
- Indonesians generally hold a formal meeting to announce an agreement.

Appointments

- Schedule business visits for dates in September through June. (July and August are popular vacation months.)
- In Islamic tradition, a day begins at sunset, not midnight. When scheduling evening dates and times, be sure to specify both the calendar date and the day of the week.
- When making appointments, be prepared to be flexible. Always take into account the heavy traffic, unpredictable phone service, Indonesian executives' busy travel schedules, numerous public holidays, and the different pace of the culture.
- Regular business hours are 9:00 AM to 5:00 PM, Monday through Friday (some offices may close for an hour for lunch). Some businesses are open 9:00 AM to noon on Saturdays.
- Try to avoid scheduling meetings for Fridays. Business and government offices close on Fridays at midday to allow Muslim employees to worship.
- Try to schedule appointments for mornings. In the afternoon, visit offices to personally reconfirm future appointments.

Communication

- In business, many Indonesians speak English. If an interpreter is necessary, visitors are responsible for providing one (although companies in Jakarta may provide one).
- Because Indonesians want to keep the boss happy at all costs, you must encourage them to report problems. When they do, never show displeasure or anger.
- Try not to ask yes-or-no questions. To avoid causing disappointment, Indonesians may answer questions untruthfully (see pages 24–25 to read more about indirect language).
- Indonesians are sensitive to status. Those of higher rank behave formally and authoritatively with those of lower rank. A boss that's too egalitarian and friendly may bewilder employees who expect a dignified distance.
- E-mail is popular in Indonesia. Many Indonesians believe the informality of e-mail better masks their poor English language skills. Plus, correspondents can craft replies carefully to best avoid confrontation.
- Don't use red ink in correspondence. Red connotes death.

Business Cards

- Present your business card to the receptionist immediately upon arrival. (If you don't, you risk waiting a long time for your appointment.)
- Exchange business cards upon introduction. Present and receive cards slowly and with your right hand. Show much interest in someone's business card before carefully putting it away in your briefcase.
- Cards in English are acceptable.

Be Aware

- Avoid conflict as much as possible. The Indonesian workplace values harmony, understanding, and mutual respect.
- To build a successful business relationship, you must visit Indonesian clients and colleagues often. Several visits are usually necessary to successfully negotiate, draft, and sign a contract.
- Always show interest. Indonesians want to work with people who show keen interest in Indonesian culture. They'll interpret indifference as dislike or disrespect.
- Because Indonesians strongly believe outside forces (like nature, coincidences, or bad luck) control events and people, they may miss deadlines if they feel fate has raised obstacles. To gauge progress, you must frequently restate your goals, plans, and deadlines—but always use indirect language. For example, ask a manager (in private, to avoid causing loss of face), "I look forward to the completion of our project. What stage are you working on right now?"

> *Slametan* are ritual meals held to ask for divine blessings or to give thanks. Traditionally, Indonesians hold them for such reasons as to bless pregnancies, to help recovery after sickness, or to reverse bad luck.
>
> Today, companies dedicate new buildings with *slametan*, and employees may request one to overcome problems within the organization.

- Be prepared to bargain. Indonesians bargain in daily life and are proud of their bargaining abilities.
- Never pressure or rush Indonesians. To them, time is flexible.
- Although Indonesians have accepted the Western need for contracts, many still believe they're a breach of trust. To them, contracts are guidelines, not statements of duties and responsibilities.

Socializing

Socializing is important to developing relationships, and Indonesians like to entertain, most often over dinner in restaurants. If invited to an Indonesian's home, know that it's a special honor.

- Business lunches are common; however, don't invite practicing Muslims to lunch during Ramadan, when they fast from dawn to dusk.
- Indonesians often include spouses in dinners. When hosting Indonesians, always invite their spouses.
- After someone has entertained you, reciprocate with an invitation to a similar event or occasion (before you leave the country, if possible). Be generous and hospitable, but don't overdo it. Indonesians criticize lavishness.
- Let Indonesians initiate business discussions at social events.

Especially for Women

Indonesian society is male oriented, and feminism seems strange to many Indonesians.

Indonesian law mandates equality among all citizens. But compared to men, Indonesian women disproportionately suffer from illiteracy, poor health, and inadequate nutrition. The law also forbids gender discrimination in the workplace, but enforcement is rare.

Women occupy an excessively high percentage of low-ranking socioeconomic and political positions. In 2001, more than a third of civil servants were women, but fewer than 6 percent were in positions of authority. That same year, Megawati Soekarnoputri became Indonesia's first female president, but in 2002 less than 10 percent of elected representatives were women.

Polygamy (up to four wives) is legal for Muslim men, who must obtain court permission as well as permission from the first wife (although in some cases, she may not be free to refuse) before marrying additional women.

Violence against women hasn't been well documented, but experts believe the number of incidents has risen in the last decade, after the economy slowed dramatically and urbanization began rising. Female genital mutilation occurs in some parts of the country, and trafficking of women and girls for forced labor or prostitution is a major problem.

- Indonesians seldom hassle foreign women, although those with blond hair and blue eyes may attract unwanted attention. (Dressing modestly helps deflect attention.) In general, foreign businesswomen will encounter few problems if they assert their qualifications and act professionally.

- A foreign woman may invite an Indonesian man to a business lunch or dinner, but never at her hotel, which may suggest an invitation to her hotel room. If she wishes to pay the bill, she should arrange payment in advance with the wait staff.
- A foreign woman may invite an Indonesian businessman and his wife to dinner, but shouldn't insist he bring her along.
- A woman may eat alone in a restaurant without hassle. In Java, however, some men may approach a woman dining alone.
- Women shouldn't patronize local bars alone. They're not safe.

Holidays and Festivals

January	New Year's Day (1)
January/February	Chinese New Year
March/April	Good Friday
May/June	Ascension Day
August	Independence Day (17)
December	Christmas (25)

Notes: Observed Islamic and Hindu holidays vary with the Islamic and Hindu calendars. Check to see when they're observed for the year you're traveling to Indonesia.

JAPAN*

Greetings from Japan

Greetings from the Land of the Rising Sun. Our nation encompasses over three thousand islands, many of which have mountains or volcanoes, including our majestic Mount Fuji.

Japan is one of the world's most densely populated countries. Nearly 80 percent of us live in urban areas. Because we live so closely to one another, we value conformity, loyalty, politeness, personal responsibility, cleanliness, and cooperation—all traits that promote *wa*, which means "harmony." We abhor aggressiveness and prize ambition, hard work, patience, determination, and modest behavior. We consider public embarrassment or any loss of face devastating.

We revere age and tradition. Families are the foundation of our society, even though today's families are small, often with fewer than two children. We believe the welfare of the family, clan, work group, company, or country always takes precedence over the welfare of the individual.

Because we live in a highly structured society where everyone knows and understands the rules, we may be uncomfortable with *gaijin* ("foreigners"), even those who are of Japanese ethnicity. We will warm to visitors if they first learn a little of Japanese etiquette and demonstrate some knowledge of our culture.

Some Americans still view Japan as a wonderfully prosperous nation, which we were for many years. Beginning in the 1960s, our economic growth was nothing short of miraculous. But in the early 1990s, growth slowed dramatically; only in 2004 did we begin to recover. Today, we must still deal with two major economic challenges: our enormous government debt and our aging population. We rely on *gaman* ("enduring patience") to help us survive these hardships.

Today, our gross national product (GNP) is second only to the United States', despite our few natural resources. Although we import most of our raw materials (and over half our food supply), we enjoy one of the world's highest health standards with the lowest infant mortality rates and highest life expectancies.

---

* This country's name has no conventional long form.

To keep our economy globally competitive, our government is now promoting reforms to help educators teach creativity and individualism instead of conformity—a major change in our cultural mindset. Our young people are embracing Western values and challenging Japanese beliefs. More and more of them are wearing hip fashions, listening to pop music, and eating fast food. Many of us feel these changes have led to consumerism, lower moral standards, and the rise in juvenile crime—and they will eventually lead to a cultural crisis in the future.

Our politicians and teachers often disagree about how to recapture the virtues of prewar Japan without promoting the nationalist fervor that hurled our nation into World War II. "Japan has become considerably self-centered, meritocratic, and egotisic," says one former Sony executive. Many of us concur and believe that consideration of others is the most important virtue to teach our children.

Despite the constraints of our postwar pacifist constitution, we do want to help resolve global conflicts. We sent over five hundred ground troops to Iraq in 2004, the first time Japanese troops have been sent to an active battleground since World War II. Our constitution limited the soldiers to humanitarian and reconstruction missions, and when the troops were withdrawn in 2006, we declared the deployment a success.

Our country has been allies with the United States since the end of World War II. The Japanese and Americans have supported each other through economic challenges. After China, the United States is our biggest trading partner, and the success of the American economy is vital to our economic health.

> Many Japanese embrace American icons. In 2006, President Bush took a delighted Junichiro Koizumi on a visit to Graceland, where the Japanese prime minister belted out a few bars of Elvis Presley hits.

While we admire American economic practices, our "contribution-internationalism" foreign policy (*kokusai-koken*) is more akin to Canada's.

Come to Japan for business or pleasure. Enjoy a tea ceremony, visit our pagodas, delight in our famous cherry blossoms, and marvel at our miraculous technology. You will initially find us a proud, polite people. But after a few drinks, we will engage you in candid, boisterous conversations.

Keep an open mind, and we will surprise you!

Vital Statistics

Population	127,463,611
Capital	Tokyo
Area	145,883 square miles, slightly smaller than California
Government	Constitutional monarchy with a parliamentary government
Living Standard	GDP = US $41,480 per capita
Natural Resources	Negligible mineral resources, fish, industrial sector heavily dependent on imported raw materials and fuels
Agriculture	Rice, sugar beets, vegetables, fruit, pork, poultry, dairy products, eggs, fish
Industries	Among the world's largest and technologically advanced producers of motor vehicles, electronic equipment, machine tools, steel and nonferrous metals, ships, chemicals, textiles, processed foods
Climate	Tropical in south; cool temperate in north
Currency	Yen (JPY)

The People

Correct Name	noun: Japanese
	adjective: Japanese
Ethnic Makeup	Japanese 99%, others 1% (including Korean, Chinese, Brazilian, and Filipino)
Language	Japanese
Religions	Shinto and Buddhist 84%, other 16% (including Christian 0.7%)

Meeting and Greeting

- The Japanese generally bow upon greeting to show respect.
- Some people both bow and shake hands. Foreigners may offer a handshake upon meeting. The Japanese shake hands limply with little or no eye contact.
- After someone introduces you, say "how are you?" rather than "hello" (preferably in Japanese). Then state your name, title, and your relationship to the person introducing you.

- The Japanese don't smile or otherwise greet strangers on the street or in other public places.

Names and Titles

- Traditional Japanese name order is last name (surname) + first name (given name); however, many Japanese who frequently deal with Western businesspeople use "Western" name order (first name + last name). If in doubt of someone's name order, ask.

> Although the Japanese appreciate bows from foreigners, be aware that bowing is a complicated ritual. The depth of a bow depends on the relationship between the parties and the situation. Never bow in jest!
>
> Unless you're thoroughly familiar with bowing rituals, give only a slight bow to show courtesy. That is, place your heels together, bend slightly at the waist, and keep your head down. Keep your hands at your sides, and don't look at the other party.

- Regardless of someone's sex or marital status, the Japanese typically address a person by last name + "-san" (pronounced "sahn"), a suffix showing honor. Never use this suffix when referring to your own name.
- Although less desirable than using "-san," you may address a Japanese person by English courtesy title (Mr., Mrs., or Miss) + last name.
- When introducing a Japanese person, give his or her name, title, and company, then mention a relationship the parties have in common. For example, if both people know Mr. Rice, introduce one to the other with, "I would like to introduce you to Mijoshi-san, systems analyst of Sony Corporation and a colleague of Mr. Rice."
- The Japanese consider corporate titles and ranks extremely important. They address top senior executives by title instead of last name, which may mislead those who don't speak Japanese to thinking a title is a last name. For example, people address Yohei Mijoshi, company president, as Shacho-san (Mr. President), not Mr. Mijoshi or Mijoshi-san.

  If you can learn an executive's Japanese title, use it. Otherwise, address a person by the name given upon introduction and use the person's business card as a reminder of the name.
- Never address anyone—especially an older person—by first name unless specifically invited to do so. Younger Japanese people and those educated in the United States may insist you address them by first name.
- Close friends will often address one another by last name only.

Language

Japanese is one of the world's major languages, ranking ninth in number of speakers. Since the middle of the last century, Japan is the only country that uses Japanese as a first or a second language. Speaking Japanese—even just a little—is the best way to make friends in Japan.

Many Japanese can read English but can't speak it. More young people than old people speak the language. If trying to communicate in English, speak slowly and clearly, using short sentences. Writing down what you want to say may help communication.

Conversation

- Upon meeting, people may fall silent for several minutes. The silence is normal; don't disrupt it. The Japanese value non-verbal communication. To them, a person who can't interpret the silence is insensitive.
- Always let the Japanese initiate conversation. They often begin conversations with lengthy small talk. Never urge them to "get to the point."
- Speak quietly and never lose your temper.
- Never say anything that may make the Japanese lose face, especially in public.
- The Japanese may ask you personal questions as a polite way to show interest. If you'd rather not answer a question, give a vague or general answer.

The Japanese intensely dislike conflict and direct confrontation, and they don't openly express opinions and desires. Because they believe direct language is unsophisticated and insulting, you must determine true meaning from indirect language.

For example, the Japanese rarely say "no"; instead, they'll say "maybe" to mean "no." "Yes" may not necessarily indicate agreement; instead, it may mean "I hear you" or "I understand." It may even mean "no" if the speaker wants to escape confrontation.

To figure out someone's real message, pay close attention to a person's body language and listen carefully to other comments he or she makes. For example, if a clerk says, "Perhaps you would like this item instead" after you ask for something, she probably means she doesn't have exactly what you requested. If you continue to ask for the specific item, you'll come across as boorish and not very bright.

Or say, "In my country, that would be a strange question." People will detect your discomfort and drop the subject.

- After establishing a relationship, the Japanese openly display a sense of humor. Although serious in formal situations, they enjoy humor at other times. Keep in mind that Western humor, especially sarcasm, doesn't translate well into Japanese culture.

Acceptable topics
- The weather
- Food
- Family
- Hobbies
- Home regions (yours and theirs)
- Your host's hospitality: Praise it often.
- Sports, particularly baseball and golf

Unacceptable topics
- Someone's appearance (although the Japanese may comment on yours)
- Ethnic minorities
- Religion (People consider the topic too personal.)
- Criticisms of Japanese culture (compliments are welcome, however)

The Japanese are passionate about baseball (*yakyu*), but their take on the game may seem strange to Americans. Because of the cultural emphasis on the group, competition often isn't strong. The Japanese prefer close scores and don't mind tie games.

Golf is wildly popular as well, but lack of space limits access to the few extremely expensive golf courses. When the Japanese can't golf on a course, they enjoy practicing their swings at driving ranges, some of which are two stories high.

Officially, Japan is one of the world's most homogeneous societies, but there are several minority groups who are ethnically and culturally distinct from the Japanese, including indigenous Ainu, Okinawans, and Koreans.

Japan also has a substantial community (perhaps a quarter million) of immigrants who look Japanese but are ethnically Brazilian. Most of these immigrants descended from the Japanese who migrated to Brazil decades earlier.

In addition, there are approximately three million Burakumin ("hamlet people"), who are culturally, ethnically, and religiously indistinct from the Japanese—and yet the Japanese consider them a separate group and discriminate against them.

- Personal compliments, especially in public: The Japanese strive for modesty and humility. They'll take great pains to downplay any achievement or to give the credit to others. To make a good impression, do the same when others compliment you. Never brag!

Topics that require sensitivity
- Japan's relationship with Russia and other Asian nations, especially North Korea
- World War II and the decades leading up to it
- World history (Always keep in mind that the Japanese have a different perspective on history than Westerners have.)
- Work (Many Japanese think work is stressful, not a source of personal fulfillment.)

Body Language
- Nodding is important! When listening to someone speak, especially in English, nod to show you understand the speaker. If you don't, the speaker will think you don't.
- The Japanese aren't "touchers." They don't stand closely to one another, and they avoid public displays of affection, like hugging and backslapping.
- Beckon someone by extending your right arm out front, bending your hand down at the wrist, then waving the fingers together back and forth. Never beckon someone with your index finger. Never beckon older people.
- Never point at someone with all fingers extended and spread, and the thumb tucked in. This gesture is obscene.
- Never stare at anyone. The Japanese consider prolonged eye contact rude.
- Sit up straight with both feet on the floor. Never rest your ankle on your knee.
- The "okay" sign (curling the index finger and thumb to make a circle) means "money" or "okay."
- Waving your hand, palm out, from side to side in front of your face means "no" or "I don't know." (This gesture is a polite response to a compliment.)
- In Japan, a smile may mean happiness, amusement, confusion, embarrassment, anger, sadness, or nothing at all. Determine meaning from the context.

Phrases

English	Japanese	Pronunciation
Hello (used only on the telephone)	*Moshi-moshi*	(MOH-shee MOH-shee)
Good morning	*Ohayo*	(oh-HAH-oh)
Good afternoon	*Konnichi wa*	(kohn-NEE-chee-wah)
Please		
(said when asking for something)	*Kudasai*	(koo-DAH-sigh)
(said when offering something)	*Dozo*	(DOH-zoh)
Thank you	*Arigato*	(ah-ree-GAH-toe)
You're welcome	*Doitashimashite*	(DOH-ee-TAHSSH-mahssh-tay)
Yes	*Hai*	(HIGH)
No	*Iie*	(ee-EH)
Excuse me	*Gomen nasai*	(goh-MEHN nah-SIGH)
Goodbye	*Sayonara*	(sigh-YOH-nah-rah)
Pleased to meet you	*Hajimemashite*	(hah-JEE-may-mahssh-tay)
How are you?	*O genki desu ka*	(oh-GEN-kee dess KAH)

- *Domo* (DOH-moh) is a polite, all-purpose expression that can mean "hello," "goodbye," "please," or "thanks."
- *Sumimasen* (soo-MEE-mah-sen) means "excuse me, I apologize for my offense," or "please" or "thank you" when giving or receiving anything.

Dining

Unlike other Asian fare, Japanese cuisine is light and uses very little oil. It balances shapes, textures, flavors, and colors for the delight of all senses. Harmony and presentation are very important.

- *Hashi* (HAH-shee), or Japanese chopsticks, are shorter than Chinese chopsticks. (See page 41 for information on chopstick etiquette.)
- Dining in restaurants is a favorite pastime in Japan. Many restaurants serve complete Western menus.
- Menus generally aren't in English. Many restaurants display realistic plastic replicas of dishes. You may simply point to desired items.

- Often the Japanese eat several snacks with drinks instead of dinner. Beer halls serve a wide range of food.
- At meals, the Japanese seat the guest of honor in the *kamiza* area, located in front of the *takonoma* (alcove). They seat the least important guest in the *shimoza* area, located near the door. They seat the other guests in order of importance, with the more important guests near the *kamiza* area. The highest-ranking host sits at the center of the table.
- Hosts serve the guest of honor first, then serve the eldest person next. They serve the rest of the guests in the order in which they're seated. Some westernized hosts may serve all women first (after the guest of honor).
- Hosts serve green tea to signal the end of a meal.

> There are several Japanese proverbs about people that feature chopsticks:
>
> "Even stumbling chopsticks are funny" = giggling young women
>
> "It can't be picked up with chopsticks or hung on a pole" = obstinate people
>
> "He hasn't ever picked up anything heavier than chopsticks" = someone from a wealthy family

Drinking

The Japanese are known for their love of tea, and the centuries-old Japanese tea ceremony has deep historical and social roots. A tea ceremony can be an elaborate affair in a teahouse or a temple, or it can be an informal gathering. If invited to a tea ceremony, watch carefully what other guests do and follow their lead. You may want to prepare further by reading one of the numerous available books that discuss the ritual.

Coffee is also a popular beverage, especially among young women. In 2003, Japan was the world's third-largest coffee importer and the seventh-largest coffee retail market.

Hashigozake (barhopping) is a favorite pastime thought to build teamwork among bosses, subordinates, and colleagues. Here are some tips when participating:

- The Japanese often drink to excess, and drunkenness is generally accepted behavior. Never criticize someone who's drunk.
- Never decline a drink. If you must, sip or pretend to drink it.

- If you don't want another drink, always keep your glass at least half-full (discreetly fill it with water, if necessary). If someone attempts to pour you another, put your hand over your glass.
- Never pour your own drink and always pour others' drinks.
- Ordinarily, the Japanese go to high-class bars only when entertaining on a company expense account.

Typical Drinks

- Sake (SAH-kay) is Japan's national drink that's served either hot or chilled. It's a rice wine that contains about 16 percent alcohol.

- Whiskey and beer—*biru* (BEE-ruh)—are popular drinks. In 2004, the

> Some research suggests the Japanese drink an average of three or more cups of green tea daily, which may be one reason for their extraordinary longevity. A recent medical study found green tea consumption linked to lower mortality rates of all diseases except cancer.

Japanese were the world's sixth-largest consumers of beer (and the largest beer consumers per capita in Asia). You can buy beer from vending machines.
- *Mizuwari* (mee-zoo-WAH-ree) is Scotch and water.

Toasting

Toasting is important in Japan, and the Japanese offer many toasts during an evening.
- *Kanpai* (KAHN-pie) means "bottoms up" or "cheers." Here's how to give the toast:
    1. Raise your drink in front of you.
    2. Make eye contact with everyone near you.
    3. Shout "*kanpai*!" then drink. (Sometimes, all the people shout it together, clink glasses, then down their drinks.)
- *Banzai* (bahn-ZYE) means "three cheers" or "ten thousand years," and people usually give this toast at the high point of the event or at the end of the evening. Here's how to give the toast:
    1. Raise both hands above your head.
    2. Shout "*Banzai*!" three times, then drink.
- The host may give a short accompanying speech with a toast to celebrate cooperation between companies.

- At dinner, wait for the toast before drinking any alcoholic beverage.
- Reciprocate each toast with a toast of your own.

Tipping

The Japanese don't tip. In general, if someone expects gratuity, the bill will include a service charge. Here are guidelines for appropriate tips:

- Restaurants: The bill usually includes a service charge. If the bill doesn't include a service charge, one isn't expected. You may leave an additional small tip for exceptional service.
- Taxis: If the driver helps with your bags, JPY100 is appropriate. Otherwise, no tip is necessary.

Manners

The Japanese go out of their way to make guests feel welcome. Their quiet, graceful manners make them and their country a real pleasure to visit. They appreciate courteous behavior, especially when guests show respect for Japanese customs.

- Don't eat until the guest of honor has begun eating. If you're the guest of honor, wait until all the food is set on the table before beginning to eat.
- Before a meal, it's polite to say "*itadakimasu*" (ee-TAH-dah-kee-MAHSS), which means "thanks to the hostess [or cook]."
- Taste every dish. Not doing so is rude.
- Always show respect for the eldest or most senior person at the table. Pour that person's drinks, serve his or her food, and pay special attention to him or her.
- It's polite to slurp noodles. The Japanese believe doing so makes noodles taste better.
- Soups accompany meals. Never finish your soup before eating other dishes. When finished eating, replace the soup bowl lid.
- Always remember that an empty plate or glass signals a desire for more food or drink. When finished, leave a little food on your plate or your glass half-full.
- If you leave the table, bend at the waist to keep your head and shoulders slightly lower than those seated until you're out of everyone's line of sight.
- After a meal, say to your host "*gochisosamadeshita*" (go-CHEE-so-sah-mah DESH-tah), which means "the dishes were delicious and enjoyed."

- After someone has entertained you, always send a thank-you note to the hostess.
- Always cover your mouth when yawning, laughing, or using a toothpick.
- Don't chew gum, especially while conducting business. The Japanese consider gum chewing crass behavior.
- Don't blow your nose in public or at the table; always do so in a restroom, if possible.
- Never litter.
- Don't eat while walking on streets.

> Be prepared for a dramatic difference between public and private behavior. Privately, Japanese are graceful and courteous. In public, pushing and shoving are common, especially on crowded trains during rush hour (sometimes filled to three times their seating capacity). Trains even have official "pushers" (*oshiya*) who force people in so the doors can close.

- To beckon wait staff, raise your hand, make eye contact, and say "*onegaishimasu*" (oh-NAY-guy-shee-mahss), which means "please."
- See pages 75–85 for information on etiquette when visiting a temple or other holy place.

When Visiting a Home in Japan

The Japanese rarely entertain at home. Consider it a great honor if invited to a Japanese home.

- Take off your coat and shoes before entering a home. At the entrance, place your shoes with the others. Make sure they're together and face the door. If uncertain what to do, follow other guests' example.
- The host provides slippers for guests. Wear only slippers inside homes. Watch where the host family wears slippers and where they don't, and do likewise.
- Always take off slippers when entering a room with tatami mats.
- Try not to step on doorsills or borders of tatami mats.
- Doors may be low. Watch your head when entering or leaving rooms.
- Doors are often made of paper. Don't touch, push, or knock on these doors or you may damage them.
- Don't sit until your host invites to do so.

- Your host may offer you a legless chair or may invite you to sit on the floor. If possible, sit on a mat or the floor with your legs tucked under you. When invited to relax, men may sit cross-legged, and women should sit with their legs together to one side, if possible.
- Restrooms in homes may not lock. Leave your slippers outside the door to show that the room is occupied. Wear the special slippers provided for restrooms. If someone knocks, knock back to indicate the room is occupied. Be sure you don't wear the special slippers outside the restroom—doing so is like having toilet paper stuck to your shoe. Leave the slippers in the same position you found them (facing the toilet) so the next person can slip into them without using his or her hands.
- Hot bathwater is for soaking only, and several people may use it in turn. Before taking a bath, wash and rinse yourself completely with either scooped-out bathwater (a bucket is provided) or with the flexible shower hose.
- Don't wander into the kitchen, and don't ask to see other rooms your host hasn't shown you.
- Don't excessively compliment an item. The Japanese may feel obliged to give it to you.
- In gardens, don't play games or walk off paths onto grass.

When Visiting a Public Bath

Sento (public baths) and *onsen* (hot spring baths) are popular with the Japanese. There are usually two tubs: one with hot water and the other with extrahot water.

- Never take valuables to a public bath.
- Leave your shoes in a locker at the building's entrance.
- Leave and lock your clothes in a locker in the locker room. Carry the key on your wrist.
- As a Westerner, expect bathers to stare at you.
- Public baths provide individual stations (often located around the perimeter of the bath) with stools, showers, and assorted soaps and shampoos. Wash and rinse yourself thoroughly for at least ten minutes. (Some Japanese cleanse themselves for a half-hour).
- Never get into the bath with soap on you. Japanese think soapsuds floating in bathwater is disgusting.

Punctuality

The Japanese consider lateness for business meetings rude, but it's accept-able—even fashionable—to be late for social events. Visitors, however, should err on the side of courtesy and always be punctual for any occasion.

Allow ample time to get to meetings in large cities. Traffic delays are often lengthy, and even taxi drivers sometimes have difficulty finding addresses.

Dress

At all times, the Japanese dress well in modern, conservative fashions.
- The kimono (a long, wide-sleeved robe worn with a wide sash called an obi) is a traditional garment. Most modern Japanese reserve wearing kimonos for special occasions only. In general, foreigners shouldn't wear kimonos because there are many nuances to wearing them correctly.
- Because you should never wear shoes in Japanese homes or temples, try to wear shoes that you can slip on and off easily. Make sure your socks or stockings are clean and without holes.
- Many restaurants and office buildings have squat toilets. Be prepared to dress accordingly (see pages 51–53).
- For business occasions, men wear dark suits and ties in subtle colors. Women wear dresses or tailored suits with heels. Although younger Japanese women enjoy wearing the latest fashions in bright colors, conser-vative styles in subtle colors are best for foreign businesswomen. In fact, foreign women shouldn't ever wear bright colors, dangling jewelry, low-cut dresses, or heavy makeup.
- In better restaurants, men wear jackets and ties, and women wear dresses or dressy pants and blouses. (Avoid wearing tight clothing because you may be seated on the floor.) More casual establishments require less formal attire. Before dining in a restaurant, ask for its dress code.
- For casual occasions, the Japanese wear clean, neat clothing. Men wear long- or short-sleeved shirts and pants, perhaps with sport coats. Women wear blouses with skirts or dressy pants. Jeans, sneakers, and T-shirts are acceptable as long as they're neat and clean—but it's best to avoid wear-ing this attire.

- For black-tie formal occasions (invitations will specify), men wear tuxedos and women wear evening gowns. (Japanese women may wear kimonos, but Western women generally shouldn't.) If the occasion isn't black-tie, men wear dark suits and ties, and women wear chic cocktail dresses.
- Always dress smartly for parties, even when an invitation indicates the event is "casual" or "come as you are."

Gifts

In Japan, the gift giving is more important than the gift. Appearance of the package counts as much as—if not more than—its contents.

- Unless you have gifts for everyone present, give a gift only when alone with the recipient.
- If possible, give a gift personally. Give (and receive) gifts with both hands and a slight bow, perhaps saying, "Here is just a small token of my esteem."
- The recipient may refuse a gift once or twice before accepting it. Many Japanese don't open gifts in the giver's presence, but you may ask them to do so. Never open a gift yourself unless the giver invites you to do so.
- When opening a gift, never rip the gift-wrap. The Japanese select gift-wrap for its design, elegance, and significance. They consider it good form to preserve the gift-wrap when opening a gift.
- Try to have gifts professionally wrapped. The clerk will make sure the gift-wrap is appropriate for the occasion. (Gift-wrap in pastel colors is preferable. Black gift-wrap is never acceptable.)

    Formal gifts are usually wrapped in a heavy white paper called *noshigami*, tied with heavy paper cord called *mizuhiki*, and decorated with a folded paper called *noshi*.
- Avoid giving gifts that are obviously extravagant or inferior. A small, high-quality gift is better than a large, cheap one.
- Where you buy a gift is important. A prestigious department store is always a safe bet.
- When you receive a gift, thank the giver immediately and promptly send a thank-you note.
- Reciprocal gifts should equal one-third to one-half the value of original gifts.
- Never get into a gift-giving contest with Japanese colleagues; you'll always lose and embarrass everyone.

Hostess Gifts

Always bring a small gift when invited to someone's home.

Consider giving

- High-quality, brand-name gifts, like items from Tiffany or Lenox china
- Items made of white precious metals (The Japanese prefer them to gold.)
- Candy or boxed cakes, especially fruit cake
- Flowers: Always check with a florist for appropriate type and presentation.
- Wine or whiskey

Don't give

- Items in even numbers, fours, or nines
- Intimate items

Business Gifts

- Always let your Japanese colleagues initiate gift-giving.
- Be prepared to give (and receive) a gift at the end of the first business meeting. If you don't give a proper gift, you risk ruining the business relationship.
- *Oseibo* in December and *Ochugen* in late June to mid-July are gift-giving seasons. If working with Japanese colleagues during these times, present gifts to them and be prepared to receive gifts.
- Always give gifts made in your home country.

Consider giving

- High-quality, brand-name whiskey or cognac
- Recordings of music
- Books
- Golf balls
- Artwork

Don't give

- Items with your company logo printed in large letters
- Items in even numbers, fours, or nines
- Intimate items
- Gifts not made in your home country

> All Nippon Airways' planes don't have rows four, nine, or thirteen. The Japanese word for "four" sounds like the word for "death." The word for "nine" is a homonym for the word for "torture." Although the superstition against the number thirteen is based in Christianity, the airline avoids using the number.

Health and Safety

The Japanese are fastidious about hygiene and sanitation—even more so than Americans. They even take their children to play in parks with sterilized sand.

- Japan's food is generally safe and of high quality.
- The country's water purification system is one of the world's best, and tap water is safe to drink anywhere in the country.
- With that said, water pollution makes swimming in lakes, streams, or harbors near populated areas inadvisable.
- Air pollution is a problem in Tokyo and in some other major cities. People with respiratory ailments should talk to their physicians before traveling to these areas.
- Medical and dental care are excellent, and health care facilities are good. Many doctors speak English. In larger cities, there are some Western doctors.
- Hospitals and clinics require full payment at the time of treatment. Before giving treatment, some may require foreigners to prove ability to pay. Be certain to buy supplemental medical insurance that covers treatment in Japan.
- It's a good idea to carry tissues and a handkerchief wherever you go. Many Japanese restrooms don't provide toilet paper, paper towels, or hand dryers.
- Watch out for wandering hands on packed trains.
- Most taxi drivers don't speak English. Ask your hotel concierge to write your destination in Japanese for the driver, and carry a card featuring your hotel's name and address in Japanese for your return trip.

> Overall, Japan is one of the world's safest countries. Crime against foreigners is rare and usually limited to petty theft.
>
> A 2004 survey, however, showed that more than half the population characterized Japan as unsafe. The country's crime rate rose 150 percent from 1994 to 2004 (while arrest rates simultaneously dropped during at least one point in this period). While its suicide rate is high, its homicide rate is still much lower than the United States' (and much of the rest of the world's rates, for that matter).
>
> Rates of some crimes against children have increased, and many Japanese parents feel that they must become more safety conscious to protect their families.

Corporate Culture

The Japanese follow the maxim "The nail that sticks up gets hammered down." In other words, they expect conformity.

Although the Japanese don't expect foreigners to know Japanese social or business customs, they greatly appreciate—and will highly reward, personally and professionally—any knowledge of Japanese culture that foreigners show.

Structure

Business and personal relationships are hierarchical. Older people rank higher than younger people, men rank higher than women, buyers rank higher than sellers, big companies rank higher than small ones, and executives rank higher than managers.

Business in Japan is group oriented. There's no internal competition—all succeed or all fail. Decision making is slow and by consensus; all team members contribute. After decisions are made, implementation is swift.

Meetings

- The Japanese conduct meetings formally, but developing personal relationships is important. Always allow time for polite conversation before meetings begin.
- First meetings are often friendly with the goal to establish harmony and trust.
- One or more teams of negotiators may represent Japanese companies. Initial negotiations generally begin with middle managers—never go over their heads to speed up negotiations. Senior executives enter negotiations when the Japanese think it's appropriate.
- Presentations should emphasize the group, not the individual.
- Business meetings may have periods of silence. When they occur, sit quietly and don't talk. The Japanese consider silence part of conversation and communication. It's their way to ponder a question.
- It usually takes several meetings to reach an agreement. Close deals with a handshake; leave the signing of contracts to a later meeting.
- The Japanese always serve refreshments (tea or coffee) at meetings.

Appointments

- Make appointments at least two weeks in advance.
- Avoid scheduling meetings for dates from mid-December to mid-January, April 29 through May 5, and late July through mid-August. Many Japanese celebrate holidays during these times.
- Many businesspeople are in their offices from 8:00 AM to 8:00 PM, Monday through Friday. Some businesses are open 9:00 AM to noon every Saturday or one to two Saturdays a month.

Communication

Japanese businesspeople may not conduct business in English; you may need to hire a qualified interpreter (see pages 26–27). It's acceptable to use the Japanese company's interpreter in the first meeting. Once negotiations begin, hire your own interpreter.

If your Japanese colleagues understand English, speak clearly and softly. Avoid using colloquialisms, jargon, and sports analogies. In general, be yourself but mindful of the rhythm and pace of the conversation. When your Japanese colleagues speak, always nod to show you're listening attentively. Keep in mind that the people speaking English may not be team leaders.

The Japanese strive to avoid confrontation. Never embarrass anyone or cause anyone to lose face. Phrase statements and questions carefully. Try to avoid saying "no." Instead, to let your Japanese colleagues save face, say something like, "That could be very difficult, but we'll certainly explore the possibility."

The Japanese base many customs on respect for age and status. They may ask about your family, your age, the university you attended, and the degrees you earned. Ask them the same questions.

Proposals, presentations, and reports with a lot of visual aids are good communication tools. Send materials to the Japanese team well in advance of meetings. Include several copies to demonstrate your respect for the team approach. Proposals should be factual, technical, and detailed. To make a good impression, have them translated into Japanese.

Business Cards

- The Japanese may exchange business cards even before they shake hands or bow. Always present business cards correctly (see page 69); doing so will make a good first impression.
- Be certain your business card clearly states your rank. Your rank determines your negotiating counterpart.

- Try to have your information printed in English on one side of your business card and in Japanese on the other side.

Be Aware

- The Japanese conduct business only with people they trust. You must establish a relationship with the Japanese before you can sell them your company's products or services.
- Always send a representative whose rank equals that of the Japanese person you want to meet. Never send a person of lower rank.
- Unlike many of their American counterparts, Japanese business planners and top executives focus on long-term results, not on earnings in the current quarter or fiscal year.
- When making your pitch, always pay attention to the details. The Japanese will assume a sloppy presentation means a sloppy product.
- Don't change deadlines or timelines. The Japanese respect those who stick to original dates.
- Proper introductions to business contacts is essential. Make sure the person who introduces you knows both your company and the Japanese organization with which you want to do business. The introducer guarantees your trustworthiness to potential colleagues.
- Don't bring your lawyer to meetings with the Japanese. They expect to build business relationships based on trust, and a lawyer's presence suggests distrust. They also don't like complicated legal documents. Write a contract that covers only essential points.
- After establishing a solid relationship with a Japanese colleague, you can always count on him or her.

Take the time to learn and respect Japanese ways. Behaving quietly, modestly, and with dignity is the easiest way to ingratiate yourself with your Japanese colleagues. Always remember the group is the basis of Japanese society, with harmony and consensus its goals.

Socializing

- Business entertaining is crucial to business success in Japan. The Japanese judge a potential colleague by his or her behavior during and after business hours. They make many business deals in restaurants or on the golf course.

- Banquets with many courses, toasts, and gifts are common. If the host organization gives you a banquet, host a reciprocal one of equivalent expense.

- Following the signing of a contract, the host organization throws a ceremonial party or dinner. If the agreement is especially important or if the parties have a long association, the foreign organization may host a reciprocal event.

- The Japanese generally don't include spouses in business dinners, but they may invite the spouses of Western colleagues.

- At business dinners, the host picks the topics of conversation. A safe topic is your family, but be careful not to brag too much, even about your children.

- There are no business breakfasts in Japan.

- Having drinks is important for developing personal relationships. Never decline an invitation to go drinking. Take a drink when offered, even if you only sip or pretend to drink it.

- Karaoke bars are popular for business entertainment. Always join in with the group, and sing a solo when it's your turn.

- Evenings generally end at around 10:00 PM.

Especially for Women

Japan is a male-dominated society, and Japanese culture binds men and women to rigid roles that define all behavior. Because companies expect employees to work long hours, many men spend little time at home, where women are the unequivocal bosses. Women manage all domestic issues, child rearing, and the family budget. Many husbands receive allowances from their wives.

In part because of Japan's high cost of living and dropping marriage rate, more and more Japanese women are working outside the home. Women make up 40 percent of the Japanese workforce, and about 30 percent of Japanese women continue to work after having children.

Women still find it difficult to advance within some companies, especially large ones. (To justify a promotion, many believe a woman must be much better than a man.) Companies often hire well-educated Japanese women only as temporary workers (called "OL" or "office ladies"). Most high-ranking executives are men, but many people expect more women to assume top positions in years to come as the Japanese population ages and experienced employees retire.

Acceptance of Japanese businesswomen is increasing, but many Japanese businessmen may not be comfortable working with women in positions of power or socializing with them as equals.

- The Japanese view Western women as foreigners first, women second. They treat Western women politely in business, and they understand Western women hold high-level business positions. With that said, the Japanese value competence and professionalism most when dealing with foreign businesspeople. For business success in Japan, Western women must establish credibility and a position of authority immediately.

- Some Japanese men may resist women in power. Be patient. Reassure them of your position of authority.

- The Japanese will judge capability by your dress and behavior. Don't wear bright colors, low-cut apparel, dangling jewelry, or heavy makeup. Try not to stand out.

- Remember, for business success it's important to participate socially. Although you should never try to stand out, you may be the center of attention. Enjoy the experience and use it to build personal relationships.

- A foreign woman may invite a Japanese man to a business lunch or dinner. Let the man choose a restaurant in which he feels comfortable dining with a foreign woman. Arrange payment with wait staff beforehand; don't let the bill come to the table.

- Extend invitations to Japanese businessmen and their wives, but don't take offense if the wives don't come.

- Most Japanese cities are safe for a woman traveling alone, but use common sense. Although rare, a foreign woman can make a Japanese man (usually a drunken one) act lewdly. If this happens, calmly ignore the behavior and leave the area as quickly as possible.

Holidays and Festivals

January	New Year's Day (1)
	Coming of Age Day (15)
February	Founding of the Nation Day (11)
March	Vernal Equinox (20)
April/May	Golden Week (April 29–May 5), including Showa Day, Greenery Day, Constitution Day, and Children's Day
September	Respect for the Aged Day (15)
	Autumn Equinox Day (23)
October	Physical Fitness Day (10)
November	National Culture Day (3)
	Labor Thanksgiving Day (23)
December	Emperor's Birthday (23)

Note: Dates of holidays change from year to year. Check to see when Japan celebrates holidays for the year you're traveling. There may also be additional holidays celebrated in different regions.

MALAYSIA*

Greetings from Malaysia

Greetings from the beautiful land where various cultures have mingled for over a thousand years. The Chinese, Indians, and Arabs are just a few of the ethnic groups that have contributed to Malaysia's uniquely diverse, tolerant society.

Our faiths are as diverse as our ethnicities. Most Malays are Muslim (the official state religion); others are Christian. Ethnic Chinese follow Buddhism, Taoism, and Confucianism, while ethnic Indians are mostly Hindu, but some are Sikh or Christian. As a nation, we consider ourselves secular.

Over a millennium ago, our ancestors formed a Hindu-Buddhist kingdom in the Bujang Valley. Silk and gold traders helped make the area an integral part of the Sriwijaya Empire. By 1400, Arab traders influenced Malaysia's rulers to convert to Islam, which became the region's dominant religion.

As a major center of regional trade, our rich land attracted European traders just starting to circumnavigate the globe. In the early sixteenth century, Portugal took control of Malacca, our thriving trading port. Control subsequently passed to the Dutch in 1641 and to the United Kingdom in 1824. At the dawn of the twentieth century, all our land became British colonies and protectorates.

In 1957, we gained our independence. Since then, we have worked hard to reconstruct our nation into a modern industrialized economy. In 1970, we were largely an exporter of raw materials; today, we have expanded into manufacturing, services, and tourism. Between 1987 and 1997, our economy grew at an annual rate of 8 to 9 percent. As a result, today we are one of the wealthiest countries in Southeast Asia.

The lives of our people have also improved. Nearly forty years ago, almost half our population lived in poverty; today, less than 10 percent do. In that same time period, our infant mortality rate was cut roughly in half. In 1970, just over half the adults could read and write; today, nearly all adults are literate.

* This country's name has no conventional long form.

Our land boasts eleven thousand species of flowering plants and trees, nearly three hundred species of mammals, and over four hundred species of birds. Malaysia is also home to the orangutan, the last surviving great ape outside of Africa.

Kuala Lumpur is a crowded, bustling cosmopolitan city that boasts the Petronas Twin Towers, the world's second-highest buildings. Visit the capital to watch a Chinese opera, Muslims preparing for prayer, and young girls taking classical Indian dance lessons.

Unfortunately, as our economy surged in the 1970s, industrial pollution wreaked environmental damage. Today, we are trying several approaches to reversing the damage and reclaiming one of the world's most ecologically diverse regions.

Along with our Asian neighbors, we value the group over the individual, and harmony over competition. We believe family is the most important part of society. We teach our young to respect their elders, and many generations may live in the same house in rural areas. Today, we worry that consumerism and a desire for individual wealth and power are replacing traditional values.

Although ours has been a diverse nation for generations, most of us identify with our ethnic group, island, or region more than with Malaysia as a whole. People of different ethnicities do not routinely mix, and tensions exist among different groups. Malays dominate politics, the Chinese are the most wealthy, and many Indians and indigenous people live in poverty.

But we are working to change. For example, because education is the key to social status, between 2001 and 2005 we doubled the number of indigenous students enrolled in schools.

We are proud of both our traditional cultures and our modern economy. Come visit us for business or pleasure. We will welcome you!

Note: See pages 109–167 and 293–310 for additional background information on the Chinese and Indian minorities in Malaysia.

Population	24,385,858
Capital	Kuala Lumpur
Area	127,317 square miles, slightly larger than New Mexico
Government	Constitutional monarchy
Living Standard	GDP = US $5,950 per capita
Natural Resources	Tin, petroleum, timber, copper, iron ore, natural gas, bauxite
Agriculture	Peninsular Malaysia: rubber, palm oil, cocoa, rice; Sabah: subsistence crops, rubber, timber, coconuts, rice; Sarawak: rubber, pepper, timber
Industries	Peninsular Malaysia: rubber and palm oil processing and manufacturing, light manufacturing industry, electronics, tin mining and smelting, logging, timber processing; Sabah: logging, petroleum production; Sarawak: agriculture processing, petroleum production and refining, logging
Climate	Tropical: annual southwest (April to October) and northeast (October to February) monsoons
Currency	Ringgit (MYR)

The People

Correct Name	noun: Malay(s) or Malaysian(s)
	adjective: Malaysian
Ethnic Makeup	Malay 50.4%, Chinese 23.7%, Indigenous 11%, Indian 7.1%, others 7.8%
Languages	Bahasa Melayu (official), English, Chinese (Cantonese, Mandarin, Hokkien, Hakka, Hainan, Foochow), Tamil, Telugu, Malayalam, Punjabi, Thai
Religions	Muslim, Buddhist, Taoist, Hindu, Christian, Sikh, Shamanism (practiced in East Malaysia)

Meeting and Greeting

- Malaysian men customarily shake hands with one another when meeting and leaving. Among close friends, the man extending the handshake may use both hands to grasp the other man's hand.

- Malaysian women and elderly people generally don't shake hands.
- Western men should shake hands with Malaysian men, but nod or give a slight bow when greeting or leaving a Malaysian woman or older person. (They may, however, shake a woman's or older person's hand if it's offered.) Western women should greet all Malays with nod and a smile.
- Malays introduce higher-ranking or older people before lower-ranking or younger people, and women before men.
- Traditional Malays may greet one another with a salaam (low bow while touching right hand to the forehead). Foreigners shouldn't attempt this greeting.

Names and Titles

English	Bahasa Melayu	Pronunciation
Mr.	*Encik*	(IN-seek)
Mrs.	*Puan*	(POO-wun)
Miss	*Cik*	(seek)

- Address Malays by courtesy title (English or Bahasa Melayu) + first name (given name).
- Ethnic Malays don't have last names (surnames). Traditional name order is first name + bin (used for men) or binti (used for women) + father's first name.

    Examples: Ali bin Isa is the son of Isa bin Osman.

    Zaitun binti Isa is the daughter of Isa bin Osman.
- After marrying, some Malaysian women take their husbands' first names and some don't.

    Example: After Zaitun binti Isa marries Ali bin Osman and takes his first name, her name becomes Zaitun Ali. One still addresses her as Mrs. Zaitun or *Puan* Zaitun.
- The federal and state governments bestow titles on prominent Malays, who use them in business. Royalty also have special titles. Upon introduction, listen carefully for a person's title, study his or her business card, and always use the given title when addressing him or her.
- In business correspondence, use English. Salutation is Dear + English courtesy title + first name.
- Because ethnic Chinese are prominent in Malaysian business, see pages 112–113 for more information on Chinese names and titles.

Language

When Arabs introduced Islam in the fourteenth century, Malaysia's language adopted the Arabic alphabet. In the seventeenth century, Dutch and British influences prompted the language to switch to the Latin (Roman) alphabet.

Today, multiethnic Malaysia debates whether to call its official language Bahasa Melayu ("the Malay language") or Bahasa Malaysia ("the Malaysian language"). Whatever the name, Malays are torn between maintaining their native language to preserve cultural homogeneity and emphasizing English, which many see as necessary to compete in the global economy.

In addition to the official language, many Malays speak Chinese, Tamil, or numerous tribal languages. In East Malaysia, people also speak several indigenous languages, most prominently Iban and Kadazan.

Conversation

- Malays ask personal questions (income, marital status, and so on) as part of small talk. Feel free to ask them personal questions. If you're uncomfortable answering a question, give a vague answer or say, "In my country, that would be a strange question."
- You may compliment Malays, but expect them to deny the praise out of modesty.

Acceptable topics

- Family
- Work and business
- Malaysian history, food, culture, and music
- Malaysia's unique beauty
- Sports, especially football (soccer)
- Travel

> Malaysia is the only country with a rotating kingship. Unlike other monarchies, Malaysian kings change every five years. The king (whose role is mostly ceremonial) serves as an apolitical symbol of national solidarity and the defender of the Islamic faith. He's also the honorary leader of the armed forces, and all laws require his assent.

Unacceptable topics

- Implications that Malaysia is a backward, third-world nation
- Comparisons of Malaysia to other nations
- Sex and sexuality
- Gender roles

Topics that require sensitivity

- Political corruption
- Bureaucracy
- Malaysia's environmental problems
- Ethnic tensions in Malaysia, especially over preferential treatment and quotas

Body Language

- Avoid touching anyone of the opposite sex.
- Malays consider public displays of affection inappropriate.
- Never touch anyone—especially a child—on the head. Tradition holds that the soul resides there.
- Use only your right hand to shake hands, point, eat, or pass items.
- Malays bow slightly when walking by people or when entering or leaving a room. The gesture means "excuse me."
- In Malaysia, a smile or laughter doesn't indicate only happiness. It may also mean surprise, anger, shock, or embarrassment.
- It's impolite to gesture to beckon adults, especially with an index finger.
- It's obscene to pound your fist into a cupped hand.
- Be careful not to put your hands in your pockets; doing so means you're angry.
- It's rude to show the soles of your shoes or feet to anyone.
- Don't move objects with your feet or use your foot to point at another person.
- Don't cross your legs in front of elderly people. Never rest your ankle on your knee in front of anyone.

Phrases		
English	**Bahasa Melayu**	**Pronunciation**
Hello	*Apa khabar*	(AH-pah kah-BAR)
Good morning	*Selamat pagi*	(seh-LAH-maht PAH-ghee)
Good afternoon	*Selamat tengah hari*	(seh-LAH-maht teng-AH hah-REE)
Good evening	*Selamat petang*	(seh-LAH-maht peh-TAHNG)
Please	*Tolong*	(TOH-long)
Thank you	*Terima kasih*	(TEHR-ee-mah KAH-see)
You're welcome	*Sama sama*	(SAH-mah sah-MAH)

Yes	*Ya*	(ee-AH)
No	*Tidak*	(TEE-dahk)
Excuse me	*Minta maaf*	(MEEN-tah mah-AHF)
Goodbye		
(said by the person leaving)	*Selamat tinggal*	(seh-LAH-maht TEENG-gahl)
(said by the person staying)	*Selamat jalan*	(seh-LAH-maht JAH-lahn)
How are you?	*Apa khabar*	(AH-pah kah-BAR)

Dining

Malaysian cuisine is spicy and flavorful. It features spices and herbs used in a variety of neighboring countries, like India and China.

Cuisine and dining customs vary among ethnic groups. While pork is a staple of the Chinese diet, strict Muslims don't eat pork or drink alcohol. Hindus and Buddhists don't eat beef.

- Most Malays and Indians eat with spoons and hands, although some use forks and spoons and others use only their hands. (Knives aren't necessary, because people serve food in bite-size pieces.) The Chinese eat with chopsticks and spoons. (See page 41 for information on chopstick etiquette.)
- Malays seat the guest of honor to the host's right or at the head of the table.
- Before dinner, hosts give guests towels and a small bowl of water to wash their hands.
- In many homes, men eat before women do.

Drinking

- Fruit juices are popular in Malaysia, but alcoholic beverages aren't as common as in some Asian countries. Islam prohibits alcoholic consumption, and Muslims may be uncomfortable at functions that serve alcohol.
- Malays usually offer coffee and tea—often with milk added—after a meal or with dessert. They may also offer soft drinks outside of mealtime.
- Always accept and serve beverages with both hands.

Toasting

In general, Malays don't follow any toasting protocol and don't make many toasts. It's more common (and always appropriate) to give a short speech to welcome people or express appreciation.

If, however, the occasion calls for a toast, here are a couple that Malays use:
- *Minum* (MEE-noom), which means "cheers."
- *Selamat menjamu selera* (seh-LAH-maht MEHN-jah-moo seh-LEHR-ah), which means "please treat your appetite."

You may give either of these toasts before, during, or after a meal. Women may propose toasts.

Tipping

Tipping isn't customary in Malaysia, but some Malays may expect Westerners to tip.
- Restaurants: The bill often includes a 4 percent service charge. If the bill doesn't include a service charge, you may leave up to a 5 percent tip. Servers in restaurants that tourists patronize may expect an additional gratuity (up to 10 percent).
- Taxi drivers: Round up the fare to the nearest ringgit or tip small change.
- Gas station attendants: Round up the bill to the nearest ringgit.
- Bellhops and porters: Tip MYR1 per bag.
- Restroom attendants: Tip MYR1 or half that amount.
- Hair stylists and barbers: No tip is necessary, but you may give small change for exceptional service.

Manners

- When invited to someone's home for dinner, be on time. There isn't a cocktail hour in Malaysian culture; hosts serve the meal as soon as all guests have arrived.
- Before entering someone's home, remove your shoes and sunglasses.
- Don't request a tour of your host's home or wander through private areas alone.
- Never refuse any offer of food or drink. Always at least taste the dish or beverage. To refuse additional helpings, put your hand above your plate or glass and say, "No, thank you."

- Wait for the host to start eating and invite you to do so before you begin eating.
- When using a fork and spoon to eat, hold the spoon in your right hand and the fork in your left. Use the fork to push food onto the spoon. Put only the spoon into your mouth. When finished eating, set the utensils on your plate.
- When using only a spoon to eat, hold it in your right hand. When finished eating, set the spoon on your plate.
- When using hands to eat, use only the right hand to eat and pass food.
- When eating satay (marinated meat, poultry or seafood grilled on skewers and dipped in peanut sauce), use a skewer to spear and eat rice cakes.
- If you can't finish your food, don't offer it to anyone or return it to the serving dish. Once you've touched food, Malays consider it tainted. Never let the serving spoon touch your plate.
- If using a fork and spoon to eat, place them together on your plate when you're finished eating. If you don't, hosts will offer you more food.
- Never blow your nose or clear your throat while eating; leave the room if necessary.
- Malays visit others' homes unannounced; however, foreigners should always call ahead unless the relationship is very close.
- Muslim families pray between 6:00 and 7:30 PM. Respect their privacy during these hours.
- When visiting a Muslim's home, don't touch the Koran (sacred text of Islam).
- If invited to sit on mats, men sit cross-legged and women sit with feet tucked under them (to the left if possible).
- Don't stand or sit on prayer rugs.
- Always show respect for the elderly (open doors for them, offer them your seat, and so on).
- Always ask permission to smoke, but never smoke in front of elderly people or royalty (many are in business and may attend meetings with foreigners).
- Cover your mouth to yawn or use a toothpick.
- Never whistle, hiss, or shout. Malays consider such behavior rude.
- See pages 75–85 for etiquette information when visiting a temple, mosque, or other place of worship.

Punctuality

Punctuality isn't important to Malays. They consider people more important than schedules. With that said, Malays expect Westerners to be on time for social occasions and business meetings. If you'll be delayed, call with an explanation.

If a Malay is late or an event or business meeting doesn't start on time, be patient and don't get frustrated.

Dress

Malaysia's climate is hot and humid, so most people wear clothing in natural, breathable fabrics. Most Malays dress in Western fashions, although batik prints are popular.

- In general, Malaysian women wear conservative skirts and pants. They never wear sleeveless blouses, shorts, short skirts, or other revealing clothing. In some areas, Muslim women wear veils and long dresses.
- For business, men wear conservative suits and ties when meeting with government officials or for a first meeting with business colleagues. At other times, they wear white shirts with dress trousers (executives should wear ties). Women wear blouses (never sleeveless) with skirts or dressy pants.
- Before dining in a restaurant, ask for its dress code. Better restaurants require men to wear sport coats. Women wear dressy pants or skirts with modest blouses.
- For casual occasions, men and women wear clean, neat casual attire. Women may wear skirts and blouses, but slacks or designer jeans are acceptable.
- Traditionally, only royalty wear yellow clothing. Avoid wearing yellow to a palace or to formal events.

Gifts

- To save face in case a gift is inappropriate, Malays usually don't open gifts in the giver's presence.
- Always give and receive gifts with both hands. Never use only your left hand.
- Soon after receiving a gift, always reciprocate with one of equal value. A dinner invitation is an acceptable gift.
- Malays may misread the intent behind gifts from men to women. If giving a gift to a Malaysian woman, a Western man should explain that it's from his wife.

- If giving food gifts to Muslims, make sure they're *halal* (see page 83).
- Never give Muslims gifts that feature dogs or pigs or any item made of pigskin (dogs and pigs are taboo to Muslims).
- For gifts for ethnic Chinese, see "red envelopes" on page 58.
- Have gifts wrapped in pink or red gift-wrap (colors symbolize luck). Never use white gift-wrap (used for funerals only), black gift-wrap (color symbolizes death), or yellow gift-wrap (used for royalty only).

Hostess Gifts

When invited to someone's home, always bring a small gift. Also bring small gifts for children (candy, children's books from your country, and so on).

Consider giving
- Flowers, except frangipani flowers (given for funerals only)
- Fruit
- Sweets
- Perfume
- Arts and crafts from your home region

Don't give
- Money
- Liquor
- Knives, scissors, or other sharp objects (connote the severing of a relationship)

Business Gifts

In general, Malays don't exchange business gifts. If you receive one, be prepared to reciprocate with one of comparable value. Make sure the gift isn't obviously expensive. Malaysian anticorruption laws forbid bribery, and Malays may consider an expensive gift a bribe.

If you give a gift to your Malaysian contacts, do so after you complete negotiations.

Consider giving
- Items that feature your company logo
- Gifts from your hometown or region
- Pens and other desk accessories
- Books

Don't give

- Money
- Liquor
- Knives, scissors, or other sharp objects (connote the severing of a relationship)

Helpful Hints

- Most shops and larger stores fix their prices, but you can discreetly ask for a discount. Expect to bargain in street markets, flea markets, and antique stores.
- Don't wait to queue for buses. When you get on a bus, rush to a seat and hold on tightly to your belongings.
- In crowded restaurants, strangers may sit together at a table. You needn't talk to them.
- Most taxis are metered, but there may be surcharges for rides during peak hours or to congested destinations. Agree on a fare before getting into a taxi.

Health and Safety

- As a precaution, drink only boiled or bottled water in major cities (even though many claim to have safe tap water) and especially in rural areas.
- Most expatriates in Peninsular Malaysia use private hospitals in Kuala Lumpur, Ipoh, Penang, and Petaling Jaya. Those living in East Malaysia seek treatment in Kuala Lumpur or Singapore. Fees are low, but providers and hospitals often expect immediate cash payment for services. Make sure to buy supplemental medical insurance with specific overseas coverage.
- Don't drive in large cities, where traffic is chaotic. Public transportation is inexpensive and relatively easy to use. Some street signs are in Bahasa Melayu and English.
- Malaysia is a relatively safe country. Major crimes against tourists are uncommon. With that said, the U.S. State Department has warned of possible terrorist attacks in Malaysia. Before traveling to the country, check the current travel warnings.
- Beware of pickpocketing, especially on public transportation. Transvestites in Kuala Lumpur often pickpocket tourists.
- Malaysia has one of the world's highest rates of credit card fraud; closely guard your credit card numbers.
- Never buy or bring illicit drugs into Malaysia. Death is the penalty for sale or possession of illegal drugs.

Corporate Culture

Structure

Decision making in companies is authoritative, subjective, intuitive, and focused on preserving existing interpersonal relationships. Companies base promotions on a superior's respect and personal regard for an employee, not on the employee's performance.

Meetings

- At the beginning of meetings, Malays may engage in lengthy polite conversation before getting down to business.
- When business talk begins, the discussions are long and detailed.
- Make sure presentations are detailed and informative.
- In the beginning, Malays won't make many concessions and will try to pressure foreigners to make them. But the longer the negotiations continue, the more concessions they'll likely make. It usually takes several trips to conclude negotiations.

Appointments

- Before scheduling a meeting, try to send a letter of introduction from an international bank (or local affiliate) or a person acquainted with you and your potential Malaysian colleagues. Without a proper introduction, Malays may ignore your request for a meeting.
- March through July is the best time to visit Malaysia for business trips.
- Make appointments at least a month in advance.
- Avoid making appointments for dates during Chinese New Year and Ramadan.
- Regular business hours are 8:00 AM to 5:00 PM, Monday through Friday. Some businesses are open Saturday mornings. On Thursdays, Muslim offices are open only in the morning; they're closed on Fridays.

Communication

- English is usually the language of Malaysian business, especially among different ethnic groups.
- Always remember that Malays never forgive someone who makes another lose face. Never publicly criticize a person, a company, a proposal, or a report. If you must criticize someone or something, do so privately and tactfully.

- Malays don't appreciate bluntness, and sometimes avoid direct communication—especially if it's negative. Learn to listen carefully and determine true meaning from the context of the conversation, other statements, and the speaker's body language.

Business Cards
- Exchange business cards upon introduction.
- Always give and receive business cards with both hands, never with only your left hand.
- Information on your business card may be in English.

Be Aware
- Establishing rapport and trust is a must for business relationships. Malays want to get to know you before doing business with you.
- Malays are cautious to form opinions and make decisions. They believe fate or God determines successes and failures, opportunities and misfortunes. Be patient.
- To Malays, the future is vague and unpredictable. After reaching an agreement—even if it's written and signed—they may try to renegotiate and request an escape clause. They believe written contracts are less important than trust.
- Malays tend to judge people by family background, education, social position, and professional status—not by occupation.

Socializing
Socializing is an important part of Malaysian business culture.
- Malays do most business entertaining in restaurants.
- Lunch or dinner follows important meetings. Always reciprocate with a meal of equal value.
- When hosting a meal, ask your guests whether they have dietary restrictions before you plan the menu.
- Try not to invite an odd number of guests when you host a dinner. Malays believe it's good luck to invite an even number of dinner guests.
- Malays may invite spouses to dinner (never lunch) if business won't be discussed.

Especially for Women

Compared to women in many other countries, Malaysian women play prominent roles in business and public life.

Some Malays believe, however, that Muslim women must endure discriminatory rules that don't apply to non-Muslim women.

Although Malays generally accept women in business, and Malaysian women hold some influential positions, only about 47 percent of working-age Malaysian women worked in 2004. To encourage women to enter the workforce, the government has implemented several programs to increase women's status and political participation.

- Although unlikely, Western women may be hassled while doing business in Malaysia. In particular, men in East Malaysia may harass a woman if she's alone.
- A Western woman may invite a Malaysian man (with or without his wife) to a business dinner. She should arrange payment with the wait staff beforehand.
- If alone, a Western woman should eat only in hotel restaurants or lounges.

Holidays and Festivals

January	New Year's Day (1)
January/February	Chinese New Year
March/April	Good Friday
	Birthday of Prophet Muhammad
May	Labor Day (1)
	Wesak Day (changes yearly)
June	King's Birthday (5)
August	National Day (31)
October/November	Deepavali
December	Christmas (25)

Note: Malaysia also celebrates several Islamic holidays and festivals. Check when they're celebrated for the year you're visiting Malaysia.

PAKISTAN
ISLAMIC REPUBLIC OF PAKISTAN

Greetings from Pakistan

Greetings from the land of friendly people and magnificent landscapes.

We have been Pakistanis for less than a century, but our people have lived in the area for millennia. One of the world's first great civilizations began in the Indus Valley over four thousand years ago. Among its accomplishments, the people developed a standardized system of weights and measures and a symbol-writing system. By 1700 BC, the civilization had disappeared, although remnants of it survived in small communities.

In the eighth century, Arab Muslims brought Islam to the area. Two centuries later, Lahore became the capital of a Turkish Muslim empire and a major center of Islamic culture. Although as time passed other kingdoms controlled the area, our identity as a Muslim civilization grew stronger.

Along with India, we broke from British control in 1947 and became an independent nation. Since then, we have had three wars with India over territory; the last one in 1971 created the Bangladesh nation. When India first tested nuclear weapons in 1998, Pakistan soon followed. A cease-fire was called in 2003, but it was a tense standoff.

Today, Pakistan and India each claims the northern Kashmir territory, and the area's border is the world's largest and most militarized. Thankfully, talks and other measures are building confidence between our countries, and tensions are easing—especially after the devastating 2005 earthquake destroyed the lives of so many in the region. After the disaster, India offered our nation emergency supplies as well as a quarter-billion US dollars in aid, which we accepted. We hope that our mutual cooperation will further defuse tensions.

Although our constitution guarantees freedom of religion, the government imposes limits. Nearly our entire population is Muslim, and Islam is the state religion. Our constitution mandates that our president and prime minister must be Muslim and all senior officials must swear an oath to preserve Pakistan's Islamic identity. Our state funds mosques and Muslim clergy.

Unfortunately, there is conflict among religious groups. There is even violence among Muslims, especially Sunni and Shia extremists.

We are working hard to improve our people's lives. A few years ago, nearly a third of the Pakistani population lived in poverty; today, roughly a quarter of us do. Our per capita income in 2002 was higher than that of Bangladesh, but our education index was lower, and the percentage of our public spending on health and education was just over 2 percent. We know we cannot improve until we educate our people, and we are working toward making education a priority.

Although Islamic law permits men to have up to four wives, very few Pakistanis practice this form of polygamy. Our families are close; parents often live with their adult sons' families in the same home. We identify ourselves by our close relationships. In fact, we may identify more strongly with our ethnic group than our nation.

We want to show the world our beautiful country, and we are eager to develop a tourism industry. Visitors will find magnificent Buddhist monuments, Hindu temples, palaces, and mansions to tour. They can visit Khunjerab National Park to see the rare Marco Polo sheep (only a few hundred left in the world), Himalayan ibex, golden marmots, wolves, snow leopards, and other species.

Adventurers may attempt to climb K2 (sometimes also called Mount Godwin Austen or Dapsang) in the Karakoram mountain range in northern Pakistan. It's the world's second-highest mountain at over twenty-eight thousand feet.

Our nation will offer such a unique, wonderful experience for many Westerners, and our friendly, hospitable people will impress you. Come and visit us soon.

Vital Statistics

Population	165,803,560
Capital	Islamabad
Area	310,403 square miles, slightly less than twice the size of California
Government	Federal republic
Living Standard	GDP = US $790 per capita
Natural Resources	Land, extensive natural gas reserves, limited petroleum, (poor quality) coal, iron ore, copper, salt, limestone
Agriculture	Cotton, wheat, rice, sugarcane, fruits, vegetables, milk, beef, mutton, eggs
Industries	Textiles and apparel, food processing, pharmaceuticals, construction materials, paper products, fertilizer, shrimp
Climate	Mostly hot, dry desert; temperate in northwest and arctic in the north
Currency	Pakistani rupee (PKR)

The People	
Correct Name	noun: Pakistani(s)
	adjective: Pakistani
Ethnic Makeup	Punjabi, Sindhi, Pathan (also called Pashtun), Baloch, Muhajir (immigrants from India at the time of partition and their descendants)
Languages	Punjabi 48%, Sindhi 12%, Siraiki (a Punjabi variant) 10%, Pashtu 8%, Urdu (official) 8%, Balochi 3%, Hindko 2%, Brahui 1%, English (official), Burushaski, and other 8%
Religions	Muslim 97% (Sunni 77%, Shia 20%), Christian, Hindu, and other 3%

Meeting and Greeting

- Pakistanis greet people individually, beginning with the eldest. They believe group greetings are rude.
- Upon meeting, men shake one another's hands. Pathan men may also place their right hands over their hearts after shaking hands. In this case, Western men may reciprocate the gesture as a sign of respect.

    Women shake hands with one another or hug and kiss on the cheek.
- Men don't shake women's hands in public; only close relatives touch one another and only in private. To avoid offending a woman's husband or violating her sense of propriety, Western men shouldn't extend a hand to women—if a woman extends a hand, however, a man may shake it.

    Western women shouldn't extend a hand to men. If a man extends his hand to a Western woman, she may shake it. If he doesn't, she should nod politely.
- People of the same sex may hug upon meeting, even when meeting for the first or second time.

Names and Titles

- Name order is generally first name (given name) + last name (surname). Traditionally, some rural Pakistanis used only first names. Today, the government requires everyone to have a last name in order to acquire a national identification card.

- In some areas, the name(s) of a person's tribe or caste follows the last name. Heads of tribes may also use titles before their first names.

  Example: Sardar Farooq Ahmed Khan Leghari

  Sardar = title

  Farooq = first name

  Ahmed = last name

  Khan = caste or tribe

  Leghari = caste or tribe

- Address government officials and male colleagues or superiors either by first name + Sir or *Sahib* (pronounced "sahb") or by Mr. + first name.

- Courtesy titles for women in Pakistan are in flux. Ask female colleagues how you should address them. Some women prefer to be addressed by Ms. + first name; others prefer Mrs. or Miss + first name.

  Addressing a female superior or an elderly woman by Madam + first name is safe and respectful (if a bit old-fashioned), especially if you don't know her preferred title. In fact, use Madam + first name to address any woman whose preferred title you don't know.

- Never address a Pakistani by only his or her first name until invited to do so. Pakistanis often address subordinates simply by first name or occupation (for example, "gardener").

- Be aware that Muslim women don't routinely take their husbands' last names after marrying, but some add their husbands' first names after their own first names.

  Example: After Zilla Aziz marries Hamid Zahid, she may or may not choose to change her name to Zilla Hamid Aziz.

- At formal occasions (official receptions or formal embassy functions, for example), address Pakistani men by either by last name + Sir or *Sahib* (pronounced "sahb") or by Mr. + last name. Address Pakistani women by Madam or preferred title + last name.

  With that said, Pakistanis highly respect military officers. Always address retired military officers by their military titles.

- Proper form of address is often difficult to tell from a business card. Ask a person for preferred address. When in doubt, address a man by Sir or *Sahib* and a woman by Madam.

- *Yaar* (YAH-ahr) means "friend" and indicates familiarity and frankness (like the British and Australian word *mate*). Men use it as a chummy way to address one another, but Western men shouldn't use it with Pakistanis until they use it first. Women don't use the term with one another or with men.

Language

Although only 8 percent of Pakistanis speak Urdu (a language closely related to Hindi) as a first language, most people speak it as an additional language. Few Pakistanis speak English—also an official language—as a first language, but it's the lingua franca of most government and international businesspeople.

Each province has its own regional languages and dialects.

Conversation

- When conversing, Pakistanis may be loud and commanding, especially when trying to persuade others.
- Pakistanis avoid using direct language. They believe indirect communication is more sophisticated and polite. For example, they try not to say "no"; instead, they say, "*Inshallah*" (if God wills), "I'll try," or "maybe."
- Flattery is important to Pakistanis. Praise things and people effusively.
- Being sarcastic is acceptable in public, but showing anger never is.

Acceptable topics

- Male members of someone's family: Pakistani men don't discuss female family members in public.
- Travel
- Sports, including field hockey, wrestling, and especially cricket: Pakistan has some of the world's most outstanding cricket teams and players.
- Your education, profession, and family history: Pakistanis will eagerly share their own information with you.
- Local and regional history (but not British involvement in Pakistani affairs)

Unacceptable topics

- Pakistan's relationship with India
- Ethnic groups in general and someone's ethnic group in particular (unless you're very knowledgeable about Pakistan's ethnicities)
- Criticism of Islam, including Islamic law: The law severely punishes blasphemy.

Topics that require sensitivity

- Politics: Pakistanis love to talk politics, but wait until establishing a personal relationship with someone before broaching this subject.
- Pakistan's relationship with the United States
- Afghani refugees
- Terrorism

Body Language

- Among members of the same sex, Pakistanis are affectionate as a sign of friendship. They stand closely to one another and may touch one another a great deal while talking (hand on someone's shoulder, patting someone's hand, and so on). Foreigners shouldn't initiate such behavior with Pakistanis, but they may return affectionate gestures if Pakistanis offer them first.
- Physical contact between men and women is strictly taboo in public.
- Don't maintain eye contact with someone. Pakistanis consider prolonged eye contact rude. Also, women should never make eye contact with men on the street; they'll interpret such behavior as a sexual invitation.
- Try to curtail your gesturing when conversing with Pakistanis. They don't use many gestures.
- Always use your right hand to pass and receive items. Pakistanis consider the left hand unclean.
- Don't point the sole of your foot at someone. If you cross your legs, make sure the sole of your shoe doesn't face anyone. If seated on the floor, squat or sit with knees bent and both feet on the floor.
- To beckon someone (including wait staff), extend your arm (palm down), then curl and flex your fingers together.

Phrases

Urdu uses a version of the Perso-Arabic alphabet called Nastaliq. There isn't standard transliteration into English. Below are the phonetic equivalents.

English	Urdu	Pronunciation
Hello/Good morning/ Good afternoon/ Good evening	*Assalam alaikum*	(ASS-a-lahm a-LAY-koom)
Please	*Meharbaanee kar ke*	(meh-har-BAH-nee kar keh)
Thank you	*Shukriya*	(SHOOK-rih-yuh)
You're welcome	*Koee baat naheeng*	(KOH-ee baht na-HEENG)
Yes	*Jee haang*	(jee hahng)
No	*Jee na-heeng*	(jee-na HEENG)
Excuse me	*Suniye*	(suh-nih-YEH)
Goodbye	*Khoda hafez*	(koo-DAH HAH-fiz)
Pleased to meet you	*Aap se milkar*	(AHP say MILL-kur)
How are you?	*Aap kaise hai*	(AHP kay-seh HAY)

Dining

Although each Pakistani region has its own distinctive cuisine, all Pakistani food is closely related to Indian fare. Persian, Afghani, and Western foods also have influenced Pakistani dishes.

- Most urban Pakistanis use utensils to eat meals at a Western-style dining table. In rural homes, people use their hands to eat meals at a knee-high table while sitting on the floor.
- Pakistanis who eat with their hands also use chapattis (a flat bread) to soak up sauces and scoop food. See pages 39–40 for more information on eating with your hands.
- Devout Muslims (that is, most Pakistanis) don't eat pork.

Drinking

Because Islam forbids the consumption of alcohol, only non-Muslims may buy alcohol in Pakistan. (Although some Muslims do drink alcohol purchased from Christians, bootleggers, or smugglers.) To buy alcohol in the few large hotels that cater to Westerners, visitors may have to show their passports to prove they're not Muslims.

- Don't try to bring alcohol into Pakistan. Customs officials will confiscate it.
- Hotels may serve alcohol in a teapot or other inconspicuous container.
- Never drink alcohol outside the hotels that serve it.
- Other common beverages include:
  - * Water: Pakistanis serve it before or after meals, but rarely during them.
  - * Tea: Pakistanis always serve it with milk and lots of sugar.
  - * Chai (tea boiled with milk, sugar, and spices)
  - * Lassi (a yogurt-based drink)
  - * Fresh fruit juices
  - * Soft drinks

> Murree Brewery is the country's only legal alcohol factory, producing beer, gin, brandy, and whiskey.

Toasting

Pakistanis don't have a tradition of toasting. If with traditional Pakistanis, don't propose toasts. If with Pakistanis familiar with Western customs and who will receive toasts well, men or women may offer short toasts in English at special events. (The beverages will likely be nonalcoholic.)

Tipping

Because tipping contradicts the Pakistani spirit of hospitality, the practice isn't customary. But Pakistanis who often serve Westerners may expect tips, especially in larger cities.

- Restaurants: The bill in hotel restaurants and elegant establishments may include a 10 percent service charge. If the bill in any restaurant doesn't include a service charge, tip a small amount (less than PKR100).
- Taxis: Tip 5 percent of the fare.
- Bellhops, porters, hair stylists, and barbers: A sign that suggests an appropriate tip amount may be posted. If not, there's no need to tip (but if you want to give one, a PKR10 tip is appropriate).

Manners

- Always respect elders; they make decisions for families.
- When entering someone's home, remove your shoes (unless your host is wearing shoes).
- Before meals, it's polite to chat with your dining partners.
- Pakistanis serve elders first, giving them the most delectable foods. Don't start eating until the eldest person has begun eating.
- When using your hands to eat, use only the right hand. (You may tear bread with both hands.) Use the right hand or both hands to pass food.
- Your host will urge you to take second and third helpings. You may decline politely while praising the food.
- Leave soon after the meal is finished. Pakistanis socialize before meals.
- Before smoking, get permission from everyone present. Know that smoking is illegal in some public places.
- During Ramadan, don't eat, drink, or smoke in public. If hosting Muslims during this time, don't smoke, eat, or drink in front of them between sunrise and sunset.

Punctuality

Pakistanis are unconcerned with punctuality in business, but foreigners should always be on time. Although they may try to be prompt, Pakistanis will expect you to be patient if they're late.

Pakistanis also aren't punctual for social occasions. Arrive thirty minutes late for a dinner or small gathering. Arrive one hour late for a party.

Dress

Although some Pakistanis wear conservative Western fashions, most wear cotton *shalwar kameez* (loose-fitting pants and long tunics). Men's version of the outfit is generally made of plain fabric in a solid color; they may add a vest or coat for formal occasions. Women's version of the outfit may incorporate bright colors and patterns, and they may add a shawl.

- Both men and women cover their legs and arms in public. Depending on their ethnic group, men wear pillbox hats, turbans, or other headwear. Women cover their hair with scarves. Traditional women may wear a burqa (a loose robe that covers the body from head to toe).
- At restaurants and for business occasions, men wear suits and ties for first meetings, then dressy shirts and pants for subsequent meetings. Women wear conservative, loose-fitting clothing.

    For more social occasions, men and women may wear more elegant attire. For example, a man may wear stylish cufflinks, and a woman may wear a silk blouse.
- For casual occasions, men wear long-sleeved shirts and trousers. Women wear conservative, loose-fitting clothing. Women should never wear shorts, and men should wear them only to play golf or other sports. Men and women may wear sandals.

Gifts

Pakistanis don't open gifts in front of the giver, and they always present and receive gifts with both hands.

Hostess Gifts

Always bring a gift when invited to someone's home. Also bring toys or sweets for any children.

Consider giving
- Decorations for the home, especially those from your home country or region
- Fruit
- High-quality chocolates or sweets

Don't give

- Obviously expensive gifts (They'll embarrass the host.)
- Alcohol
- White flowers (for weddings only): Plus, men shouldn't give any flowers to women.
- Pork or pigskin products

Business Gifts

- Pakistanis generally exchange business gifts after the successful completion of negotiations.
- It's customary to exchange gifts on Eid al-Fitr, which commemorates the end of Ramadan. Just as American businesspeople do at Christmas, you may give sweets to office staff, send gifts to customers, and so on.
- Men should give business gifts to Pakistani women on the behalf of their wives or female relatives.

Consider giving

- Arts and crafts from your home region or books about the area

Don't give

- Alcohol
- Pork or pigskin products

Helpful Hints

- Only major tourist destinations, restaurants, and shops catering to Westerners accept credit cards.
- Bazaars and markets offer all kinds of goods, and shopkeepers will expect you to bargain. Consider hiring a local guide to help you bargain; the savings you'll get will more than pay for the guide's fee.
- Telephone service in Pakistan is spotty. Hotels and shops may charge exorbitant fees to use their telephones.
- To ensure delivery, register outgoing mail at a local post office.
- Visitors may have difficulty entering Pakistan if their passports have entry stamps to India or they have Indian visas. If you must travel to both countries, try to obtain a second passport.

Health and Safety

- Before traveling to Pakistan, check for current health precautions and travel warnings (see page 373). Extremists within Pakistan have targeted Americans and American businesses, and suicide bombings and other violent acts are threats.
- Register with your home country's embassy upon arrival.
- Don't travel outside Islamabad without checking current travel warnings. You may need official permission to travel to some areas.
- Avoid anti-Western rallies and demonstrations. Also avoid Shia gatherings during Shia religious festivals, when violence against Sunni Muslims is highly probable.
- Doing anything that offends Islam could provoke Pakistanis to violence.
- Avoid visiting public places of worship and using public transportation. Both are often targets of terrorism.
- Avoid driving. Pakistanis drive aggressively (on the left side of the road) and usually aren't formally trained. Many vehicles are in poor condition and don't have headlights. Roads are extremely crowded in urban areas and poorly maintained everywhere. Streetlights and road signs are almost nonexistent.
- It's safest to hire a reputable driver from a reputable company. If necessary, ask your hotel to call a taxi company. Before getting in a taxi, check for a meter. If it doesn't have one, be sure to agree on the fare before leaving.
- Petty crime is common throughout the country. In urban areas, carjacking, armed robbery, and other violent crimes are common. Always be aware of your surroundings, and try not to travel after dark.
- Medical care is adequate in major cities but almost nonexistent in rural areas. Facilities require prepayment for medical services. In case you need emergency health care, make sure your health insurance covers travel to places outside Pakistan.
- Make sure to bring medications with you. American brand-name medicines aren't widely available, and local medicines are of questionable quality.

Pakistan is no stranger to natural disasters. Earthquakes are common and frequently severe, especially in the north and west. The Indus River, the country's longest river, floods during the monsoon months.

- Always drink boiled or imported (never domestic) bottled water. Make sure the seal on bottled water is intact. Don't consume tap water anywhere in Pakistan, including ice cubes and water to brush your teeth.
- Avoid drinking milk (it's not pasteurized), and eat only cooked and peeled vegetables and fruits.
- Even with these food and drink precautions, most visitors eventually catch some stomach illness. Sanitation in restaurants isn't up to American standards.
- Wear insect repellent. Mosquitoes carry diseases like dengue fever and malaria.

Corporate Culture

The Pakistani government has worked with the International Monetary Fund to develop policies for economic development, and the nation has made substantial progress over the last few years. In 2006, the industrial production growth rate was a steady 6 percent.

Unfortunately, Pakistan's conflict with India, internal political disputes, and entrenched corruption are major obstacles to the continued improvement of its economy.

Before doing business with any Pakistani company, investigate it thoroughly. Check its legitimacy with the Securities and Exchange Commission of Pakistan (http://www.secp.gov.pk).

Structure

- Pakistani companies have several layers of bureaucracy. Private businesses may have a more participatory management style, but government and public organizations are likely to be hierarchical.

Asking for baksheesh (a "polite" bribe) before doing a service was once common in Pakistan. People phrased their requests courteously and indirectly; for example: "It will take three months to fix your telephone, unless you pay a small service charge, and then it will be fixed by the end of this week."

Today, as Pakistan works to improve efficiency and adopt Western business customs, some businesspeople believe that asking for baksheesh is a dying practice. Many Pakistanis consider the word *baksheesh* an insult.

If, however, someone asks you for baksheesh, remember that under no circumstances should you offer a bribe. Instead, ask your local contact to intervene. (See page 67 for more information on hiring a local agent.)

- Management by consensus isn't common; managers give direct orders. Pakistanis expect managers to be decisive.
- Family networks are important, and nepotism is expected. Pakistanis prefer doing business with family members or people of their ethnic background.

Meetings

- Meetings begin with small talk, usually about family and health. At first meetings, Pakistanis may not even discuss business.
- Employees commonly walk in and interrupt meetings, starting a new discussion. Be patient.
- Pakistanis may hold meetings to gauge opinions and gather information, but top executives make decisions.
- If hosting a meeting, be sure to offer tea and refreshments.

Appointments

- Regular business hours are 9:00 AM to 5:00 PM, Monday through Thursday and Saturday, and 9:00 AM to noon on Friday.
- Working late and on weekends is common (but employees expect compensation). Pakistanis don't like to leave the office while the boss is still there.
- Make appointments several weeks in advance and confirm them by fax or letter afterward. You won't be able to "drop in" on potential business contacts.
- Try not to plan business trips for dates during Ramadan. At that time, workdays are shorter, and Pakistanis can't offer refreshments—an important part of doing business—during daytime meetings.

Communication

- Face-to-face communication is important. Pakistanis want to do business with people, not telephones or computers. You'll need several visits to establish a relationship.
- Employees may have difficulty correcting or complaining to managers. They won't offer feedback unless asked politely.
- Be aware of the number of questions you ask. Pakistanis may view those who ask a lot of questions as inexperienced or uneducated.
- Always remain calm and polite during negotiations, even if your Pakistani counterpart becomes loud or sarcastic.

Business Cards

- Present and receive business cards with both hands or with the right hand only.
- Make sure your business card includes any degrees and your full professional title. Both will help determine your status.
- Your information may be only in English, or it may be in English on one side of the card and in Urdu on the other side.
- When you receive someone's business card, read it carefully before placing it neatly into your business card case.

Be Aware

- Pakistanis highly value education and experience, but they don't want to do business with people they don't know. Personal networks are vital for business success. Have a respected third party introduce you to potential Pakistani clients.
- Be patient. Don't let the Pakistani slow business pace frustrate you.
- Be prepared to be flexible. Pakistanis don't strictly enforce deadlines and schedules.
- Family loyalty always takes top priority—even over business obligations.
- Pakistanis don't like to be rushed. Don't push for quick decisions and don't use high-pressure tactics.
- Pakistanis establish relationships among people, not companies. If your company replaces a key negotiator, it'll have to restart negotiations.

Socializing

Meeting outside of work for social functions is important to establishing relationships. Pakistanis enjoy hosting guests and take great pride in their hospitality.

- Pakistanis do business entertaining both in restaurants and in homes.
- They generally don't invite spouses to formal business dinners, but they may invite them to less formal events.
- Because many Pakistani men don't socialize with women who aren't relatives, men and women may be segregated at events.

Especially for Women

Pakistanis' interpretation of Islam gives men great power over women. Many consider women the property of their male relatives, and women don't receive the same opportunities for education and advancement. Men make all decisions about education, marriage, work, and travel for their families.

The rape of women is common. In Pakistani law, there's no category for rape; only adultery or fornication. In 2006, however, Pakistan's National Assembly passed a law that allowed judges to try rape cases under criminal law, not Islamic law. Previously, victims had to provide four witnesses to prove the charge.

The same law also discontinued the death penalty and flogging as sentences for consensual nonmarital sex. (The sentence is now a fine and five years in prison).

Personal and family honor are fundamentally important. In order to restore the family's honor, families may kill a female member who engages in illicit behavior or otherwise brings shame on her family (or is suspected of doing so). Even expressing a desire to choose her own spouse may result in an honor killing. In 2004 there were at least six hundred honor killings recorded. Many more go unreported, and of those that are reported, authorities rarely punish the killers.

Attempts to make laws less discriminatory and dangerous for women have met resistance from conservatives who want to preserve laws made in the name of Islam. For example, only in 2005 was a law passed to stop the practice of offering girls in marriage as compensation for crimes.

Although all Pakistani adults may vote, women's rates of voting historically have been lower than men's. For example, during the 1997 elections, in some areas not a single female vote was cast. Families and clans may strongly influence women not to vote or otherwise participate in public life.

Pakistani women have made some advancements. Benazir Bhutto was prime minister of Pakistan from 1988–1990 and 1993–1996. She was the first female elected leader in an Islamic nation. In 2006, the Pakistani Air Force and Navy inducted their first female pilots and sailors.

Many Pakistani women live sheltered lives. A friend once told me this story: "When our second son was born in Pakistan, one of my husband's work colleagues, who was a very traditional Pathan, visited our home. His wife and young son accompanied him, and we had a nice visit.

"We found out later that ours was the first nonfamily home his wife had visited since their wedding over a decade earlier."

- Western women will have difficulty doing business in Pakistan. Be prepared and persistent, without flouting local cultural norms—a delicate but doable balancing act.
- Women shouldn't walk alone at any time, day or night.
- A Western woman may invite a Pakistani man to a business dinner at a restaurant. She should make certain he understands they won't be dining alone; a group will attend. She should also arrange payment with the wait staff beforehand.

Holidays and Festivals

March	Pakistan Day (23)
May	Labor Day (1)
August	Independence Day (14)
September	Anniversary of Qaid-i-Azam's Death (11)
November	Allama Iqbal's Birthday (9)
December	Qaid-i-Azam's Birthday and Christmas (25)

Note: Pakistanis also celebrate several Islamic holidays that follow the lunar calendar. Check when they're celebrated during the year you're traveling to Pakistan.

PHILIPPINES
REPUBLIC OF THE PHILIPPINES

Greetings from the Philippines

Greetings from the Pearl of the Orient. The astounding beauty of our more than seven thousand islands makes our country a special place to live and visit.

Our location puts us squarely at Asia's crossroads. In the fifteenth century, Muslim missionaries strongly influenced our ancient island traditions. Roughly a century later, the culture of the Spanish colonists, who followed Ferdinand Magellan's arrival in 1521, dominated for over the next three hundred years. As a result, today we have the Spanish passion for food, fiestas, and life. In fact, we consider ourselves more Latin than Asian.

In 1898, we demanded our independence. Our proclamation of a republic made us the first Asians to try to escape European colonialism. Warring with Spain, the United States soon took control of the Philippines—an event that we initially resisted. In the 1930s, we became an American commonwealth, and our independence was finally recognized on July 4, 1946.

The extended family is the basis of our society. To us, family is more important than the individual, and interdependence is more important than independence. *Bayanihan* is our communal spirit that enables us to help one another at a moment's notice.

We value personal and family honor as well as dignity and pride. We accept what comes our way and bear it with hope and patience. For example, we marry our spouses for life; divorce is illegal.

We love socializing and always offer visitors the best we have. Each village has a plaza where we meet to mingle, dance, and play basketball. Political events and meetings also take place here.

Filipinos prize education. Families make great sacrifices to educate their children. Many people in low-level jobs are often highly educated, but cannot get higher-paying jobs.

We know that we have an image problem in the international community. Imagine the geographic and infrastructure issues we must manage in order to govern almost ninety million people speaking more than a hundred different dialects across numerous islands.

Our government is committed to solving our country's problems, and we have made progress in improving our lives. We are healthier than we were fifty years ago, and we are doing a better job fighting diseases, including malaria and tuberculosis.

Many challenges remain—namely, disparities between urban and rural people, corruption and cronyism, internal conflicts (for example, Communist and Muslim uprisings against the government), income inequalities among regions, and high levels of poverty and malnutrition. While we have worked to improve our human rights record, we understand there is much room for improvement.

Environmental problems are another area for improvement. The expansive clearing of our lush rainforests may have worsened the devastating 2006 landslide in Leyte that killed hundreds.

A number of our citizens (some highly educated) are emigrating to other nations to work. Filipino doctors and nurses working in the United Kingdom and the United States, as well as low-paid Filipino domestic workers employed all over Asia, send home billions of dollars every year to support their families. While our economy depends on these funds, we resent the need for our trained people (especially nurses) to leave our land.

Despite our troubles, we are a wonderful place to visit for business and pleasure. Come see our fantastic reefs and sea life, eat our uniquely delicious cuisine, and enjoy our friendly, helpful, and fun-loving people. We will welcome you!

Vital Statistics

Population	89,468,677
Capital	Manila
Area	115,831 square miles, slightly larger than Arizona
Government	Republic
Living Standard	GDP = US $1,380
Natural Resources	Timber, petroleum, nickel, cobalt, silver, gold, salt, copper
Agriculture	Sugarcane, coconuts, rice, corn, bananas, cassavas, pineapples, mangoes, pork, eggs, beef, fish
Industries	Electronics assembly, garments, footwear, pharmaceuticals, chemicals, wood products, food processing, petroleum refining, fishing
Climate	Tropical marine; northeast monsoon (November to April); southwest monsoon (May to October)
Currency	Philippine peso (PHP)

The People

Correct Name	nouns: Filipino(s) (people collectively or men only), Filipina(s) (women)
	adjectives: Philippine or Filipino (people or nation collectively), Filipino (men), Filipina (women)
Ethnic Makeup	Tagalog 28.1%, Cebuano 13.1%, Ilocano 9%, Bisaya/Binisaya 7.6%, Hiligaynon or Ilonggo 7.5%, Bikol 6%, Waray 3.4%, other 25.3%
Languages	Two official languages: Filipino (once called Pilipino, based on Tagalog) and English; eight major dialects: Tagalog, Cebuano, Ilocano, Hiligaynon or Ilonggo, Bicol, Waray, Pampango, and Pangasinan.
Religions	Roman Catholic 80.9%, Evangelical 2.8%, Iglesia ni Kristo 2.3%, Aglipayan 2%, other Christian 4.5%, Muslim 5%, other 1.8%, unspecified 0.6%, none 0.1%

Meeting and Greeting

- Filipinos customarily use English greetings.
- They may ask, "Have you eaten?" instead of "how are you?" Answer "yes" (even if you haven't eaten).
- Filipinos shake hands (limply, compared to American handshakes) with everyone upon meeting and leaving; however, men wait for women to extend a hand. Men may also pat one another on the back.
- Filipinos greet elders first as a sign of respect.

> Before 1987, the official language was Tagalog, and the word *Filipino* was spelled *Pilipino* because there was no "f" sound in the Tagalog alphabet. Foreign words like *Philippines*, which is based on the English spelling for King Philip of Spain, were changed to fit the Tagalog language. In 1987, the official language became Filipino, and the letter *F* came into official use.

- The "eyebrow flash"—raising the eyebrows quickly—is a casual Filipino greeting. Out of respect, Filipinos don't use it to greet elders or superiors.
- As a sign of respect, Filipino children may take a visitor's hand and press it against their foreheads.

Names and Titles

- Because of three centuries of Spanish rule, most Filipino families have Spanish last names (surnames).
- Filipinos often introduce another by full name, including his or her middle name. Always introduce a Filipino by his or her full name.
- Until specifically invited to use first names (given names), address a Filipino by English courtesy title (Mr., Mrs., or Miss) or appropriate professional title + last name. Engineers, architects, lawyers, doctors, and others use professional titles (for example, Attorney Maria Gavino or Engineer Paz Tiongson).
- Even after developing a relationship with elders or superiors, always address them by Sir, Ma'am, or courtesy title + last name.
- Upon marriage, many women don't take their husbands' last names. Some add their husbands' last names to their own with a hyphen. If *vda* appears between a woman's maiden name and her husband's last name, she's a widow.
- In written correspondence and in conversation, address a woman with a hyphenated last name by Mrs. + husband's last name. For example, address Mrs. Maria Bacani-Aquino as Mrs. Aquino.

Language

Escalating nationalism in the 1960s and '70s forced the Philippine government to review its language policies, which it soon changed to promote Filipino. Some ethnic groups resisted the change because Filipino was based on Tagalog—a language they didn't speak. Nonetheless, Filipino became the national language in 1987, and today about half of Filipinos speak it.

Although Filipino is a required subject in schools, English is the main language for higher education and is the lingua franca for government and business. The Philippines is the world's third-largest English-speaking country (behind the United States and the United Kingdom).

Tagalog was originally written in the Baybayin alphabet (derived from a southern Indian alphabet), but today Tagalog uses the Latin alphabet and Filipinos use Baybayin mainly for ornamental purposes.

Tagalog speakers often use English words and phrases, creating a language called "Taglish" that's often incomprehensible to native English speakers.

Conversation

- Filipinos ask personal questions as a way to show interest. They'll expect you to ask them personal questions, especially about family. If you're uncomfortable answering a question, give a vague answer or say, "In my country, that would be a strange question."
- Never criticize anyone or anything, especially in public. Don't express personal opinions that may offend someone.
- Filipinos prefer indirect language, and they don't like to say "no" directly. To avoid making someone lose face, don't ask direct yes-or-no questions.
- Don't give insincere compliments.
- Filipinos may laugh at sad or unfortunate events. To them, laughter relieves tension and embarrassment.
- Filipinos enjoy humor in private, but not during business. Know that they don't appreciate dry, sarcastic humor.
- Speak softly and control your emotions. Filipinos consider loud voices uncouth.

Acceptable topics
- Family (yours and theirs)
- Your home country and region: If possible, bring postcards of the area to show your hosts.
- Filipino culture
- Sports, especially basketball, baseball, softball, football (soccer), tennis, horseracing, and cockfighting

Unacceptable topics
- Divorce
- Artificial contraception
- Abortion

Topics that require sensitivity
- Religion, especially the Catholic Church
- Muslim insurgents
- Ethnic and religious minorities in the Philippines
- Local politics, especially issues that involve corruption
- American involvement in Filipino affairs during the last century: Let your Filipino colleagues bring up the subject. Some Filipinos appreciate American influence; others don't.

Body Language

Filipinos are open, friendly people. They smile, show emotion, and touch one another more readily than do people of other Asian cultures. They're familiar with North American gestures.

- As a sign of friendship, people of the same sex may hold hands in public.
- If Filipinos don't understand a question, they open their mouths. They raise their eyebrows to signify recognition or agreement.
- In social situations, Filipinos extend their arms to the front and stoop when passing in front of people.
- Jerking your head upward means "yes"; jerking it downward means "no." Because Filipinos rarely say "no," they sometimes say "yes" while making the gesture for "no" (they mean "no").
- Although Filipinos consider staring rude or a challenge, they may stare at or even touch foreigners, especially where foreigners are uncommon.
- Standing with hands on hips expresses anger.
- Never beckon someone with your index finger. Instead, extend your arm (palm down), then curl and flex your fingers together.
- To indicate two of something, raise your ring and pinkie fingers.
- To get someone's attention, touch his or her elbow lightly. Don't tap a shoulder.
- Don't point with a finger. Instead, shift your eyes toward an object or purse your lips and point with your mouth.
- Filipinos seldom queue (form a line). You may have to push to get ahead.

Phrases		
English	**Filipino**	**Pronunciation**
Hello (literally, "long life")	*Mabuhay*	(mah-BOO-high)
Good morning	*Magandang umaga*	(mahg-NDAHNG oo-MAH-ga)
Good afternoon	*Magandang tanghali*	(mahg-NDAHNG than-GAL-ay)
Good evening	*Magandang gabi*	(mah-NDAHNG ga-BEE)
Goodbye	*Paalam*	(pah-AH-lahm)
Please	*Pakisuyo*	(pah-kee-SU-yoh)
Thank you	*Salamat*	(sah-LAH-maht)

English	Filipino	Pronunciation
You're welcome	*Walang anuman*	(wah-LAHNG ah-noo-MAHN)
Yes	*Oo*	(oh oh)
No	*Hindi*	(HIN-day)
Excuse me	*Patawad po*	(pat-OW-ahd POH)
Pleased to meet you	*Ikinagagalak kong makilala kayo*	(ihn-ahg-AHL-ak kong mahk-ee-LA-la kye-OH)
How are you?	*Kumusta ka*	(kuh-MOO-stah kah)

Dining

Filipinos love to eat, and food is the focus of most social activity. Many cultures have influenced the country's diverse cuisine, which is flavored with a variety of herbs and spices. Americans will likely detect a Spanish influence.

- A typical meal includes boiled rice, fried fish, vegetables, and fruit.
- Filipinos eat with forks and spoons. They hold the fork in the left hand and the spoon in the right, then use the fork to push food onto the spoon. They put only the spoon into their mouths.
- Hosts generally serve all dishes at once.

Drinking

- Lambanog is a potent Philippine liquor with a high alcohol content. It's distilled from the sap of unopened coconut flowers and comes in several different flavors.
- Filipinos enjoy beer (*serbésa*), especially beer brewed locally in San Miguel, and more Filipinos are drinking wine. They also enjoy high-quality Scotch like Chivas Regal or Johnnie Walker Black Label, but many can't afford it.
- Never offer a Filipina an alcoholic beverage. Women in the Philippines rarely drink alcohol in public. Instead, they generally drink soft drinks or juices.
- The Philippines offers many exotic and delicious fruit juices, including jackfruit and calamansi (a local citrus fruit).

- The Philippines produces coffee, but not enough to satisfy domestic demand. Filipinos prefer instant coffee, but the demand for brewed coffee is growing.
- Filipinos drink iced tea, often mixed with fruit juice.
- In restaurants, it's common to have a drink (alcoholic or not) before ordering dinner.
- Don't get drunk—Filipinos consider drunkenness greedy behavior.

Toasting

Toasting isn't a traditional part of Philippine business culture, but some Filipinos offer toasts.
- It's appropriate for the host or senior visitor to initiate a toast during dinner.
- *Mabuhay* (mah-BOO-high) is a Philippine toast that means "long life." People offer it during a meal.
- Toasts in English are also appropriate.
- Women may propose toasts.

Tipping

Although tipping isn't a Filipino tradition, it's becoming common in hotels and restaurants that cater to foreigners. Filipinos especially appreciate tips in American dollars.
- Restaurants: The bill usually includes a 15 percent service charge. If the bill doesn't include a service charge, leave a 15 percent tip. You can leave small change as an additional gratuity for excellent service.
- Taxi drivers: Round up the fare to the nearest PHP5 or PHP10; for a large fare, tip 10 percent. Always carry bills in small denominations. Taxis may not have change for large notes, and in remote areas it may be difficult to provide change for even PHP100 notes.
- Doormen, bellhops, and porters: Tip PHP5 to PHP10.
- Hair stylists and barbers: Tip 10 percent of the bill.

Manners

Filipinos are hospitable and strive to make their guests feel at home.
- Don't immediately accept a verbal invitation. Wait to be invited two or three times before accepting.

- When entering a person's home, you may have to remove your shoes. Some Filipinos wear shoes in their homes; others don't. Follow your host's lead.
- Don't peek into the kitchen or wander through someone's home unaccompanied. Ask your host for permission to use the bathroom.
- Never refer to the woman of the house as the "hostess." For example, never say, "You're such an excellent hostess." Filipinos associate the word with prostitutes.
- Be sure to sincerely compliment the host's home décor, flower arrangements, and so on. Especially compliment the food.
- Never refuse an offer of food or drink. Eating and drinking a lot best compliments your host.
- When finished eating, leave a small amount of food and your utensils on your plate.
- Leave a weekday dinner party at 10:00 PM; leave a weekend party at approximately midnight.
- Filipinos appreciate thank-you notes; promptly send one after someone entertains you.
- Shortly before hosting an event, you must invite guests at least once again to show that the invitation is sincere, even if they've accepted your initial invitation. To save face, Filipinos may use a third party to decline an invitation.
- If hosting an event, always offer refreshments.
- At a restaurant, the person who extended the invitation pays the bill.
- To beckon wait staff, raise your hand with fingers together. Address waitresses by "Miss" and waiters by "Boss."
- Always show respect for the elderly. Greet them first, offer them your seat, and so on. Never disagree with them.
- Never disgrace or dishonor a person. Doing so would be a disaster not only for the individual, but also for his or her family.
- Always ask permission before photographing anyone.

Punctuality

Filipinos have a relaxed attitude toward time. Meetings often begin late, but they expect foreigners to be on time.

Arrive fifteen to twenty minutes late for social affairs.

Dress

Often wearing Western fashions, Filipinos are some of the smartest dressers in Asia. They judge a person's status and competence by his or her appearance. To make a good impression, always dress well.

- April and May are the hottest months in the Philippines. Men seldom wear suit coats during this time. Women always dress modestly; they never wear skirts with hemlines above the knee or low-cut or sleeveless tops. Men and women wear shorts only at the beach, pool, or resort—never on the street.

- The rainy season extends from June through November. If visiting the Philippines during this time, make sure to bring raingear.

- For business, men wear suits and ties at initial meetings. At subsequent meetings, they may remove coats and ties. (Foreigners may remove theirs only if Filipino colleagues do so first.) Some Filipino men wear barongs (also called barong Tagalogs), which are loose shirts worn outside the trousers; foreigners shouldn't wear them.

  Women wear dresses or skirts with blouses. Elegant pantsuits are also appropriate. Filipino women wear bright-colored clothing. Foreign women may wear high-quality, conservative styles in bright colors.

  Government offices, banks, and other companies may require employees to wear uniforms.

- At restaurants, men wear suits or barongs or shirts with ties and dress trousers. Women wear cocktail dresses or stylish skirts or pants with blouses.

- For casual occasions, men wear cotton shirts and pants. Women may wear stylish slacks or jeans with blouses.

Gifts

- Filipinos don't expect gifts, but they appreciate the thought behind giving them.

- Filipinos don't open gifts upon receipt. Instead, they thank the giver and set the gift aside to open later.

- Be prepared to give small, inexpensive gifts to friends and colleagues at Christmas.

- Have gifts elegantly wrapped.

Hostess Gifts

- Remember never to use the word *hostess*. Filipinos associate it with prostitutes.
- Always bring a small gift when visiting someone's home, or send one following a dinner.
- Families greatly appreciate sweets or small toys for any children.

Consider giving
- Flowers
- Candy or pastries
- Specialty foods from your home region
- Perfume

Don't give
- Liquor

Business Gifts

- Bring a small gift to your first meeting. Give more expensive gifts only after signing contracts.
- Give a gift to each person present or give a group gift. If there's just one recipient, give the gift when alone with the person.

Consider giving
- Specialty foods or arts and crafts from your home region
- Books about your home region
- Scotch (Chivas Regal or Johnnie Walker Black Label) or other liquor (for men only)
- Perfume (for a woman)
- High-quality pen sets
- Items that feature your company logo

Don't give
- Items made in the Philippines
- Obviously ostentatious gifts (may be considered bribes)

Helpful Hints

- Feel free to bargain everywhere except in large department stores.
- Always remember that Filipinos feel obliged to return a favor.

- Filipinos may assign visiting American men a "Guest Relation Officer" (a woman to accompany you during your visit) upon arrival. You may politely decline by saying, "Thank you, but I am fine on my own."
- Most businesses accept American dollars.

Health and Safety

- Before traveling to the Philippines, check current health precautions, especially for malaria. Also check current travel warnings. (See page 373.) Terrorist threats against Americans aren't uncommon, especially in the southern Philippines. Be sure to register with your embassy upon arrival.
- Although tap and well water is likely safe, it's safest to drink only boiled or bottled water. Also, drink only bottled beer and soft drinks served with caps on. Avoid using ice cubes.
- Avoid eating raw produce, dairy products (they're often not pasteurized), and food served in unsanitary conditions.
- To avoid contracting schistosomiasis and other parasitic diseases, wear shoes at all times and avoid swimming in fresh water.
- The Philippines has a fairly good health care system, especially in larger cities. If you're seriously ill or injured, go to Manila if possible.
- Most hospitals provide 24-hour emergency care and have pharmacies. Many deluxe hotels provide medical and dental services for their guests.
- Most common medications are available, but be sure to pack less common prescriptions.
- Crime is a serious problem in the Philippines. Kidnapping for ransom is on the rise, and foreigners are often targets. Islamist extremist groups have abducted Americans in recent years. Check with authorities before traveling to remote areas, and never tell strangers where you're staying.

> Natural disasters are frequent in the Philippines. The islands contain several active volcanoes, and the government announces volcano alerts when necessary. In addition, earthquakes, typhoons, and flash floods are common.

- Public transportation may be unsafe, and driving is often difficult (heavy traffic, poor roads, and so on). If possible, hire a driver. If not, have your hotel call a reputable cab company for you. Avoid hailing taxis on the street—some visitors have reported cab drivers who extorted or threatened them.

- Avoid showing anger, shouting, or being rude, even if you have cause. Back away from trouble to avoid an attack with a knife, bottle, or other weapon. If mugged, give the muggers your belongings; don't resist.

Corporate Culture

Spain, China, and especially the United States have strongly influenced Filipino business culture. Many of the country's business and government leaders were educated in the United States, and American business practices are common.

In 2005–2006, the Philippines had the best performing currency in East Asia.

Structure

"Benevolent autocracy" best describes the management style. Employees expect their employers to take care of them.

Filipinos identify with their clan, community, or company. In return, companies have a sense of loyalty to their customers and suppliers. Foreigners may have trouble breaking into the market.

Meetings

- Filipinos begin meetings with casual conversation. Don't expect to discuss business immediately.
- Make sure proposals are practical and conservative.
- Filipinos negotiate at a much slower pace than Americans do. Be patient.
- If negotiations become sticky, bringing in a trusted third party may help achieve compromise.
- Don't let meetings last too long. Filipinos love to eat, and their attention and enthusiasm wane when hungry.

Appointments

- Regular business hours are 8:00 AM to 5:00 PM. Many offices close for lunch from noon to 1:00 PM. Some offices may be open Saturday mornings.
- January through March and October through November are the best times to travel to the Philippines for business. Avoid scheduling appointments for dates during Christmas and Easter, when many Filipinos are on vacation.
- Make appointments at least a month before your trip.
- To initiate business contacts more easily, have a mutual friend or business associate introduce you to potential clients or colleagues.

Communication

- English is the language of Filipino commerce. All communication is courteous, regardless of content. People present the truth diplomatically, allude to controversial matters vaguely, and always take the listener's perception into account. They often view excessive candor as uncouth.
- Filipinos find it difficult to disagree, reject, or be confrontational, especially when a superior is involved. They'll give ambiguous or indirect answers in order to please and avoid confrontation. Be prepared for apparent agreements that never produce results, or for projects to begin but never be completed.
- Phrase questions simply and avoid asking yes-or-no questions. Especially avoid asking negatively phrased questions, such as "Won't you join me for dinner?" You may receive an affirmative answer, but the meaning may be "Yes, I won't join you for dinner."
- Criticize Filipinos only in private. Don't be pushy or back anyone into a corner.
- Filipinos prefer face-to-face interaction. Communication by mail or telephone is unreliable at best, and letters and e-mails may go unanswered.

Business Cards

- Filipinos exchange business cards upon introduction.
- Use both hands to give and receive business cards.
- Your information may be in English. Be sure to include your title.

Be Aware

- Filipinos equate age and experience with wisdom and authority.
- Ethnic Chinese are a tiny minority but major players in the business community.
- Traditionally, nepotism, cronyism, and favoritism have outweighed ability and performance. But as a new generation of Western-trained managers takes charge, the importance of competence is growing.
- Filipinos' slow pace may lead them to ignore deadlines. They complete tasks, but perhaps not as quickly as foreigners would like.
- Because failure could bring shame, Filipinos consider innovation, change, and competition risky. They attribute success to fate as much as to ability and effort.
- When they're selling, Filipinos often have a "take it or leave it" attitude on price. They may make concessions, but only after an extended period.
- Trust, loyalty, sincerity, and patience are essential to business success in the Philippines.

Socializing

- Filipinos do most business entertaining in clubs or restaurants, preferably a restaurant in an international hotel.
- Business lunches are acceptable.
- Filipinos generally don't discuss business during meals, but they do at other social occasions.
- Singing is common during business entertaining, and your Filipino colleagues may ask you to join in. It's best to accept the invitation.
- Invite people to lunch and dinner engagements personally. Remember to extend the invitation two or three times (see page 251).
- Uninvited people may turn up at a dinner, and Filipinos include them graciously. If hosting a dinner, be sure to welcome "party crashers."
- If invited to dinner, reciprocate with a meal of equal lavishness before you leave the country. Be sure to extend the invitation to colleagues' spouses.

Especially for Women

Women enjoy greater equality with men in the Philippines than do women in other parts of Southeast Asia. Filipina women are just as literate as Filipino men, and they compose about 40 percent of the workforce. They're active in government, business, and other professions. Women are often in charge of financial operations at home and in businesses, even those headed by men. Nearly half the nation's scientists, engineers, and research and development workers are women.

- Western women won't likely have problems doing business in the Philippines.
- A Western woman may invite a Filipino man to a business lunch or dinner, but she should let him pay the bill. Insisting on paying will insult him and harm the business relationship.
- Men may make rude comments to women walking on the street. Just ignore them.
- While it's not unusual for a Filipina woman to travel alone, a Western woman traveling alone must be careful. Never walk alone after dark; instead, take a taxi with someone you know well.
- Filipina women rarely smoke or drink in public but Western women may do so if they wish.

Holidays and Festivals

January	New Year's Day (1)
March/April	Easter (Thursday–Sunday)
April	Day of Valor (9)
May	Labor Day (1)
June	Independence Day (12)
August	National Heroes' Day (last Sunday)
November	All Saints' Day (1)
	Bonifacio Day (30)
December	Christmas (25)
	Rizal Day (30)

Note: Filipinos celebrate the first day of the Islamic holiday Eid al-Fitr. Check to see when it's celebrated for the year you're traveling to the Philippines.

SINGAPORE
REPUBLIC OF SINGAPORE

Greetings from Singapore

Greetings from the small country that is Southeast Asia's business giant. Our culture and values are unmistakably Asian, and our infrastructure and business practices are among the world's most modern, sophisticated, and prosperous.

Singapore has few natural resources, but thousands of multinational companies have offices here to take advantage of our favorable business climate. Our thriving port is one of the world's busiest, and our multicultural, multilingual population is one of the world's best workforces and is a wonderful testing ground for products and services intended for the rest of Asia.

Ours is a highly disciplined society that encourages—even demands—high ethics and moral standards. Family is central to all Singaporeans, and we emphasize unity, loyalty, and respect. We require our citizens to adhere to the law. In Singapore, voting is a legal obligation, not just a right.

Our government is highly organized and proactive—some critics claim it micromanages our society and is only marginally democratic. But we believe the government's actions have our best interests in mind. Our system works for us.

For example, when the SARS (severe acute respiratory syndrome) epidemic damaged our tourism industry in 2003, the government distributed postcards to every household and asked us to send them to family and friends living overseas, encouraging them to visit.

Singapore has one of the world's highest population densities, but we enjoy the same (or better) standard of living as do the four largest Western European countries. We consider our educational system to be among the world's best. In 2004, our fourth and eighth graders ranked at the top in the Trends in International Mathematics and Science Study.

Despite this accomplishment, we are not resting on our laurels. We are constantly finding ways to improve. For example, to better compete globally our educational system is considering focusing on diversity, flexibility, and resilience instead of uniformity, rigidity, and conformity.

In the past, our ethnic diversity has led to conflict, but today we work toward racial harmony and national unity. Each Singaporean works hard to maintain his or her ethnic traditions while building a modern cohesive society.

Our people think of themselves as Singaporeans first and Chinese, Malays, or Indians second.

Our country is a great introduction to Asian culture. We love to make money and enjoy life. We are proud that modern technology coexists with feng shui and ancestor worship. Come and experience all we have to offer.

Vital Statistics	
Population	4,492,150
Capital	Singapore is a city-state. There are essentially no rural areas.
Area	267 square miles, about the same size as the city of Chicago
Government	Parliamentary republic
Living Standard	GDP = US $32,030
Natural Resources	Fish, deepwater ports
Agricultural Products	Rubber, copra, fruit, orchids, vegetables, poultry, eggs, fish, ornamental fish (Agriculture as an industry is negligible in Singapore.)
Industries	Electronics, chemicals, financial services, oil drilling equipment, petroleum refining, rubber processing and rubber products, processed food and beverages, ship repair, offshore platform construction, life sciences, entrepôt trade (in which merchandise can be imported and exported without paying import duties)
Climate	Tropical; hot, humid, rainy; two distinct monsoon seasons: northeastern monsoon (December to March) and southwestern monsoon (June to September); between monsoon seasons: frequent afternoon and early evening thunderstorms.
Currency	Singapore dollar (SGD)

The People

Correct Name	noun: Singaporean
	adjective: Singaporean or Singapore
Ethnic Makeup	Chinese 76.8%, Malaysian 13.9%, Indian 7.9%, other 1.4%
Languages	Mandarin 35%, English 23%, Bahasa Melayu (Malaysian) 14.1%, Hokkien 11.4%, Cantonese 5.7%, Teochew 4.9%, Tamil 3.2%, other Chinese dialects 1.8%, other 0.9%
Religions	Buddhist 42.5%, Muslim 14.9%, Taoist 8.5%, Hindu 4%, Catholic 4.8%, other Christian 9.8%, other 0.7%, none 14.8%

Meeting and Greeting

- Singaporeans shake hands firmly upon meeting and leaving.
- Men usually wait for women to extend a hand before shaking it.
- Chinese Singaporeans and older people may also bow slightly while shaking hands. They'll appreciate a slight reciprocal bow.
- Rank comes before age or sex. Singaporeans introduce the highest-ranking person first, (or the oldest person, if everyone is of equal rank), and they introduce women before men.

Names and Titles

Address all Singaporeans by English courtesy title (Mr., Mrs., Miss, or Ms.) + appropriate name. Here's a brief guide to name usage for each of the three main cultures. For more information, see pages 214, 112–113, and 152–154.

Malaysian

- Ethnic Malays don't have last names (surnames). Traditional name order is first name (given name) + bin (used for men) or binti (used for women) + father's first name.

  Examples: Ali bin Isa is the son of Isa bin Osman.

  Zaitun binti Isa is the daughter of Isa bin Osman.

- Upon marriage, some Malay women take their husbands' names and some don't.
- Address Malays by English courtesy title + first name.

Chinese

- Traditionally, Chinese name order is last name + first name. Some may print their names in "Western" order (first name + last name) on business cards. Listen carefully to how others address the person to make sure which is the first name and which is the last. (As a reminder, you may want to note this information on the person's business card at a later time.)
- Ethnic Chinese address one another by last name + courtesy title or government or professional title, if applicable. Never address a Chinese Singaporean by only his or her last name.
- Be aware: It's difficult to distinguish women's first names from men's. Also, ethnic Chinese women use their maiden names after marrying. For example, Mrs. Wang may be married to Mr. Li.

  In addition, most ethnic Chinese women don't wear wedding rings. Don't assume someone is single because she lacks a wedding ring.

Indian

- Most Indian Singaporeans are of Tamil ancestry and don't have last names. Name order is first initial of father's first name + first name.
- Upon marriage, ethnic Indian women may replace their fathers' first initial of first name with their husbands' initial.
- Address Indian Singaporeans by English courtesy title + first name.

Language

Singapore has four official languages: Chinese, Tamil, Bahasa Melayu (Malaysian), and English, the main language of instruction and business. In addition, most public signage is in English.

Several Chinese dialects are spoken in Singapore. In 1979, in an attempt to improve communication, the government mounted a "Speak Mandarin" campaign encouraging all Chinese to learn and speak Mandarin. The campaign is still ongoing.

Most Singaporeans are bilingual; some are trilingual.

Conversation

Singaporeans are well educated and well traveled. They're comfortable conversing with people from other cultures and will likely forgive any cultural mistakes you make.

- Singaporeans may ask personal questions. If you're uncomfortable answering them, give vague answers or say, "In my country, that would be a strange question."
- Don't get angry or raise your voice; if you do, your Singaporean host or colleague will lose face.
- Avoid telling jokes until you've established a personal relationship with Singaporeans. They likely won't understand or appreciate Western humor.
- Be aware: Singaporeans may smile or laugh to cover embarrassment.

Acceptable topics
- Food: Compliment local cuisines.
- Someone's health, career, or family: Don't, however, ask about someone's wife.
- Travel
- Art

Unacceptable topics
- Disputes with Malaysia
- Singapore's laws: Don't criticize them or imply that America's approach to crime and punishment is better or more civilized. In particular, don't mention the 1994 incident in which the Singapore courts sentenced an American teenager to caning for vandalism. American leaders pressured Singapore for leniency, and the courts ultimately reduced the sentence from six to four strokes of the cane.

> Singaporean government enforces morality and cultural traditions. For example, because of Singaporeans' traditionalist stance, unwed mothers don't receive the same tax benefits as do married mothers, and they can't purchase low-cost housing unless they apply for an exception.

Topics that require sensitivity
- Ethnic differences
- Mandatory military service
- Religion and politics (especially the People's Action Party): Let hosts initiate these topics.

Body Language
- Singaporeans consider public displays of affection inappropriate.
- Never touch anyone—especially a child—on the head. Tradition holds that the soul resides there.

- Singaporeans consider the foot unclean because it's the lowest part of the body. When sitting, never rest your ankle on a knee. It's best to sit up straight with both feet on the floor. Never let the soles of your shoes face or point at another person.
- Don't tap your foot or swing your leg while sitting. Doing so suggests nervousness or lack of interest.
- To get someone's attention, raise your hand. Never point at someone with your index finger.
- It's obscene to pound your fist into your open palm.
- As a show of friendship, a woman may hold hands with another woman when walking on streets.

Phrases

See pages 117 and 216–217 for Chinese and Bahasa Melayu (Malaysian) phrases. Be aware that the Indian dialect spoken in Singapore is primarily Tamil, not Hindi. Consult a Tamil phrase book to learn useful Tamil phrases.

Dining

The world knows Singapore for its excellent Chinese, Indian, and Malaysian food. The delicious cuisine isn't available only at exclusive restaurants. Some of the country's best food is at hawker centers, where vendors sell tasty fare to pedestrians.

- Dining habits and etiquette vary according to the cuisine and the culture or religion of the people eating it. For example, Hindus and some Buddhists don't eat beef, and Muslims don't eat pork.
- Most Singaporeans use chopsticks (see page 41), but foreigners can easily find Western-style utensils.
- Singaporeans usually serve all dishes at once to share. Most meals include rice or noodles.
- Cocktails and appetizers are uncommon, although Western-style restaurants may serve them.
- To ensure good fortune, Singaporeans aim to have an even number of people at the table.

Following is a brief guide to dining customs for each of the three main cultures. For more information, see pages 117–119, 217, and 156–157.

Chinese

- Chinese Singaporeans may host a banquet. Always reciprocate with a banquet of equal value before leaving the country.
- Although they sometimes use Western-style utensils, Chinese Singaporeans use chopsticks to eat most food and use spoons to eat soup.
- The host and hostess usually sit opposite each another at a round table. They seat the guest of honor at the place facing the entrance, to the host's left.
- Although hosts will invite you to begin the meal, let them start first.
- Most Chinese Singaporeans spit bones onto their chopsticks, then set the bones on the table. Don't use your fingers to remove a bone from your mouth.
- When finished with your meal, place chopsticks on the chopstick rest. Don't set them on your plate (doing so means you're not done eating).
- Hosts usually apologize for the quality of meals. Always assure them the meal was excellent and appreciated.

Malaysian and Indian

- Most Malays and Indians eat with spoons and hands, although some use forks and spoons and others use only their hands. (Knives aren't necessary because people serve food in bite-size pieces.)
- When using a fork and spoon, hold the spoon in your right hand and the fork in your left. Use the fork to push food onto the spoon, then eat. Put only the spoon into your mouth. When finished eating, set the utensils on your plate.
- Wait for the host to start eating and invite you to do so before you begin eating. Traditionally, men eat before women do.
- If you can't finish your food, don't offer it to anyone or return it to the serving dish. Once you've touched food, people consider it tainted. Never let the serving spoon touch your plate.
- Never refuse any offer of food or drink. Always at least taste the dish or beverage. To refuse additional helpings, put your hand above your plate or glass and say, "No, thank you."
- When finished, place your spoon and fork together on your plate. If you don't, hosts will offer you more food. To show you're finished eating when using a banana leaf, fold the leaf in half with the fold toward you.

Malaysian

- Be on time for dinner in a Malaysian home. Malays don't usually offer drinks or appetizers before a dinner; they serve the meal immediately upon guests' arrival.

- Hosts seat the guest of honor either to the host's right or at the head of the table.
- Before dinner, hosts give guests towels and a small bowl of water to wash their hands.

Indian
- Don't offer Indian women alcoholic beverages; they rarely drink.
- Indians always wash their hands before and after a meal.
- After meals, expect to stay for approximately an hour of conversation.

Drinking

- Coffee and tea are both popular in Singapore. At *kopi tiams* (traditional coffee shops), you can purchase both. Singaporeans often drink coffee heavily laced with sweetened condensed milk.
- Devout Muslims don't drink alcoholic beverages or serve them to guests.
- As a sign of respect, pass or accept a drink with both hands. With someone of obviously lower rank (wait staff, for example), you may use only your right hand.
- See pages 119, 157, and 217 for more information on Chinese, Indian, and Malaysian drinking customs.

Toasting

Toasting isn't common in Singapore, although ethnic Chinese, Malays, or Indians may propose them. See pages 120, 158, and 218 for examples.
- Stand to offer a toast. Also stand when receiving a toast; after the toast, thank the person who gave it.
- Singaporeans make toasts while holding the glass with both hands and looking the recipient in the eye. Recipients hold the glass with the right hand only.

Tipping

Singaporeans don't expect tips and often discourage tipping. Here are guidelines for appropriate tips:
- Restaurants: The bill usually includes a 10 percent service charge. No extra tip is necessary. If the bill doesn't include a service charge, tip 10 percent.
- Taxi drivers: Round up the fare to the nearest SGD.
- Bellhops and porters: Tip SGD1 or SGD2.

Manners

- Always respect elders. Open doors for them, offer them your seat, and so on.
- Remove your shoes upon entering someone's home.
- Bow slightly when entering or leaving a room or passing people.
- Compliment the host's home and family, the food served, and so on. The host will appreciate the comments, but likely won't verbally accept them out of modesty.
- Try not to clear your throat or blow your nose at the table. If you can't avoid doing either, do so discreetly.
- Cover your mouth when using a toothpick.
- At restaurants, let hosts order all the dishes.
- To beckon wait staff, raise your entire hand (not just an index finger). Never whistle, hiss, or shout to get their attention.
- When eating at food stalls in an outdoor market, don't mix utensils from a Muslim stall with those from a Chinese stall. (Muslims don't use utensils that have touched pork.)
- See pages 75–85 for etiquette information when visiting a temple or other place of worship.

Punctuality

Singaporeans expect punctuality for business and social occasions. They view tardiness as disrespectful. Call if you're delayed.

Dress

Singapore's modernity and ethnic diversity make many different kinds of attire acceptable. Most Singaporeans dress in Western "smart casual" fashions (see page 52), usually made of lightweight cotton to accommodate the tropical climate. Despite the heat, don't be tempted to wear safari suits; they're not chic in Singapore.

- For business occasions and at restaurants, men wear white shirts with ties and trousers. Jackets aren't usually required for business, although some restaurants may require them. When meeting government officials, Singaporeans dress more formally. Foreign men should wear jackets at initial meetings, and especially when meeting with government officials. (At subsequent meetings, they can follow their hosts' lead about wearing jackets.) When being entertained for business, foreign men should wear jackets, with or without a tie.

Women wear pantsuits or skirts and blouses (with sleeves). They never wear short skirts or revealing clothing.

- At trendy nightspots, men commonly wear suits and women wear evening gowns.
- For casual occasions, men wear shirts and trousers, often with ties. Women wear pantsuits or skirts and blouses (with sleeves).

Gifts

The Chinese, Malays, and Indians have different gift-giving traditions. See pages 123–125, 161–162, and 220–222 for more information. Here are some general guidelines to follow:

- Singaporeans don't open gifts in front of the giver. They thank the giver and set aside the gift to open later.
- Use both hands to give and receive a gift.
- Always give high-quality, brand-name gifts.
- Have gifts elegantly wrapped.
- Always bring a gift when invited to someone's home.
- Be careful that recipients don't misinterpret a gift—even a small one—as a bribe. Never give a government official a gift.
- Singaporeans don't usually exchange business gifts.

Helpful Hints

- Singapore is a shopping marvel. There are numerous shopping malls, and prices are competitive. Haggle for prices in small shops—but not in large department stores.
- Pay for items in cash; credit card purchases often carry a surcharge.
- In crowded restaurants, strangers may sit at your table. You needn't talk with them.
- Be prepared for notoriously talkative cab drivers who share their opinions on the government and many other issues. You can politely debate with them if you know what you're talking about and as long as you never criticize Singapore, its people, or its government. If you can't give informed opinions, ask questions and listen politely.

Health and Safety

- Singapore's Western-based health care system is excellent, but the people also patronize traditional medicine practitioners. The country has among the world's lowest infant mortality rates and highest life expectancies.
- Medical providers require immediate payment for services.
- Hospitals can fill prescriptions day or night, but locally registered doctors must write prescriptions. Pharmaceuticals are available at supermarkets, department stores, hotels, and shopping centers.
- Avoid driving in Singapore. Traffic is often heavy, and road construction is constant. Traffic rules are strict, and breaking them may lead to an arrest. Use public transportation or taxis to travel. Both are safe and convenient.
- Although crime rates have risen in recent years, many still believe Singapore is safer than many other countries, including the United States. Watch out for pickpocketing and other petty crimes, especially in crowded areas.

  The U.S. Department of State, however, warns that Americans should be alert and aware of their surroundings. Singapore has detained dozens of members of Jemaah Islamiyah (a terrorist group active in Asia and affiliated with Al Qaeda) who were suspected of planning attacks in Singapore. Check current travel warnings before your trip.
- Be aware of Singapore's strict laws. The country imposes strict penalties for what Americans may think are minor offenses. If arrested, you won't be read any rights and you may be detained without trial. The government doesn't offer legal assistance except in capital cases. There are no jury trials—judges hear trials and decide sentencing.

  With these facts in mind:
  * Don't jaywalk.
  * Don't smoke in outdoor eating areas, air-conditioned buildings, or nightclubs. (Some bars have designated smoking rooms).
  * Don't spit on the sidewalk.
  * Don't litter.
  * Don't try to smuggle in chewing gum. It's legal to chew gum only with a medical prescription (nicotine gum, for example). The penalty for smuggling in chewing gum is a year in jail and a SGD10,000 fine.
  * Don't try to smuggle in pornographic materials or reproductions of copyrighted publications, like videotapes, CDs, DVDs, records, or cassettes.

* Don't try to smuggle in firearms or anything that can be considered a weapon, including kitchen knives and handcuffs.
* Don't, under any circumstances, try to smuggle illegal drugs into the country. Possession of illegal drugs can bring a death sentence. Always carry prescriptions for all medications.

Corporate Culture

Most prominent businesspeople in Singapore are of Chinese ancestry. See pages 126–131 as well as 145–147 and 307–309 for additional information on Chinese business practices.

Structure

The Singaporean government finances many large corporations. The bureaucratic system is highly efficient and corruption free. From 1995–2005, the Political & Economic Risk Consultancy, Ltd. named Singapore Asia's least corrupt country in which to do business.

Smaller firms use a traditional Chinese management style, with a loose structure and centralized decision making. Most larger firms, however, use a Western management style (that is, more collaborative decision making and more direct communication).

Meetings

- Parties enter meeting rooms according to rank, with the senior person leading.
- Once meetings begin, Singaporeans discuss business immediately.

Appointments

- Schedule appointments well in advance of your visit.
- March through July is the best time to do business in Singapore. Avoid scheduling appointments for November through February, a common time for vacations.
- Regular business hours are 9:00 AM through 5:00 PM, Monday through Friday.

Communication

- Singaporeans speak English in business.
- Always speak directly and to the point with Singaporeans.

- With that said, don't correct anyone in front of others. Doing so will cause embarrassment and loss of face.
- Singapore has an outstanding telecommunications infrastructure. The broadband network reaches 99 percent of the population.

Business Cards

- Singaporeans exchange business cards during introductions. After you're introduced, exchange business cards with both hands.
- Because of the number of official languages spoken in Singapore, it's best to have your information printed only in English on business cards.
- Include your business card in all written correspondence.

Be Aware

- Singaporeans will expect you to deliver reports, correspondence, products, and services when promised.
- Take the time to get acquainted before scheduling meetings to discuss business. It may take several years to develop business relationships, but personal contact is important for Singaporean business success.

> Singaporeans are fiscally minded. Here are three prime examples:
> - Credit cards are available only to those with a designated minimum salary.
> - The government has made home ownership a priority, and in the 2000 census 92 percent of Singaporeans owned their homes.
> - To encourage care for the aging, the government gives financial incentives to people who live with their elderly parents.

- Singaporeans have excellent entrepreneurial instincts and make decisions quickly. They drive hard bargains on costs and deadlines.

Socializing

- Singaporeans do most business entertaining in restaurants, usually at dinner. It's a time to socialize and build relationships, not discuss business details. Don't be surprised if your hosts schedule business dinners for every night of your trip.
- Business lunches are popular, but business breakfasts aren't common. Business lunches are for discussing business, not for socializing.
- Singaporeans don't include spouses at business lunches or dinners.

Especially for Women

In Singapore, women enjoy many of the same opportunities as men do. In 2003, just over half of university students in Singapore were women. Also that year, more than half of Singaporean women were in the workforce.

The Singaporean government mandates a twelve-week maternity leave and provides tax benefits and financial support for child rearing.

- Singaporeans generally accept Western businesswomen, but some women may encounter sexist comments or chauvinistic behavior. Keep your sense of humor and never get angry.
- Women can travel alone safely in Singapore, but use common sense.
- A Western woman may invite a Singaporean man to a business dinner. She won't have any trouble paying, but it's good manners to arrange for payment with the wait staff beforehand.

Holidays and Festivals	
January	New Year's Day (1)
January/ February	Chinese New Year (Many Chinese firms close for the week.)
March/April	Easter (Friday through Sunday)
May	Labor Day (1)
May/June	Vesak Day
August	National Day (9)
December	Christmas (25)

Notes:
- Observed Islamic and Hindu holidays vary with the Islamic and Hindu calendars. Check to see when they're observed for the year you're traveling to Singapore.
- When a holiday falls on a Sunday, the following Monday is a public holiday.
- Singapore also has many spectacular annual festivals, like the Singapore Food Festival, Great Singapore Sale, and Thaipusam (a Hindu festival of penance and thanksgiving).

SOUTH KOREA
REPUBLIC OF KOREA

Greetings from South Korea

Greetings from the "Land of the Morning Calm." Maintaining harmony is one of our highest values.

Although few of us officially practice Confucianism, it influences every Korean's behavior. Confucianism teaches us virtue, morality, and parental devotion. We expect our children to respect their parents and defer to them.

Status and social order are important to us. Age, sex, education, family background, wealth, and occupation all determine one's status. At business meetings and social gatherings, status determines who we greet and seat first, where we sit, and even who pours the wine.

We segregate our children by sex, beginning in early childhood. Men and women have separate duties to perform and ethics to observe. We believe maintaining proper relationships between men and women is vital for our society's harmony.

We speak modestly and accept honors or compliments reluctantly. We never want to lose face. We believe no one has the right to upset another person or make him or her lose face. Always remember that we strive for harmony.

We enjoy our culture and arts, especially our folk music, drum dances, mask dances, mask theater, and puppet theater. We also enjoy sports, particularly baseball, basketball, football (soccer), volleyball, swimming, tennis, bowling, and golf.

Our population is largely urban; almost 50 percent of us live in the greater Seoul-Inchon area, the world's third-largest metro area with roughly twenty million people. If you visit our cities, know that traffic is a horrendous problem. But we are improving transportation to other parts of our country. Our new bullet train—with speeds up to 185 miles per hour—began operation in 2004.

We work very hard. South Korea has the world's longest average workweek, and only one out of ten of us works part-time. Our work ethic and commitment to education contribute to our strong economy. In the last half-century, we have risen out of poverty to become one of the world's largest economies— a remarkable achievement!

Despite our economic success, we still have problems. It is a fact that a few wealthy families control a huge sector of our economy. The thirty largest family-owned enterprises (*chaebols*) control almost 40 percent of the economy. Our remarkable success has convinced some that these families are worthy stewards. But recent scandals are making us re-examine their competence. Shareholders are now demanding accountability.

As our economy improved, our birth rate dropped to the lowest in the developed world. Within a generation, half our population will be over age fifty. The Korean Development Institute warns that if we do not raise the birth rate, our economy will slow by 2010. We struggle with how best to encourage more births.

Relations with Japan are problematic. We have demanded that Japan apologize for colonizing our nation during the last century; the Korean "comfort women" (women who were sexually enslaved by the Japanese military and their supporters) also want an apology. There are also several islands whose control we dispute with Japan.

But we are making attempts at friendship: South Korea and Japan jointly hosted the 2002 World Cup, and South Korean entertainers are becoming celebrities in Japan.

Please use our correct country name when visiting us. Formally, our nation is the Republic of Korea, but South Korea is our common name. Anything associated with our nation or government since 1953 is South Korean.

As a people, however, we are Korean—just as are our family and neighbors to the north. Millions of us have family in North Korea, and we want the freedom to visit them whenever we want. Since 2000, there have been just a handful of government-sanctioned meetings between the residents of the Koreas. But our government is working toward union with all our people.

Although our young people today follow pop culture and wear Western fashions, we honor our traditions. Our food, language, and culture differ from those of other Asian countries. If you do not respect that distinction, we will not work with you. And remember: At all costs, maintain harmony. If you do, we will enjoy working with you.

Vital Statistics

Population	48,846,823
Capital	Seoul
Area	38,023 square miles, slightly larger than Indiana
Government	Republic
Natural Resources	Coal, tungsten, graphite, molybdenum, lead, hydropower potential
Living Standard	GDP = US $20,240 per capita
Agriculture	Rice, root crops, barley, vegetables, fruit, cattle, pigs, chickens, milk, eggs, fish
Industries	Electronics, telecommunications, automobile production, chemicals, shipbuilding, steel
Climate	Temperate, with heavier rainfall in summer
Currency	South Korean won (KRW)

The People

Correct Name	noun: Korean(s)
	adjective: Korean
Ethnic Makeup	Korean (except for about 20,000 Chinese)
Languages	Korean (official), English (widely taught in school)
Religions	No affiliation 46%, Christian 26%, Buddhist 26%, Confucianist 1%, other 1%

Meeting and Greeting

- Koreans traditionally bow upon meeting and leaving. The depth of a bow depends on the relationship between the parties and the situation. Unless you're thoroughly familiar with bowing rituals, give only a slight bow to show courtesy. That is, place your heels together, bend slightly at the waist, and keep your head down. Keep your hands at your sides, and don't look at the other party.
- Among men, handshakes often follow bows upon meeting.
- Korean women generally don't shake hands after bowing; instead, they usually nod slightly. Western women, however, may extend handshakes to Korean men, but should nod to Korean women.

- Koreans shake hands less firmly than Americans do. To show respect when shaking hands, hold your right forearm with your left hand.
- Younger people greet older people first.
- Lower-ranking people bow first to higher-ranking people. But higher-ranking people extend handshakes to lower-ranking people.
- Younger people may wave when leaving instead of bowing.

Names and Titles

- Korean name order is last name (surname) + two-part first name. Family members of the same generation sometimes share the first part of the first name. The second part is the person's given name.

  Example: Last name   Generational name   Given name
               Lee   Dong   Sung
- When Koreans address other Koreans, they may use the honorific *sonsaengnim*, which means "teacher," either by itself or after the last name. Unless you speak Korean fluently, don't use this address.
- In most cases, address Koreans by English courtesy title (Mr., Mrs., Ms., or Miss) + last name. Never address them by given name unless invited to do so.
- When addressing a senior executive or other high-ranking person, use the person's professional title + last name. You may also use English courtesy title + professional title.
- After you've established a personal relationship, you may address someone by given name + "-shi" (pronounced "shee"). For example, address Lee Dong Sung as "Sung-shi."
- Some Koreans may mistake your first name for your last name (or find your last name unpronounceable) and address you by English courtesy title + first name. Never correct Koreans unless they specifically ask for help.

    If someone realizes that he or she has been calling you by your first name, minimize the gaffe and allow the person to save face by saying, "In my country, we call one another by first name all the time."
- After marrying, most Korean women don't take their husbands' last names.
- The most common Korean last names are Kim, Lee, and Park.
- Be aware: Westerners may have trouble distinguishing whether a Korean first name is for a man or a woman.

Language

The Korean language is unique and includes six main dialects. Many scholars (but not all) place Korean in the Ural-Altaic family of languages, the same one that includes Japanese as well as Hungarian and Finnish.

China's influence prevails in the Korean language. Koreans used Chinese characters millennia ago, and today they still use some characters (*Hanja*) along with a phonetic alphabet called *Hangeul*, invented in the fifteenth century. Today, about half of the Korean vocabulary derives from Chinese words (although Koreans pronounce them differently than do the Chinese).

Korean translates into English with various spellings. In general, words with different spellings that are pronounced the same probably have the same meaning. Some consonant pairs are interchangeable in English spellings: *p* and *b*, *k* and *g*, *t* and *d*, and to some extent *ch* and *j*. The vowels *u* and *oo* also are interchangeable.

Conversation

- As a way to show polite interest in someone, Koreans may ask personal questions; for example, they may ask what your parents' occupations are. If you're uncomfortable answering them, give vague answers or say, "In my country, that would be a strange question."
- Never confuse Koreans with the Chinese, Japanese, or other Asians. Doing so is a grave insult.
- Never upset someone or damage his or her reputation; never criticize or disagree with someone in public. *Kibun* (basically, "peace of mind") is important to Koreans, and they view someone's disrupting it as bad form.
- Never laugh or talk loudly in Seoul. In other regions, boisterous conversation is more common.
- Speak clearly and precisely, but not exceedingly slowly (or else you may appear patronizing).
- Resist the urge to move your face close to a Korean's in an attempt to understand his or her English. Koreans respect personal space.

> Families are important to Koreans, and they love to celebrate familial events in style. For example, to pay for a relative's sixtieth birthday party, family members form a *gye* (an agreement among a group of people to save money for a celebration). Families also form *gyes* to pay for funerals, weddings, first birthdays, and other special occasions.

- Never say *fellow*, *guy*, *this man*, or *that man*. Koreans consider these words demeaning.
- To save face, Koreans often won't admit they don't know the answer to a question. Instead, they may give a wrong answer or an answer they think you want to hear.

> South Korea's film industry is gaining international respect. In recent years, South Korean movies have won awards at film festivals in Berlin and Venice as well as at Cannes. Koreans are also proud that their pop culture is becoming wildly popular across Asia.

- In South Korea, *yes* doesn't necessarily indicate agreement. It may mean "I hear you" or "I understand you."
- Koreans may not appreciate sarcastic or ironic humor.
- When embarrassed, afraid, angry, or surprised, Koreans often laugh.

Acceptable topics
- Korea's accomplishments
- Hobbies (yours and theirs)
- Family (yours and theirs)
- Your Korean colleagues' health

Unacceptable topics
- A specific Korean person or Korean customs and culture, even if to make complimentary remarks (Koreans find compliments embarrassing.)
- Politics
- Korean War
- Relations with North Korea, Japan, and China

> The Korean War (1950–1953) and the subsequent split with North Korea are still painful to South Koreans. Never bring up these tense topics. Their relationship with North Korea is complex, and they don't appreciate outsiders' input. If Koreans discuss them, listen carefully and ask sensitive questions. (Be sure to read up on both countries' current events.)

- Praise of another region in South Korea: Some Koreans may discriminate against those from other regions.

Topics that require sensitivity
- American troops stationed in South Korea
- Religion

Body Language

- Avoid hugging, backslapping, or otherwise touching Koreans. Koreans consider touching distasteful except among relatives or close friends. They believe touching older people and those of the opposite sex particularly inappropriate; however, more young people are holding hands and kissing in public, especially on university campuses.
- Koreans rarely use gestures. Try to restrain your gesturing.
- Korean sense of personal space generally matches North Americans', but acquaintances usually stand and walk closely to one another. Koreans believe it's rude to make someone walk behind you. Close Korean friends of the same sex may hold hands or walk with a hand on the other's shoulder.

> In Korea, direct eye contact is usually impolite—even in business situations. But with increased international contact, direct eye contact is becoming more common among Korean businesspeople.

- Korean women cover their mouths when laughing. Men usually don't.
- Good posture is important. Always sit and stand up straight. Don't cross your legs or stretch them out in front of you. Keep your feet flat on the floor—never rest them on furniture.
- Never beckon someone with your index finger or say "come here." Doing so is rude. To beckon someone, extend your arm (palm down) then curl and flex your fingers together.
- Tilting your head back and sucking in air between your teeth means "no" or "very difficult."

Phrases		
English	**Korean**	**Pronunciation**
Good morning/good afternoon/good evening (said in formal situations)	*Annyong hasimnika*	(AHN-yohng hah-SHEEM-nee-kah)
Hello (said in informal situations)	*Annyong haseyo*	(AHN-yohng HAH-say-oh)
Thank you	*Kamsa hamnida*	(KAHM-sah HAHM-nee-dah)
You're welcome	*Chon-man-e Mal-sum-im-ni-da*	(CHON-mahn-AH-yo mahl-SOO-eem-nee-DAH)

English	Korean	Pronunciation
Yes	*Yě*	(YEE-eh)
No	*Anio*	(AH-nee-yoh)
Excuse me	*Che-song-ham-ni-da*	(CHAY-song hahm-NEE-dah)
Goodbye		
(said by a person departing)	*Annyonghi kesipsiyo*	(AHN-yohng-hee kah-SIP-sih-yoh)
(said by a person staying; also said by two or more people leaving at the same time)	*Annyonghi kasipsiyo*	(AHN-yohng-hee kay-SIP-sih-yoh)
Pleased to meet you	*Man-na-so pan-kap-sum-ni-da*	(MAHN-nah-so pahn-gop-SOOM-nee-dah)

The polite way to say "please" is to add *yo* (pronounced "yoh") at the end of the sentence. Many Koreans understand the English word *please*, and foreigners may use it.

Dining

Cuisine is an essential part of Korean culture. The fare is generally spicy, although some dishes are milder. Kimchi (pronounced "KIM-chee") is cabbage fermented with hot chilies and sometimes with onion, garlic, or anchovies. It's the most well-known Korean food, and everyone has a favorite kimchi recipe.

Korean meals are simple—rice, meat or fish soup, vegetables, and kimchi.

- Korean dishes are eaten with chopsticks (see page 41 for information on chopstick etiquette), although spoons are used to eat soup. Westerners may ask for utensils, but wait staff in many restaurants will bring utensils to Westerners without being asked.

- Before meals, your host may give you a towel (hot or cold) to wash your face and hands.

- Hotels serve dishes by course—as many as twelve. They serve appetizers first, followed by meat, vegetables, and *ssam*, which are various leaf vegetables. (Roll the meat and vegetables in a leaf to eat.) They usually serve soup with the main course.

- Korean restaurants serve all dishes at once. You may eat the dishes in any order, but be sure to taste each one.

- Western cuisine is available everywhere in South Korea. In large cities, American chain restaurants are as common as in the United States.

Drinking

- Koreans drink green tea, but in general they drink far less tea than the Chinese and Japanese do. Since 1967, the Myung Won Cultural Foundation has worked to revive Korea's millennia-old tea ceremony.
- Coffee has become popular in South Korea, and local and international chains have opened numerous coffee shops in the last few years. The world's largest Starbucks (five stories high) is in South Korea.
- Drinking alcohol is a popular pastime in South Korea, and food usually accompanies alcohol, as do singing performances. (Be prepared to sing a solo.)
- While drunkenness is acceptable, loud, aggressive behavior isn't.
- Koreans' favorite alcoholic drinks include Scotch, vodka, and beer.
- Men don't pour their own drinks, but will offer to pour for others. Women may pour their own drinks as well as men's drinks, but never other women's drinks.
- When someone pours a drink for you, lift your glass to a level convenient for the pourer. When pouring for someone, support your forearm with your other hand.
- Hosts refill empty glasses. If you don't want more, leave some liquid in your glass.
- Koreans often serve coffee with cream and sugar added. They may ask you how you like your coffee before serving it, but if they don't, drink (or pretend to drink) at least a few sips.

Toasting

- At formal occasions, the host offers the first toast and the guest of honor reciprocates. At informal occasions, anyone may give the first toast.
- Use your right hand to lift your glass during a toast. To show respect for the recipient, support your right forearm with your left hand.
- People may or may not clink glasses during toasts. (Follow others' lead.)
- The toast *wihayo* (wee-hah-yoh) means "for our health and prosperity." Koreans generally use it at formal occasions only.

- The toast *konbae* (GOHN-beh) means "bottoms up." Raise your drink with your right hand; everybody toasts and clinks glasses. Be certain you don't mistakenly say the Japanese toast *kanpai* (KAHN-pie).
- Women may propose toasts during dinner, but they shouldn't at a bar. To avoid making a social gaffe, women should make toasts only if other women in the group do so (and the group receives the toasts warmly).

Tipping

In general, Koreans find tipping offensive, but it's becoming expected in hotels frequented by foreigners. Don't tip anyone if you see a "no tipping" sign posted.
- Western-style restaurants and hotel restaurants: The bill always includes a 10 percent service charge. You can leave small change as an additional gratuity for excellent service.
- Other restaurants: The bill doesn't include a service charge, and no tip is necessary.
- Taxis: Round up to the nearest KRW 1000. Additionally, tip the equivalent of US $1 if the driver helps with your luggage.
- Porters: Hotels usually post a schedule; tip according to it.
- Hotel bellhops: Many hotels officially prohibit bellhops from accepting gratuities, but bellhops may nevertheless expect a tip the equivalent of US $1.
- Hair stylists and barbers: No tip is necessary.

Manners

- Always knock before entering a room.
- Always pass and receive items with both hands or with your right hand (have your left hand support your right forearm).
- Always let your host seat you. If given the seat of honor (the one facing the entrance), it's polite to protest slightly before sitting. The host sits to the left of the guest of honor.
- Hosts serve the elderly first and children last. Don't eat until the most senior person at the meal begins eating.
- Never pick up food with your hands, even fruit (use a toothpick to eat fruit pieces). Never raise a bowl or dish to your mouth.
- Regardless of how exotic the dish, graciously taste it. Never show any distaste.

- Never refill your own glass or soy sauce dish. Always refill your neighbors' glasses and soy sauce dishes.
- When finished eating, place your spoon in your soup bowl or lay it across your rice bowl. Place chopsticks on the chopstick rest or directly on the table; never plant them in your rice. (That's how Buddhists offer rice to deceased ancestors.)
- Keep conversation to a minimum during meals. Koreans don't like to converse while eating. They appreciate silence during meals, and they socialize only after the meals.
- Leave a dinner party shortly after the meal or entertainment concludes.
- When dining socially, the oldest person usually pays the bill. When dining for business, the person who extended the invitation pays (although it's polite for the guests to offer to pay).
- To beckon a waiter, say "Yo-gi-yo" (yoh-gee-yoh), which means "here, please."
- Cover your mouth when yawning or using a toothpick.
- Don't blow your nose in public. Never put a used tissue in your pocket; dispose of it immediately.
- Keep your hands out of your pockets.
- Don't eat while walking on streets.

> In crowds, expect Koreans to push and shove. They don't queue (stand in line). Be aggressive or you won't get anywhere!

- Remove sunglasses when speaking to someone.
- Show great respect for the elderly—hold doors for older people, give them your seat, stand when they enter a room. In particular, acknowledge elderly men as the most important figures in Korea.
- Always stand at attention during the South Korean national anthem.
- See pages 75–85 for information on etiquette when visiting a temple or other holy place.

Punctuality

Koreans expect Westerners to be punctual for business and social occasions. Call with an explanation if you'll be delayed.

Foreigners, however, should prepare to wait. Korean executives' busy schedules as well as heavy traffic may make them up to a half-hour late for business meetings. For social occasions, many Koreans follow "Korean time," which means they arrive up to a half-hour late.

Dress

Koreans pay special attention to appearance and dress well in conservative Western fashions. They rarely dress casually—even college students. Men dress soberly, and women dress modestly; they never wear tight, short, or revealing clothing, including sleeveless blouses. Visitors should dress accordingly to show respect.

- For business, men wear dark suits with white or light-blue shirts and conservative ties. Women wear tailored suits or dresses; they rarely wear slacks.
- For formal occasions and at restaurants, men wear dark suits with white shirts and ties. Women may wear tailored suits, but evening gowns or dresses in conservative colors are preferred.

> Plastic surgery is common among South Korean women, regardless of age. By some estimates, half the country's women in their twenties have had some kind of plastic surgery.

- For casual occasions, men wear conservative slacks and shirts. Women wear skirts, sweaters, and blouses. Slacks are acceptable.
- If visiting in the winter, pack very warm clothing.
- Wear shorts only at the beach or at very casual occasions at which no elders are present.
- Koreans often seat guests on the floor. Make sure to wear appropriate clothing.
- Never go barefoot.

Gifts

- Exchanging gifts is common in South Korea, but Koreans never open gifts in front of the giver.
- Offer and receive gifts with both hands.
- After receiving a gift, reciprocate with a gift of similar value.
- It's important that gifts are elegantly wrapped. If possible, hire a professional wrapper; this person will know the appropriate presentation for the occasion. If wrapping a gift yourself, never use red gift-wrap (red symbolizes China and Communism) or dark-colored gift-wrap (dark colors symbolize death).

Hostess Gifts

Always bring a gift when invited to someone's home.

Consider giving
- Candy, cakes, or cookies
- Flowers
- Fruit

Don't give
- Liquor: Koreans don't give liquor to women.

Business Gifts

- Koreans commonly exchange gifts at first meetings. Let your host initiate gift giving.
- Employers frequently give cash gifts to their employees at Korean Thanksgiving and New Year's Day.

Consider giving
- Liquor or wine (to men only): Koreans especially enjoy red wine, and they prize high-quality Scotch, especially Ballantine's 30 Year Old.
- Fruit
- Desk accessories
- Items from France or Italy (convey status)
- American regional arts and crafts

Don't give
- Obviously expensive gifts (Koreans will feel obliged to reciprocate with a gift of equal value.)
- Knives, scissors, or other sharp items (connote the severing of a relationship)
- Green headwear (signifies that somebody in the recipient's family is an adulterer)
- Items with red writing (Red connotes death.)
- Shoes (connote running away from one another)
- Gifts in sets of four (The number four connotes death.)

Helpful Hints

- Except in stores marked "one price," feel free to bargain.
- Keep to the left on sidewalks and stairs. In South Korea, people tend to walk to the left (unlike in the United States, where people tend to walk to the right).

- South Korea is a homogeneous society, and Koreans may find foreigners curious (and perhaps distrustful). Expect people to stare at you, especially if you have red or blond hair. They may even try to touch your hair.
- Korean strangers in stressful situations (a traffic accident, for example) may show more anger than Americans would expect. Among colleagues and friends, however, they're always calm and controlled.
- In crowded restaurants, you may be seated with strangers. You needn't converse with them.

Health and Safety

- In case of an emergency, keep your hotel business card (information in Korean) with you at all times.
- To avoid contaminants, eat only peeled and cooked fruits and vegetables.
- Tap water in cities should be safe for drinking, but many Koreans boil their water. To be safe, drink only boiled or bottled water—even in major hotels with their own filtration systems. Always drink only boiled or bottled water outside cities.
- Health care facilities and providers in South Korea are good. If necessary, your hotel can refer a suitable physician or clinic.
- Providers and hospitals may expect immediate cash payment for services.
- Koreans label many medications completely differently than Westerners do. It may be difficult to locate exact equivalents of Western medicines. Make sure to pack any necessary medications. If you must buy medications in South Korea, consult a pharmacist.
- South Korean streets are generally safe for visitors (but use common sense). The crime rate is low, and yellow signs identify police stations on all major streets.
- Student demonstrations occasionally occur, but Westerners rarely encounter any violence from them.

Corporate Culture

Structure
- The founding families still run the huge conglomerates.
- Although employees expect decisiveness in managers, open communication and decision making are becoming important. Younger Koreans especially appreciate a manager who's open to suggestions and feedback.

- Middle managers have considerable authority, but departmental consensus often determines decisions, which are then communicated to the senior level for approval. All appropriate departments implement decisions.

Meetings

- First meetings are for establishing trust, not discussing business. They often take place over a meal.
- A "tea girl" serves tea, coffee, or soft drinks before meetings. Accept the beverage with both hands.
- Let your Korean hosts seat you at meetings. They seat the highest-ranking foreigner opposite the entrance and seat the rest of the foreign team opposite their Korean counterparts.
- Act formally in meetings until the Korean delegation relaxes. Then you may act more casually.
- Make presentations brief and support them with highly detailed reports.
- Koreans generally start negotiations with an unreasonable position and are prepared to compromise. They're tough negotiators and admire a firm, persistent opponent—but don't be too aggressive.
- Meetings often extend beyond normal business hours.
- Negotiations are generally protracted and may require several trips.

Appointments

- It's vital to find a Korean contact who can formally introduce you to potential clients and colleagues. Without such a contact, you may be unable to schedule appointments.
- Have a senior executive of your company schedule the first meeting with the Korean company's senior executive. For subsequent meetings, send representatives of the same level as the Korean counterparts.
- Regular business hours are 9:00 AM to 5:00 PM, Monday through Friday, and 9:00 AM to 1:00 PM on Saturday. Many people arrive at work early and frequently stay late. Workers rarely leave before the manager does. For these reasons, South Korea has one of the world's longest average workweeks.
- Make appointments well in advance to give Koreans time to research your company and prepare for your visit.
- February through June is the best time for business appointments. Avoid scheduling appointments for July and August (common times for vacations) and the second half of December through early January (Christmas/ New Year's holidays). Also avoid scheduling appointments for the weeks around the Lunar New Year and Harvest Moon (see page 291).

Communication

- Many Korean businesspeople speak English, but they may need an interpreter for clear understanding. If they require an interpreter, your Korean hosts will usually provide one. Check before the meeting to learn whether you need to provide an interpreter.
- Always show respect and never criticize or embarrass a Korean, especially in front of others. Being patronizing or condescending will destroy any chance of a business relationship.
- To show attentiveness and sincerity, listen carefully to Koreans and maintain eye contact when listening and speaking. Never smile; Koreans consider smiling during negotiations frivolous.
- Don't be surprised if Koreans repeatedly ask a question. Always give a consistent answer.
- Try to avoid asking yes-or-no questions. To avoid conflict, Koreans don't say "no," and "yes" doesn't necessarily indicate agreement.
- With that said, Koreans can be blunt, even aggressive, during negotiations. They may interrupt you mid-sentence to argue. Don't lose your cool.
- Never boast about your company. Use professionally written reports to show your company's abilities and achievements.
- Do your homework and be prepared. You'll embarrass Koreans if you can't answer a question, and your ignorance could damage your credibility.
- Reply promptly to written and electronic correspondence.
- You may have trouble getting Koreans to report problems. Remember: their culture steers them to avoid conflict.

Business Cards

- Businesspeople meeting for the first time usually exchange business cards. Present and receive business cards with both hands.
- Have your information printed in English on one side of your card and in Korean (using either *Hangeul* or *Hanja*; see page 277) on the other side. Never use Japanese! Koreans still resent the Japanese occupation of last century.
- Koreans are impressed by education and experience. Make sure to include degrees and achievements on your business card.

Be Aware

- Certain Korean universities are more prestigious than others, and their graduates have more status and respect.

- The Korean market is tough to enter. Hire a consultant or lawyer with a good track record to help you break into the market.
- Networking is important for success in South Korea. Koreans want to get to know you before doing business. They want to learn all about your company and your position within it.
- Koreans are cautious and sometimes go to great lengths to avoid making mistakes.
- They highly value friendship. Friends rely on one another in both their personal and business lives.
- Koreans don't like detailed, inflexible contracts. To them, mutual trust and benefits are more important than legal documents.
- Who signs a legal document is of vital importance to Koreans. Having the most senior person sign documents proves a company's commitment. Never sign a contract with red ink, which connotes death.
- Koreans believe written contracts are always subject to renegotiation.
- Quality, price, and service are essential to Korean business success. Always deliver promises in a timely manner. Koreans greatly value after-sale service.
- Koreans strive to meet deadlines, because asking for an extension means losing face.

Socializing

Business success depends directly on building trust and relationships. Sharing a meal or drinks after business hours is essential to sealing the deal. Many Koreans believe a proper evening out has three destinations: a restaurant, a bar, and a nightclub, for example. If planning an evening for Korean colleagues, keep this belief in mind.

- Koreans do most business entertaining in restaurants.
- Business dinners are most common; business lunches are less so. Business breakfasts are rare.
- The meal generally precedes any business discussion or other conversation. Show appreciation for the food. Let your Korean hosts initiate business discussions.
- Koreans often consume large quantities of alcohol at business dinners. Be warned: They'll hold you to any promises you make when drinking.
- Singing usually follows dinner. Be sure to take your turn. (Songs with English lyrics are acceptable.)

- After dinner, the host generally invites guests to go drinking at a bar or nightclub, where a hired hostess serves drinks and snacks (to allow guests to concentrate on socializing). Never refuse this invitation.
- After dining, an evening often ends at a *kisaeng* house, an expensive restaurant where beautiful, talented women talk with guests and play music. These women flirt, sing, and talk—they're *not* prostitutes. (Koreans rarely invite Western businesswomen to *kisaeng* houses.)
- Koreans generally invite only colleagues or the negotiating team to dinners. They rarely invite spouses. When hosting an event, don't invite spouses.
- After someone entertains you, reciprocate with comparable entertainment when he or she visits you at your home.

Especially for Women

Traditionally, Korean society is strongly male oriented. Men come first in almost everything. (Koreans even address audiences as "gentlemen and ladies.") Men make all the decisions, and women defer to them. Women let men enter rooms first, help men put on their coats, and pour drinks for men (but rarely do so for other women).

Not surprisingly, women haven't held prominent positions in South Korean businesses and government. Women generally have lower-ranking jobs, make less money, and have fewer opportunities for advancement than men do.

The government has implemented measures to increase women's status and opportunities in the workplace, including establishing the Ministry of Gender Equality. But the nation has a long way to go to achieve gender equality.

- Western women may have difficulty doing business in South Korea (although Koreans will try to respect that Western women are used to equality). Older Koreans may prefer negotiating with men. To gain acceptance and respect, make your title as impressive as possible and be prepared to demonstrate your knowledge.
- Wait for men to begin negotiations. Generally, women let men make the first move in Korea.
- Always make sure your behavior is elegant, refined, and demure. Never act aggressively, and don't talk or laugh too loudly. Dress conservatively.
- South Korea is generally safe for women traveling alone, but use common sense, especially in Seoul.
- A foreign woman may invite a Korean man to a business dinner, but she should be clear that she's hosting ("I would be honored if you would allow

me to host you for dinner") and then give a specific time and place. She should arrange payment with the wait staff beforehand. If the bill comes to the table, a Korean man will feel obliged to pay.

> Korean women generally don't smoke on the street, and Koreans may give women dirty looks if they do so. (It's more acceptable for women to smoke in a restaurant or in private.) Nonetheless, some Korean women smoke on the street simply to show assertiveness and strength.

- Although much less common today than in the past, men and women may socialize in separate rooms. If this situation occurs, women may approach men to talk, especially about business.

Holidays and Festivals

January	New Year's Day (1)
January/February	Lunar New Year*
March	Independence Movement Day (1)
April	Arbor Day (5)
May	Children's Day (5)
	Buddha's Birthday*
June	Memorial Day (6)
July	Constitution Day (17)
August	Liberation Day (15)
September/October	Harvest Moon (Chusok)*
October	National Foundation Day (3)
December	Christmas (25)

* These holidays follow the lunar calendar. Check when they're observed for the year you're traveling to South Korea.

TAIWAN
REPUBLIC OF CHINA

Greetings from Taiwan

Greetings from the Republic of China on Taiwan (ROC), the name that formally separates us from the People's Republic of China (PRC), also known as Mainland China.

In 1945, the Cairo agreement gave Mainland China administrative control of our island, after fifty years of Japanese colonial rule. Four years later and near the end of a civil war, Communist forces in Mainland China drove the Nationalist Chinese to our land, where many stayed.

Today, although we and Mainland China both consider Taiwan a province of China, we disagree on the location of China's legitimate government. We consider the capital to be Taipei; they believe it to be Beijing.

Taiwan was the United Nation's (UN) official designate of China until 1971, when the UN gave the role to Mainland China. Presently, only two dozen countries recognize us as the government of China.

Our government set up the National Unification Council in 1990 as part of its official policy toward working for unification with Mainland China. But the council was disbanded in February 2006; a year later, the government dropped *China* from the names of two state-owned companies. Many observers see these moves as steps toward officially declaring Taiwan an independent nation.

The government may be reflecting the will of the citizens of Taiwan, many of whom no longer want to pursue unification. At least one recent poll indicates that half our people want to abandon the status quo and declare independence. For more than a half-century, we have been working to distinguish ourselves as a democracy with a capitalist economy and a unique culture. Today, our leaders are promoting the study of our history, geography, and languages.

We understand that declaring our independence would have complex consequences that the rest of the world would rather avoid. For example, Mainland China has vowed it will use force to keep us from becoming officially independent. (It currently has more than seven hundred missiles targeted at us.)

We do not take the current peace for granted. We require young men to serve nearly two years in our military. Those unsuited to regular military service perform other services to fulfill the obligation.

As a country, Taiwan is modern and industrialized. As a people, we are highly motivated, hardworking, patient, friendly, and respectful. Schools and government promote group and community participation. We are proudly preparing to host the World Games (the world's second-largest international sporting event after the Olympics) in 2009.

We consider our family unit more important than the individual, and many extended families live together, especially in rural areas. We expect our children to obey their parents; however, as in the rest of the world, older people fear the young are abandoning traditional values in favor of material possessions and a westernized lifestyle.

We enjoy good health. Taiwan has had universal health coverage since 1995, and our infant morality rate and life expectancies are the same as in the United States. Our spiritual health is also sound. Most of us practice a combination of Taoism, Buddhism, and Confucianism—the philosophy of the last faith orders our relationships and is the foundation of our value system.

Although our history and current status are complex, we are a wonderful place to visit for business or pleasure. Our country hosts wonderful festivals and has spectacular mountains, forests, and coastline that everyone should see.

All we ask is that visitors take the time to read about our past and present before traveling to Taiwan. If you do not, you will not be able to understand us.

Vital Statistics

Population	23,036,087
Capital	Taipei
Area	13,892 square miles, slightly smaller than Maryland and Delaware combined
Government	Multiparty democracy
Living Standard	GDP = US $17,520
Natural Resources	Small deposits of coal, natural gas, limestone, marble, and asbestos
Agriculture	Rice, corn, vegetables, fruit, tea, pigs, poultry, beef, milk, fish

Industries	Electronics, petroleum refining, armaments, chemicals, textiles, iron and steel, machinery, cement, food processing, vehicles, consumer products, pharmaceuticals
Climate	Tropical; marine; rainy season during southwest monsoon (June through August); persistent and extensive cloudiness all year
Currency	New Taiwan dollar (TWD)

The People

Correct Name	noun: Correct noun form in Taiwan can be tricky. *Taiwanese* generally applies to those who lived in the country before 1949 and their descendants. *Chinese* or *Taiwan Chinese* usually refers to the Nationalist Chinese who came to Taiwan in 1949 and in the years afterward. Because the Taipei regime still considers itself the legitimate government of China, always use the term *Chinese* when speaking with government officials.
	adjective: The term *Taiwanese* is appropriate only when referring to Taiwan's geographic features and cultural matters (food, history, art, and so on) and when referring to those who lived in the country before 1949 and their descendants.
Ethnic Makeup	Taiwanese (including Hakka) 84%, Mainland Chinese 14%, aborigine 2%
Languages	Mandarin (official), Taiwanese (Min), Hakka dialects
Religions	Mixture of Buddhist, Confucian, and Taoist 93%, Christian 4.5%, other 2.5%

Meeting and Greeting

- Introductions are important in Taiwan. If possible, have a respected third person introduce you to new people. At a party or business meeting, have the host introduce you before you greet others. At a banquet, however, you may introduce yourself to others at your table.

- Residents of Taiwan give a nod or slight bow as a greeting. Only men who are friends greet one another with a handshake.

- Always greet the eldest person first.

- To show respect to the elderly, greet them by placing your right hand over your left fist and raising both hands to heart level. Also, if you're wearing glasses, remove them before greeting.

Names and Titles

- Name order in Taiwan is last name (surname) + middle name (generational name, given to all siblings in a family) + first name (given name). Residents of Taiwan usually hyphenate their middle and first names.
- Because titles indicate rank and status, they're extremely important in Taiwan. Whenever possible, use a person's correct business or professional title. You may use English titles, but learning and using their Chinese translations will impress colleagues in Taiwan. Address people by English professional title + last name, or by last name + Chinese professional title. If you don't know a person's professional title, use the appropriate courtesy title.

    Examples: President Kuo or Kuo *jing li* (pronounced "jeeng-LEE")
- Some businesspeople in Taiwan adopt an English first name for foreigners to use. In this case, they'll use the name order first name + last name.
- Don't address people by first name only until they specifically invite you to do so.
- In Taiwan, there isn't a standard method of transliteration from Chinese to English. Different people may spell the same name in different ways. For example, someone may spell *Wang* as *Wong* or *Wan*.
- Women in Taiwan don't routinely take their husbands' last names after marrying, and they use their maiden names on business cards and socially. If you don't know a woman's maiden name, address her by Mrs. + husband's last name.
- After marrying, women may use the courtesy title Madam (Mdm).

English	Chinese	Pronunciation
Mr.	*Xiansheng*	(shee-ehn-SHUNG)
Mrs.	*Taitai*	(TIE-tie)
Miss (also used to politely address a waitress, female cashier, or female elevator attendant)	*Xiaojie*	(shee-OW-jyeh)

Language

Although Mandarin is the official language of Taiwan and spoken in most formal situations, about 70 percent of the citizens speak Taiwanese (Min), a local Chinese dialect similar to the dialect spoken in Fujian (where many of the original settlers of Taiwan hailed from).

For many decades, schools banned the use of Taiwanese and the media limited its use. The government lifted many of these restrictions in the 1980s, and today several schools teach the language. Some companies even use it as their official language.

In Taiwan, Mandarin is written in classical Chinese characters instead of the simplified characters used in Mainland China.

The people of Taiwan believe that speaking English is an important skill in today's international marketplace. Many speak some English but are dissatisfied with their grasp of the language. Teachers of English are in great demand, and the language is a required subject in schools, beginning at the elementary level. Many parents also pay for additional English instruction for their children.

Conversation

- Be aware: In Taiwan, saying "yes" can indicate either understanding or agreement. Saying "maybe" or "I am not sure" often means "no."
- You may compliment people, although they'll likely decline compliments. When you receive a compliment, be self-effacing. Don't say "thank you" or else you may appear immodest.
- When in Taiwan, always refer to the People's Republic of China (PRC) as "Mainland China" (but never use this term when in the PRC).
- Never embarrass anyone or cause someone to lose face.
- Residents of Taiwan don't appreciate bluntness. Don't speak too directly.
- While in Taiwan, be prepared for people to ask personal questions. If

In the 1970s, a government program encouraged the traditionally large families of Taiwan to have fewer children. By 1984, the country's birthrate fell below replacement level. For a population to grow by reproduction, its replacement level must be more than two to one—that is, on average each woman must bear at least two children.

Today, with its population aging, Taiwan has begun to worry about its extremely low birthrate.

you're uncomfortable answering them, give vague or humorous answers. For example, if asked how much money you make, answer "Enough that my mother brags about me."

- Don't be offended if someone calls you fat or skinny. They're just stating a fact as they see it; they don't mean to insult you.

Acceptable topics
- Weather (in Taiwan and your home region)
- Taiwanese cuisine: Ask your colleagues for restaurant recommendations.
- Someone's health
- Local sights, like the abundant temples and churches or the world-renowned National Palace Museum (It'd take twelve years to see the more than half-billion pieces in its collection.)
- Travel
- Sports, including baseball and basketball (Taiwan has professional leagues for both), football (soccer), badminton, and table tennis
- Family: Be sure to ask about any children. Show photos of your family; your hosts will likely show you photos of their families.
- Compliments of Taiwan

Unacceptable topics
- Suggestions that Taiwan isn't part of China
- Implications that the Beijing regime—not Taipei—is China's legitimate government
- Money

Because the People's Republic of China (PRC) won't let other nations jointly recognize it and the Republic of China, Taiwan has diplomatic relations with few countries.

Diplomatic ties between the United States and Taiwan were severed in 1979, when the United States officially recognized the PRC. Unofficial relations, including trade ties, continue through the American Institute in Taiwan and the Taipei Economic and Cultural Representative Office (Taiwan's representative in the United States).

In 2005, Taiwan was the United States' eighth-largest trading partner. It's also a major exporter to the United States and importer of American goods.

Taiwan enjoys informal relations with many other nations and has become an economic powerhouse—despite its diplomatic status.

- Comparisons between Taiwan and the United States
- Unification with China

> Never discuss unification with China with a resident of Taiwan. People have strong views on this subject and can be quite hostile to those who hold different opinions.

Topics that require sensitivity

- Local politics
- Relations between Taiwan and Mainland China
- Taiwan Independence Movement
- Taiwan's diplomatic relations with other countries
- Ethnic tensions between native Taiwanese and ethnic Chinese: Although the government claims it's committed to recognizing indigenous cultures (who share a common heritage with those of the South Pacific islands), natives still receive lower wages and have a higher unemployment rate than other citizens of Taiwan.

Body Language

In Taiwan, respect the following rules:
- Stand and sit up straight; people admire good posture.
- Never touch anyone, especially a baby, on top of the head. People believe that's where the soul resides.
- People don't approve of public displays of affection. Young women, however, commonly hold hands with one another in public.
- Don't put your arm around another person's shoulder. People aren't comfortable with such familiarity.
- Never use your feet to move or point to an object. People consider feet dirty because they're the lowest part of the body.
- Place your hands in your lap when sitting. People don't use many hand gestures.
- Men don't cross their legs; they keep both feet on the floor. Women cross their legs at the knee, taking care that their soles aren't exposed.
- Don't point with your index finger; doing so is a rude gesture. Instead, use an open hand.
- Moving your hand (palm face out) from side to side means "no."
- Never wink—people consider the gesture rude.
- To refer to themselves when speaking, people point to their noses.
- To beckon someone, extend your arm (palm down) then curl and extend your fingers together.

Chinese is a tonal language. That is, a word's meaning depends not only on pronunciation, but also on pitch.

The following phrases are only approximations. (The complexities of Chinese pronunciation are beyond the scope of this book.) Your colleagues in Taiwan will appreciate any attempt you make to speak a few words of the language. You'll pick up the nuances of common words' pronunciations by listening carefully and practicing at every opportunity. If you want to learn how to speak Chinese more accurately, use audio language sources or a comprehensive phrase book.

Note: No standard method of transliteration of characters exists in Taiwan. Different cities and municipalities have adopted different methods. Note, too, that spelling and pronunciation of the Chinese words and phrases in this chapter may differ slightly from those you encounter in Taiwan.

English	Chinese	Pronunciation
Hello/good afternoon/ good evening	*Nin hao*	(NEEN how)
Good morning (until 10:00 AM)	*Zao an*	(zaow AHN)
Goodbye	*Zaijian*	(dzeye JYEN)
Please	*Qing*	(chyeeng)
Thank you	*Xie xie*	(SYEH syeh)
You're welcome/ not at all	*Bu xie*	(boo SYEH)
Excuse me		
(when asking a question)	*Qing wen*	(chyeeng WEN)
(to get by someone)	*Lao jia*	(lay-ow JYEE-ah)
(to mean "I'm sorry")	*Duibuqi*	(doo-EE-boo-chyee)
Yes	*Dui*	(doo-EE)
No	*Bu shi*	(boo SHEE)

Dining

In general, dishes in Taiwan are less spicy than Szechuan food but more spicy than fare from northern China. Unlike chefs of the elaborate Shanghai or Guangdong cuisines, cooks in Taiwan prepare ingredients only once, then serve them.

In Taiwan, the people take great pride in their cuisine. Always show appreciation for the food.

- Most people in Taiwan eat with chopsticks and flat spoons (to eat soup). See page 41 for information on chopstick etiquette.
- Dining in Taiwan can be elaborate; banquets can offer up to twenty courses. (Be sure to pace yourself—eat first courses sparingly.)
- The host seats the guest of honor at the place facing the entrance. The host always sits opposite him or her.
- Hosts serve guests the first course. Guests help themselves to additional courses.
- Hosts often place food on a revolving tray on the center of the table.
- Restaurants in Taiwan serve excellent and relatively inexpensive food in a wide variety of Chinese cuisines. There also are many Western-style establishments.

Drinking

- Hosts commonly serve tea, juice, and rice wine (*Shaoxing* is a popular variety). They often serve whiskey or cognac during and after dinner.
- Coffee consumption is growing briskly in Taiwan, and the country has a small but prestigious coffee-growing industry. Locally produced beans are quite expensive.
- Beer brewed in Taiwan is good, and imported beer is available.
- Be careful if drinking *kaoliang*, a potent sorghum liquor.
- To thank someone who pours you a drink, tap the table next to the glass three times with your middle finger.
- Hosts may consider it their duty to get guests intoxicated. If you don't drink, or when you decide you've had enough, politely decline with an excuse (for example, "My health does not permit me to drink" or "I have to drive").

Toasting

Toasting is common in Taiwan. People propose toasts with wine or liquor before and during meals. Foreigners should pace themselves—toasting can go on for hours.

- To make a toast, the host raises a glass with both hands, one hand supporting the bottom of the glass.

- The toast *gan bei* (gahn bay) means "dry cup" or "bottoms up." After the toast, people drain their glasses, then turn them upside down to show they're empty. Participate in a few of these toasts to delight your hosts, but don't overdo it! In business situations, women especially should exercise restraint (perhaps participate in just one or two toasts to show respect).
- Hosts may propose a toast to someone and pass the person an empty glass, which the hosts then fill. People expect the person to toast the hosts and drain the glass.
- When you're the recipient of a toast, maintain direct eye contact with the person who is toasting you. Do the same when you're toasting someone.
- If you prefer not to drain your glass, immediately say *suei yi* (SWAY-yee), which means "to your liking," then drink the amount you want.
- It's acceptable for women to propose toasts.

Tipping

- Restaurants: The bill often includes a 10 percent service charge. If the bill doesn't include a service charge, a 10 percent tip is appropriate at expensive Chinese and Western restaurants. In small restaurants, tipping is unnecessary. You may leave small change for excellent service.
- Taxis: No tip is necessary, although you may give small change for good service or for handling luggage.
- Bellhops and porters: Tip TWD15 per piece of luggage.
- Hair stylists, barbers, and drivers: Tip TWD50 to TWD100.
- Restroom attendants: Tip TWD5 to TWD10.
- Coat-check attendants and maids: Tip TWD10 to TWD50.
- Ushers and gas station attendants: No tip is necessary.
- Guides and translators: Tip an amount appropriate to the amount of time and level of service. Ask your hotel concierge or a knowledgeable colleague for advice.

Manners

People in Taiwan are reserved, refined, and quiet. Never engage in loud, boisterous behavior when with them.
- Arrive on time for a dinner party. In Taiwan, there usually isn't a cocktail hour.

- Remove shoes upon entering a home. Hosts will provide slippers.
- Hosts usually offer guests beverages or candy. Out of politeness, take at least a few sips or bites.
- The hostess may spend most of a meal in the kitchen. Don't ask to help her or wander into the kitchen uninvited.
- Other guests and the host wait to eat any dish until the guest of honor has sampled it.
- It's appropriate to pick up your bowl and hold it close to your mouth when eating; don't let it rest on the table when eating from it.
- Compliment the hostess on the food. She'll likely decline the praise, but will appreciate it.
- When not using your chopsticks, place them on the chopstick rest or together on the table—never across the rim of your bowl.
- Never place bones or seeds in your rice bowl. Place them on a plate or on the table, if a plate isn't provided. In Taiwan, people may spit bones and seeds on the table or floor. They consider doing so more sanitary than removing them with fingers.
- When you're full, always leave some food in your bowl. If you empty your bowl, your host will refill it.
- Hosts often consider it a compliment for guests to belch at the end of a meal.
- Hosts serve tea to signal the end of the meal or party. Your hosts may invite you to stay longer, but they're just being polite. The guest of honor should leave first, with the other guests following promptly.
- As guests leave, hosts generally walk with them a distance. Guests should insist the hosts return home, but thank them for their effort.
- Always promptly send a thank-you note to your hosts after they've entertained you.
- Don't eat while walking on streets.
- When using a toothpick, cover your mouth with your hand.
- Stand as older or higher-ranking people enter a room.
- Revere the elderly. Hold doors for them, offer your seat to them, and so on.
- Give and receive items with both hands.
- At restaurants, the person who extended the invitation pays the bill. Out of politeness, guests will offer to pay (but they won't insist).
- See pages 75–85 for etiquette information when visiting a temple or other place of worship.

Punctuality

The people of Taiwan appreciate punctuality, but they don't mind when others are a few minutes early or late. They may be late for business meetings (often blaming traffic), or they may even skip them. Foreigners must be patient and flexible.

For social occasions, being "fashionably late" by fifteen to thirty minutes is acceptable, especially for weddings.

For a dinner party or a banquet, always arrive on time or early. For more information on banquet etiquette, see pages 38–39.

Dress

The people of Taiwan commonly wear conservative, neat clothing in Western styles. They often wear red and gold attire (colors symbolize luck and prosperity).

- Comfortable, lightweight clothing is best for summer months. Heavier clothing is necessary during the winter and in the mountains.
- For business occasions and at banquets, men wear suits and ties. They may remove jackets during meetings (foreigners should follow their hosts' lead). Women wear conservative tailored suits, dresses, pantsuits, or blouses with skirts—with little or no jewelry.
- At restaurants, men wear dressy pants and shirts. Women wear stylish pantsuits or dresses.
- For casual occasions, men wear slacks and cotton shirts. Women wear skirts or pants with modest blouses.
- To make a good impression, wear only clean high-quality shoes. Traditionally, only farmers wore sandals; avoid wearing them for a business or social occasion.
- Never wear black clothing to a wedding or red clothing to a funeral.
- Shorts are acceptable at the beach, but people generally consider them appropriate only for young people or when exercising.

Gifts

- The people of Taiwan don't open gifts in front of the giver. They thank the giver and set aside the gift to open later.
- When offered a gift, it's polite to refuse at least once and as many as three times. Immediate acceptance implies greed or arrogance. When giving

gifts, keep politely insisting that the recipients accept. When they finally do, say, "I am so pleased."
- Make sure to reciprocate a gift with one of equal value.
- Always give and receive a gift with both hands.
- Many people exchange "red envelopes." See page 58 for more information.
- Have gifts wrapped with great care in pink, red, or yellow gift-wrap (never white gift-wrap—for funerals only). A gift's presentation is as important as the gift itself.

Hostess Gifts

Always bring a small gift when invited to someone's home.

Consider giving
- Flowers in even numbers
- Books or arts and crafts from your home region
- American ginseng

Don't give
- Clocks (connote death)
- Knives (connote the severing of a relationship)
- Umbrellas (A homonym for the Chinese word for "umbrella" means the recipient's family is going to disperse.)
- Food gifts (imply your hosts aren't generous)
- Handkerchiefs (connote grief)

Business Gifts
- In Taiwan, it's common to exchange gifts at initial meetings and at the successful conclusion of negotiations.
- Always bring a small gift for your business host, who will certainly have one for you. Also bring a gift for each person on the host team, or bring the team a group gift.
- Be aware: Your colleagues from Taiwan give (and expect to receive) expensive gifts. Don't give token or poor-quality gifts.

Consider giving
- High-quality Scotch
- American ginseng
- Desk accessories

Don't give

- Clocks (connote death)
- Knives (connote the severing of a relationship)
- Umbrellas (A homonym for the Chinese word for "umbrella" means the recipient's family is going to disperse.)
- Items manufactured in Taiwan

Helpful Hints

- When traveling by taxi, take your hotel's business card (information written in Chinese) with you so the driver has the hotel's address for the return trip.
- Avoid using triangles (in your company logo, for example). In Taiwan, the triangle connotes negativity.
- Be prepared: People push and shove in lines for buses, trains, and taxis.
- At crowded restaurants, strangers may sit at your table. You needn't speak with them.

Health and Safety

- Before traveling to Taiwan, check current health precautions. Also check current travel warnings. (See page 373.)
- Health facilities in Taiwan are fully adequate for routine treatment and emergencies.
- Providers and hospitals may require immediate cash payment for services.
- Drink only boiled or bottled water. Hotels and major restaurants provide guests distilled or boiled water.
- Outside hotels and better restaurants, avoid eating raw fruits and vegetables.

> Taiwan is no stranger to natural disasters. In September 1999, an earthquake of 7.6 on the Richter scale shook the central region. More than nine thousand aftershocks followed, and more than two thousand people died.
>
> The country's often harsh typhoon season runs from April to October, but storms typically begin in July.

- Taiwan has abundant open-air food stalls, but their cleanliness varies. Eat only at those recommended by a trusted local person.

- To avoid contracting schistosomiasis and other parasitic diseases, wear shoes at all times and avoid swimming in fresh water.
- Taiwan is generally a safe country for visitors traveling alone, even at night—but use common sense.
- Avoid driving in Taiwan; traffic is terrible. Public transportation is generally safe.
- Be careful when crossing streets; drivers don't always stop for pedestrians.

Corporate Culture

Taiwan's business climate is competitive and its economy strong. Its unemployment rate is low, and the country has the world's third-largest foreign reserves.

Businesspeople in Taiwan are savvy about Western business customs. They believe this knowledge distinguishes them from their counterparts in Mainland China.

In 2004, eight of the top twenty-five companies in *Business Week*'s Info Tech 100 were based in Taiwan. Taiwan finished thirteenth in the rankings of the World Economic Forum's 2006–2007 Global Competitiveness Report, ahead of Canada and France.

Tensions between Taiwan and Mainland China haven't inhibited trade relations. Mainland China is Taiwan's largest export market and its third-largest source of imports.

Structure
- Most companies in Taiwan are small to medium-size. Many are family owned. Usually the patriarch makes final decisions, but businesses consult other family members and relatives for major decisions.
- Most businesspeople in Taiwan strive to own their own businesses.

Meetings
- Don't enter the room until your hosts invite you to do so.
- Even when the key decision maker isn't at the negotiating table (which is likely), always give presentations as though he or she were present. Participants will convey the information to him or her.
- Even though businesspeople in Taiwan generally get down to business in meetings, be prepared to engage in polite conversation before beginning serious discussions.
- To show respect, address comments to the group as a whole.
- Make presentations slowly and clearly, repeating key points.

- Don't push too hard or too fast when trying to reach an agreement. Let your hosts set the pace.

Appointments
- It's best to schedule meetings for dates between April and September. Always avoid scheduling meetings for the weeks before and after Chinese New Year.
- Your colleagues in Taiwan may appreciate meetings that begin no earlier than late morning (11:00 AM to 4:00 PM is the best time), because they may have entertained you late the previous night.
- Traffic is terrible in Taiwan. Allow plenty of time to get to appointments.
- Regular business hours are 8:30 AM to noon and 1:00 PM to 5:00 PM, Monday through Friday. Businesses are open Saturdays 8:30 AM to noon.

Communication
- Many businesspeople in Taiwan speak some English. Check in advance whether an interpreter is necessary. To prevent confusion and misunderstanding, speak slowly and use simple words and short sentences.
- Although more open and candid than other Asians, businesspeople in Taiwan avoid saying "no." They may say "we'll try" instead, or leave "no" unsaid.

Business Cards
- In Taiwan, people exchange business cards upon first meeting.
- Have your business cards printed in English on one side and in classical Chinese characters on the other. If planning to visit Mainland China, which uses simplified characters, mark the boxes of business cards in some way to avoid using cards with classical characters in Mainland China and simplified characters in Taiwan.
- On business cards, many people in Taiwan write the order of their names on the English side in the Western style (first name + last name). To make sure you don't mistake a last name for a first name (and vice versa), ask the person how you should address him or her.
- When arriving for a meeting, present your card to the receptionist.

Be Aware
- Taiwan is a large, competitive market. Pricing and after-sale service are crucial to success.
- It's common in Taiwan to get approval from a feng shui master before opening an office or factory. See pages 86–87 for more information.

- Lawyers aren't part of negotiations in Taiwan. People settle conflicts by arbitration, not through the courts.
- To avoid conflict, international organizations sometimes call Taiwan "Chinese Taipei."
- *Guanxi* (GWONG-she) is the web of relationships and obligations that ties people and businesses together. It's vital to any successful business arrangement in Taiwan.

     If negotiations with your colleagues break down, don't formally end them. Instead, to save face you (or your colleagues) should say, "Let's temporarily cease negotiations." If the deal ultimately falls through, never speak ill of your colleagues. Doing so may poison your *guanxi*.
- Personal relationships are essential to business success in Taiwan. People want to know you personally before doing business with you. Show commitment, sincerity, and respect for your hosts. Visit often and invite them to visit your home.

Socializing

- People in Taiwan do most business entertaining in restaurants, often well into the night. Choosing the right restaurant and entertaining well can greatly enhance your chances of business success.
- Don't discuss business during dinner unless your hosts bring up the subject. Dinners are an opportunity to build trust and rapport. Never regard them as a waste of time.
- After someone hosts a dinner for you, reciprocate with a invitation to a dinner of equivalent value.
- You may invite spouses to a business dinner. They may or may not attend.
- Banquets are an important part of business in Taiwan. See pages 38–39 for more information.

Especially for Women

Women in Taiwan play a more traditional role than do women in Europe or North America, but that role is changing rapidly. In 2003, Taiwan finished nineteenth in the world and first in Asia in the United Nation's Gender Empowerment Measure, which evaluates gender inequality in the economic and political spheres.

     Nearly half the women are in Taiwan's workplace. Women's educational achievement in Taiwan is equal to men's through the university level. More men, however, graduate from postgraduate programs. There are also few female elected officials in Taiwan.

- Foreign women can do business easily in Taiwan.
- If a foreign woman invites a man to business lunch or dinner in Taiwan, she should pay. The man will offer to pay (even though he'd rather not). To avoid a misunderstanding, arrange payment with the wait staff beforehand.
- To be safe, women should avoid traveling alone at night.

Holidays and Festivals

January	Founding Day of the Republic of China (1)
January/February	Chinese New Year*
February	Peace Memorial Day or 228 (28)**
April	Tomb Sweeping Day (5)
June	Dragon Boat Festival*
September/October	Mid-Autumn Festival*
October	Double Tenth National Day (10)

* The days of these holidays follow the lunar calendar. Check when they're celebrated for the year you're traveling to Taiwan.

** In 2005, 1.5 million residents formed a human chain nearly five hundred kilometers long to commemorate the 1947 massacre of tens of thousands of civilians and to promote peace.

THAILAND
KINGDOM OF THAILAND

Greetings from Thailand

Greetings from the "Land of the Free"—the Thai definition of *Thailand*. Our pleasant, humble, and patient people have earned our country another meaning: "Land of Smiles."

The Thai expression *mai pen rai* means "never mind," and it characterizes our general approach to life. Although we are productive and hardworking, we believe life is to be enjoyed.

We tolerate individualism, but find comfort and security in groups. Our families are the basis of our society. In rural areas, several generations may live under the same roof. Elders have superior status, and family members offer them humility, obedience, and respect.

Most of us are devout Theravada Buddhists. We expect our men over age twenty to serve as Buddhist monks for at least a few months, and many do. Buddhist philosophy guides every aspect of our lives. Even those of us who worship Hindu gods and animist spirits conform to Buddhist philosophy.

At the beginning of the twentieth century, our country (known then to foreigners as Siam) was the last territory not colonized by imperialist nations. Our astute diplomacy, shrewd accessions, and ability to play foreign powers against one another preserved our independence.

Today, Thailand is a constitutional monarchy, and we believe it is the most democratic nation in Southeast Asia. In 1997, we amended our constitution to make voting compulsory, encourage greater political participation, and reduce corruption.

In the past, we received international and American aid; today, we proudly donate to the global community. We sent troops to the international peace-keeping effort in East Timor and to Afghanistan and Iraq for reconstruction work. We also provide more aid (as a percentage of our income) to poorer countries than do many European countries.

Within our own borders, since 2000 we have cut the number of people living in poverty in half, and enrollment in primary education is almost universal. We are now working to decrease our poverty rate to 4 percent by 2009.

Controlling the AIDS epidemic has been a huge challenge for our nation, but we have had some success. By 1990, there had been 150,000 new cases of the disease every year. In 2004, thanks to numerous education programs and initiatives, that figure dropped to 25,000 annually. We have also worked to reduce the number of mother-to-child transmissions of HIV, and we have used surveillance, monitoring, and evaluation to help prevent and treat infections.

Despite our success, we know we still face many problems. For example, an ongoing Islamic separatist movement in southern Thailand has instigated a number of violent attacks. The distribution of wealth and resources between rural and urban, rich and poor, is uneven. Rapid economic growth has harmed our environment, and the damage makes sustainable economic growth a formidable challenge. Air pollution in our cities is among the world's worst.

These problems should not keep foreigners from visiting our wonderful country. We are proud of our culture and history. If you want to succeed in business here, you must study our ways. Do not attempt to westernize us or otherwise attempt to change us. If you accept us as we are, we will happily accept you.

Vital Statistics

Population	64,631,595
Capital	Bangkok
Area	198,457 square miles, slightly more than twice the size of Wyoming
Government	Constitutional monarchy
Living Standard	GDP = US $3,420 per capita
Natural Resources	Tin (world's third-largest producer), rubber, natural gas, tungsten (world's second-largest producer), tantalum, timber, lead, fish, gypsum, lignite, fluorite, arable land
Agriculture	Rice, cassava (tapioca), rubber, corn, sugarcane, coconuts, soybeans
Industries	Tourism, textiles and garments, agricultural processing, beverages, tobacco, cement, and light manufacturing like jewelry and electric appliances, computers and parts, integrated circuits, furniture, plastics, automobiles and automotive parts
Climate	Tropical; rainy, warm, cloudy southwest monsoon (mid-May to September); dry, cool northeast monsoon (November to mid-March); southern isthmus always hot and humid
Currency	Baht (THB)

The People

Correct Name	noun: Thai(s)
	adjective: Thai
Ethnic Makeup	Thai 75%, Chinese 14%, other 11%
Languages	Thai (official), English (secondary language of the elite), ethnic and regional dialects
Religions	Buddhist 94.6%, Muslim 4.6%, Christian 0.7%, other 0.1%

Meeting and Greeting

- In Thailand, introductions are common only in formal situations (for example, initial business meetings or meetings with government officials). A respected third party usually makes introductions, but if you must introduce yourself, make sure to give your first and last names. At social functions, you may introduce yourself by first name only.

- Thais always introduce people of lower rank first. For example, they introduce children before parents and secretaries before bosses.

- Thais traditionally greet one another with a *wai* (pronounced "why"), a gesture that means "hello," but can also mean "thank you," "I'm sorry," or "goodbye." A *wai* is a slight bow with the palms pressed together close to the chest (fingers together and pointing upward). The closer to face level the hands are, the more respectful the gesture. Subordinates may raise their fingers to eye level (but never above).

- Thais don't expect foreigners to initiate *wais*, but they appreciate foreigners' returning the gesture if given one.

- Thais don't use *wais* to greet children, servants, street vendors, or laborers. Never return the gesture to children, wait staff, clerks, or other people of lower rank. Simply nod and smile in response.

  Similarly, while Thais will offer a *wai* to monks, monks won't return the gesture.

- Thai businesspeople often shake hands with foreigners instead of offering *wais*. If not offered a *wai*, shake hands with men, and smile and nod to women.

Names and Titles

- Thai name order is first name (given name) + last name (surname). Nicknames are common.
- Titles and ranks are important. When possible, address Thais by military, professional, or academic title + first name.
- If there isn't a military, professional, or academic title, Thais address one another (men and women) by the courtesy title *Khun* (pronounced "koon") + first name. If you don't know a person's first name, address him or her simply by *Khun*.
- In correspondence, use Dear + *Khun* + first name.
- Thai last names are difficult to pronounce, even for Thais. (Families didn't use last names until 1913, when King Rama IV required everyone to adopt a last name.) They use last names in address only for very formal occasions and written communications.
- Thais often address foreigners by courtesy title + first name (not out of familiarity but out of ease).
- Don't address a Thai by just his or her first name unless specifically invited to do so.

Language

Thai is a tonal language with five distinct tones. That is, a word's meaning depends not only on pronunciation, but also on pitch. Thais don't expect foreigners to speak the tones correctly, but they appreciate foreigners' attempts to speak Thai. Even when you speak the tones incorrectly, Thais will tell you, "*Poot Thai geng geng*," which means "You speak Thai very well!"

International businesspeople and other educated Thais often speak relatively fluent English. Especially in Bangkok, most Thais employed in the travel industry usually speak some English. (The exception is taxi drivers.)

There isn't a standard way to transliterate the Thai alphabet (which was likely invented by King Ramkhamhaeng in 1283) into English. As a result, there are often multiple English spellings for the same Thai word. For example, *krap* may also be spelled *krub*.

Written Thai doesn't put spaces between words; spaces indicate the end of a clause or sentence.

Conversation

- Don't speak loudly or show your temper.
- Never criticize anyone publicly.
- If a Thai criticizes Thailand (its pollution problem, for example), don't agree. Instead, reply, "It's fine."
- Be aware that Thais prefer indirect language and don't appreciate bluntness.
- Thais may ask your age or your income as a way to express interest. If you're uncomfortable answering the question, give a vague answer or say, "In my country, that would be a strange question."
- Thais have a wonderful sense of humor. Enjoy it with laughter and smiles.

Acceptable topics

- Someone's family—but only after you've developed a relationship: Don't compliment babies or children; some Thais believe praise attracts evil spirits.
- Travel
- Your positive experiences in Thailand
- Local cuisine
- Sports and games, especially football (soccer), tennis, *muay thai* (Thai boxing), *takraw* (similar to volleyball), and *makruk* (similar to chess)

Unacceptable topics

- Criticisms of Buddhism or its practitioners
- Criticisms of the monarchy: It's a crime to criticize or defame the royal family.
- Thailand's war against illegal drugs
- Personal problems

> In 2006, King Bhumibol, the world's longest-serving monarch, celebrated his sixtieth year on the throne. His constant concern for his people has led Thais to declare him the "soul of our nation." They consider him inviolable and sacred—almost a deity.

- Thailand's sex trade: All prostitution is illegal in Thailand, and the government is using domestic and international resources to destroy the trade that has tarnished the country's reputation. Most Thais adhere to a strict Buddhist code of conduct and don't want to discuss a topic that contradicts their beliefs so extremely.

Body Language

- Thais disapprove of public displays of affection.
- People of the same sex touch one another more often in Thailand than in many other Asian countries; however, touching someone of the opposite

sex is taboo. Traditional Thais believe a woman loses face if a man touches her in public.

- Never touch anyone on the head or pass something over a person's head. Tradition holds that the soul resides there.

- Thais consider the foot unclean because it's the lowest part of the body. Never point your feet at anyone or use your feet to move anything or touch anyone. Also, don't cross your legs in the company of others, especially elderly people or monks (you may inadvertently show the sole of your shoe).

- From a desire to maintain harmony, Thais smile to express embarrassment, remorse, resignation, fear, or even anger. As a result, Thais often smile at seemingly inappropriate situations.

- Don't wave your hands while talking. Thais will think you're angry.

- Never gesture or pass anything with your left hand. Instead, when giving or receiving an object, use your right hand and hold your right forearm with your left hand.

- Never point with an index finger. To indicate the direction of an item, casually motion your open right hand in the appropriate direction.

- To beckon someone, extend your arm (palm down) and flutter your fingers.

- Be prepared to have people stare at you, especially if you have fair skin, blond hair, and blue eyes. Don't be offended; they're just curious.

Phrases

The following phrases are only approximations. (The complexities of Thai pronunciation are beyond the scope of this book.) Your Thai colleagues will appreciate any attempt you make to speak a few words of the language. You'll pick up the nuances of common words' pronunciations by listening carefully and practicing at every opportunity. If you want to learn how to speak Thai more accurately, use audio language sources or a comprehensive phrase book.

English	Thai	Pronunciation
Hello/Goodbye*		
(said by men)**	*Sawatdee krap*	(sahw-waht-DEE KRAHP)
(said by women)	*Sawatdee kha*	(sahw-waht-DEE KAH)
Hello (literally, "Where are you going?")	*Pai mai*	(pie-MY)
For a walk (polite response to *Pai mai*)	*Pai theo*	(pie tay-OH)

English	Thai	Pronunciation
Goodbye		
(said by a man leaving)	*Lah gawn krap*	(law-gahn KRAHP)
(said by a woman leaving)	*Lah gawn kha*	(law-gahn KAH)
Please	*Dai proad*	(die-PROO-nah)
Thank you		
(said by a man)	*Kawp-kun krap*	(kawp-KOON KRAHP)
(said by a woman)	*Kawp-kun kha*	(kawp-KOON KAH)
You're welcome		
(said by a man)	*Mai pen rai krap*	(MY-pen-rye KRAHP)
(said by a woman)	*Mai pen rai kha*	(MY-pen-rye KAH)
Yes		
(said by a man)	*Chai krap*	(chye KRAHP)
(said by a woman)	*Chai kha*	(chye KAH)
No		
(said by a man)	*Mai chai krap*	(my-CHYE KRAHP)
(said by a woman)	*Mai chai kha*	(my-CHYE KAH)

* Thais use these expressions as a general greeting at any time of day and also as a farewell when they're the ones staying.

** As a polite way to show respect to the listener, men say *krap* at the end of most expressions, and women say *kha*.

Dining

Thai food may be sweet, sour, hot, salty, or spicy—it's never bland. Almost every meal includes rice, and many dishes include herbs and spices like lemon grass and coriander. Many use dried red peppers, which are among the world's most piquant and can overwhelm the Western palate. People new to Thai cuisine should request "medium" spicing, not "hot."

- Thais eat food with forks and spoons. They hold the spoon in the right hand and the fork in the left, and use the fork to push food onto the spoon. Put only the spoon into your mouth.

- Thais don't eat directly from the serving dish; they eat from individual bowls.
- Restaurants in better hotels serve Western and continental dishes as well as Thai cuisine.
- Thai buffets are informal. Hosts expect guests to serve themselves.
- Hostesses may wait until everyone else has eaten to eat their own meals.

Banquets

- Hosts customarily serve banquets in a teak-paneled room, usually beginning at 8:00 PM.
- Thai dancers perform before and during the meal, and the guest of honor sits at the table closest to the dancing.
- The host may or may not sit near the guest of honor.
- Hosts serve rice first, then place several dishes on the center of the table. Guests serve themselves; they don't pass dishes.
- Thais eat only one dish at a time with their rice. Don't mix different dishes on your plate.
- Use your spoon to cut food.
- It's impolite to leave a lot of food on your plate. Leave just a few bites to show you've had enough to eat.

Drinking

- Fruit juices and soft drinks are widely available. Ask for Pepsi or cola (Coca-Cola), and you'll usually get one or the other.
- Thais enjoy coconut water (the liquid from the center of a coconut). Freshly prepared and chilled, it's delicious.
- Although the Thai government regulates how and when alcohol may be advertised, alcohol consumption has risen in recent years. Beer is popular but expensive by Thai standards. Many consider Singha beer, Thailand's first original beer, one of Asia's best. Its slightly bitter taste complements spicy Thai food.
- Be careful if drinking *lao khao*, a potent distilled rice liquor.
- Some devout Buddhists don't drink alcohol, and most Thais don't drink to excess in polite company; drunkenness violates the Buddhist sense of humility and reserved behavior.
- Thais consume most of the tea grown in Thailand. They often serve iced tea flavored with cinnamon and star anise or ground tamarind. They commonly

serve hot tea with sweetened condensed milk. Tea served in restaurants may be much weaker than Americans are used to.

- Thais drink coffee (often instant rather than brewed) laced with sweetened condensed milk.

Toasting

Toasting isn't a Thai tradition, but Thais don't oppose the custom. In fact, the guest of honor should propose a toast to thank the host sometime during the meal.

- When proposing a toast, preface it with "Please allow me to express my happiness about [our friendship, our partnership, or other appropriate subject]." Then give one of these Thai toasts:
  * *Chok-dee* (choke-DEE), which means "good luck."
  * *Chai yo* (CHYE yoh), which also means "good luck." Among friends, when one person shouts *chai*, the rest of the group may respond with *yo*.
- At a bar, Thais may give the toast *Chon gow* (CHOHN gah-oh), which means "hit glasses." Everyone then clinks glasses before drinking.
- Toasts in English are acceptable, as are short, personal accompanying stories.
- Women may propose toasts.

Tipping

- Hotels: The bill normally includes a 10 to 15 percent service charge.
- Restaurants: The bill may include a 10 to 15 percent service charge. If the bill doesn't include a service charge, leave a 10 percent tip. Also leave loose change, but only if it totals more than THB1. Thais consider a tip up to THB1 an insult.
- Taxis: Tip 10 percent of the fare. Bargain for the fare before entering a taxi.
- Bellhops: Tip the equivalent of US $1 to US $2.
- Porters: Airports and railway stations post signs specifying charges.
- Hair stylists and barbers: Tip 10 percent of the bill.

Manners

- Carefully step over the threshold when entering a home. Tradition holds that souls reside in thresholds.
- After entering someone's home, remove your shoes if your host isn't wearing shoes.

- If the host sits on the floor, do the same but don't expose the soles of your feet or shoes.
- Don't begin eating until the host invites you to start.
- Don't refuse an offer for food. If you don't like a dish, discreetly avoid it, but don't express displeasure. Thais appreciate visitors who like Thai food. Hosts usually serve guests second helpings and insist they eat more.
- Don't use your left hand to pass items or eat.
- Never eat the last servings of any dish. Thais offer servants leftovers.
- When finished eating, leave a small amount of food on your plate and place your fork and spoon side by side diagonally across the upper right quadrant of your plate.
- Make sure you don't excessively praise an item. If you do, the owner may feel obliged to give it to you as a gift.
- Don't put your hands in your pockets while talking to someone.
- Don't drape an arm on the back of a chair when someone is sitting in it.
- Cover your mouth when using a toothpick.
- Never step over someone lying on the floor or sidewalk.
- Don't photograph anyone, especially a Buddhist monk, without permission.
- To beckon wait staff, extend your hand (palm down) and flutter your fingers. Never snap your fingers or raise your voice. Address wait staff by *nong* (pronounced "nohng").

> I know a Thai family who once hosted an American exchange student. When the Thai son began avoiding the exchange student, the American boy asked his host brother what he had done. The Thai boy burst into tears and explained that the American had embarrassed him at school. Every morning, while the Thai national anthem was played, the young American would tap his foot. Thais view such behavior as disrespectful to the king and the Thai people.

- At a restaurant, the person who extended the invitation pays the bill. Never offer to split the bill; doing so will insult the host. (At food stalls, however, Thais generally split the bill.)
- Always show great respect for the royal family. Stand still when the Thai national anthem is played.
- See pages 75–85 for etiquette information when visiting a wat or other places of worship.

Punctuality

In Thailand, there are two senses of time: *nat farang* or "foreign time," which implies punctuality, and *nat Thai* or "Thai time," which implies a more relaxed attitude toward time.

Thais aren't in a hurry. They appreciate foreigners' punctuality but are often late themselves. If they're late, don't show disapproval. Thais believe establishing relationships is more important than being punctual.

Dress

Many Thais wear clothing in Western styles. In general, their attire is stylish and lightweight (to accommodate Thailand's hot, humid climate). It's informal but always neat and clean.

- For business occasions, men wear dressy trousers and shirts, with or without ties and sometimes with lightweight jackets (which add status). Senior executives wear lightweight suits. Women wear tailored suits.
- For casual occasions and at most restaurants, men wear cotton trousers and shirts (often batik shirts) without ties. Women wear skirts or pants with cotton blouses.
- Especially for formal occasions, Thais dress to match their social stations. They greatly admire wealth, and upper-class Thais often overdress. Thai women, in particular, always dress extremely well in Thai silks and designer clothing—but never anything that's revealing, like sheer or low-cut dresses or miniskirts. These garments offend the Buddhist sense of modesty.

  Men wear dark suits or formal Thai shirts and ties. Top international restaurants and formal banquets may require men to wear this attire.
- Always take a sweater, shawl, or lightweight jacket to air-conditioned restaurants. They're often too cool.
- Never wear black at a party in someone's home. Black is the color of mourning.
- Always dress modestly when in or near any temple, including its compound.
- Shorts are appropriate to wear only at beaches or resorts.

Gifts

Gift giving in Thailand is less formal than elsewhere in Asia.
- Thais generally don't open gifts in front of the giver unless invited to do so.
- Always give and receive gifts with your right hand only. Also offer a *wai*, if appropriate (see page 20).

Hostess Gifts

Always bring a small gift when invited to someone's home. The family will also appreciate small gifts for any children.

Consider giving
- Fruit baskets
- Flowers, except carnations and marigolds (for funerals only)
- Pastries or candy
- Brandy or other liquor
- Recordings of music

Don't give
- Knives, letter openers, or other sharp objects (connote the severing of a relationship)
- Personal items

Business Gifts

- Thais may exchange small gifts after the successful conclusion of negotiations.
- If you want to bring a gift to an initial meeting, tell the Thai company secretary or protocol officer when scheduling the meeting. Doing so prepares your hosts so they can give you a reciprocal gift and save face.
- Bring a small gift for anyone who works for you regularly.

Consider giving
- Brandy or other liquor
- Pastries
- American arts and crafts
- Books
- Desk accessories
- Items that feature your company logo

Don't give
- Knives, letter openers, or other sharp objects (connote the severing of a relationship)
- Personal items

> Thais may invite you to a religious ceremony, perhaps in conjunction with the opening of an office or factory. Give the host an envelope with money (THB100 to THB200) at the ceremony to please the spirits.

Helpful Hints

- Bargain everywhere except in major department stores. Merchants' first price is often two to three times the fair price. They expect shoppers to bargain with them.
- Watch out for "friendly" strangers who offer to guide you to a vendor selling overpriced gems. Don't fall for this scam, which claims too many victims every year. Contact the Tourism Authority of Thailand (http://tatnews.org) to find current advice on buying gemstones in Thailand.
- Before getting into a *tuk-tuk* (three-wheeled automotive taxi), agree on a fare with the driver.
- At crowded restaurants, strangers may sit at your table. You needn't speak with them.

Health and Safety

- Drink only bottled water or water that's been boiled for at least ten minutes. Avoid using ice.
- Avoid eating dairy products like milk and ice cream. Most aren't pasteurized.
- Except in first-class hotels and restaurants, avoid eating raw or unpeeled fruits and vegetables. Make sure meats have been cooked thoroughly.
- Several people have died of avian influenza (bird flu) in Thailand since 2003. While visitors aren't likely to contract the disease, avoid contact with live poultry and poultry feces (for example, on farms or at markets), and eat only fully cooked poultry and eggs.
- Thailand's air quality is poor, especially in Bangkok. People with respiratory ailments should talk to their physicians before traveling to Thailand.
- Medical treatment in Thailand is generally good, especially in Bangkok. Many newly built hospitals provide 24-hour emergency services. Call your embassy or consulate for advice on providers, clinics, or hospitals.
- Providers and hospitals often expect immediate cash payment for services.
- Bangkok has numerous pharmacies, but prescriptions must be written in Thai.
- Be aware: the composition of over-the-counter medications may not be the same as those in the United States.
- To avoid contracting schistosomiasis and other parasitic diseases, don't go barefoot outdoors and avoid swimming in fresh water.

- Be careful when swimming in the ocean. The undercurrents can be incredibly strong. Some beaches use a flag system to indicate the danger of undercurrents: green is safe, yellow is caution, red is dangerous.
- Drug sale and use is illegal in Thailand, and the penalties are severe (from heavy fines to harsh prison sentences to death). Never accept offers from people who claim they can get drugs for you.
- Thailand is relatively safe for foreigners, but petty crimes like pickpocketing are common in areas where tourists gather, particularly on buses and near hotels. Travelers should be careful when arriving at New Bangkok International Airport, particularly at night.
- Don't travel outside metro areas (especially to southern Thailand and the Thai/ Burmese border) without current information about military or insurgent activity in the regions.
- Ask trustworthy people to recommend reputable bars and nightclubs. Don't leave your drink or food unattended. Unscrupulous people may drug the food or beverages of victims, then rob them.
- Avoid driving in Thailand. Traffic is very heavy in metro areas. Rent a car service, hire a taxi, or take public transportation.
- Ask your hotel to call a reputable taxi company for you. Don't get into a taxi that has anyone other than the driver in it.
- Use overhead walkways to cross roads whenever available. Even with a green light, look both ways and be alert while crossing a street.
- Be wary of traveling by boat in Thailand. Ferries and speedboats can be overcrowded and often don't carry enough life preservers.

> Critics have raised concerns about Thailand's strict drug trafficking laws, but Thais are unmoved. The country is located along a major route for heroin trafficking, and opium production has been a problem.
>
> Thailand's zero-tolerance policy for drug offenses has minimized the nation's opium production, and Thais strongly believe they must continue to do whatever is necessary to keep drugs out of their country.

Corporate Culture

Structure

- Many companies are privately held, and top executives are members of the owning families.

- Businesses make decisions slowly and cautiously. All levels of management weigh in on options, but top executives make final decisions.

Meetings

- Be prepared for extended negotiations. First meetings are generally for getting acquainted; Thais consider discussing business with strangers rude behavior. Second meetings usually include an invitation to a meal.
- During presentations, modestly explain your firm's successes. Use charts, graphs, photos, blueprints, and other data necessary to establish credibility.

Appointments

- Large companies prefer or insist on scheduled appointments. Propose several dates for initial meetings.
- Normal business hours are 8:00 AM to 5:00 PM, Monday through Friday. Many businesses are open Saturdays until noon.
- Try to schedule meetings for between 10:00 AM and 3:00 PM. Avoid scheduling earlier or later appointments; rush hour traffic is horrendous.
- November through March is the best time for a business trip to Thailand. Try not to schedule business trips for dates in April and May (when Thais typically take vacations), during the Songkran Festival in April, or around Christmas.
- Always allow ample travel time to appointments. Traffic is a major problem, especially in Bangkok. Try to stay in a hotel that's close to where you'll be doing business.

Communication

- Thai is the official language, but many businesspeople speak English. Check in advance whether an interpreter is necessary. If discussing particularly important issues, use an interpreter to help avoid confusion.
- Always remember that Thais prefer indirect language and don't appreciate bluntness. Don't expect direct answers, and be subtle when disagreeing.
- Have contracts written in both Thai and English.
- Personal contact is essential to developing business relationships in Thailand. If possible, hire a reliable local agent to represent you in your absence.

Business Cards

- Business cards are important in Thai business.
- Have your information printed in Thai on one side of your card and in English on the other side.

- Upon introduction, hand your business card (Thai-side up) to the most senior Thai person first.
- Receptionists may ask visitors for their business cards.

Be Aware

- Thais keep their business and personal lives separate, but family comes before business.
- If possible, have a well-connected Thai introduce you to potential colleagues or clients. Thais place a lot of weight on whom you know.
- Status is important in Thai companies. Workers may seek prestigious titles more than salary increases.
- Thais prefer to work late into the evening rather than early in the morning.
- Although ethnic Chinese compose only about 10 percent of the Thai population, they dominate the business community and their money dominates politics.
- Thailand encourages foreign investment. The foreign investment board grants lucrative tax incentives to foreign investors.
- Thai negotiators get what they want while appearing shy, retiring, and hospitable. Don't ever underestimate these savvy businesspeople.

Socializing

Entertaining is essential to doing business in Thailand.
- Thais do most business entertaining in restaurants, usually at dinner. It's an honor to be invited to a Thai's home.
- Minimize business talk while eating; meals are social events.
- Thai companies may host a lunch shortly after meeting colleagues or clients. The meal is for getting acquainted, not for discussing business.
- After a dinner in Bangkok, Thai businesspeople may take visitors to visit the famous Patpong Road district.
- Traditional evenings out are for men only, with fancy dinners, nightclubs, and dancing with charming hostesses. Wives aren't included.

Especially for Women

Although the 1997 constitution improved the legal status of women in Thailand, there are still inequities in specific laws, including divorce laws. Although the Thai government abolished polygamy in 1935, a man may still have an "unofficial" second wife. Trafficking of Thai women is a serious problem.

Women compose nearly half the Thai workforce, but there's still discrimination in the workplace. Men conduct most business.

Thai women are nevertheless advancing. A 2005 survey on gender equality ranked Thailand best in the Asia-Pacific region, beating Australia and New Zealand. More women than men are enrolled in post-secondary education in Thailand, and more Thai women are holding executive positions, especially in banking and finance.

- Foreign businesswomen can succeed in Thailand, but they should be prepared to defer to men.
- A foreign businesswoman may invite a Thai man to a business dinner. She shouldn't invite his spouse and should arrange payment with the wait staff beforehand.
- Try to travel with others at night or in remote areas.

Holidays and Festivals	
January	New Year's Day (1)
February/March	Makha Bucha*
April	Chakri Day (6)
	Songkran Festival
May	Labor Day (1)
	Coronation Day (5)
	Visakha Bucha*
July	Buddhist Lent*
August	Queen's Birthday (12)
October	Chulalongkorn Day (23)
December	King's Birthday (5)
	Constitution Day (10)
	New Year's Eve (31)

* The dates of these holidays follow the lunar calendar. Check when they're celebrated during the year you're visiting Thailand.

VIETNAM
SOCIALIST REPUBLIC OF VIETNAM

Greetings from Vietnam

Greetings from a stunningly beautiful land whose people have an indomitable spirit. We Vietnamese value harmony and work hard to establish and maintain pleasant relationships.

Our history has challenged our desire to keep the peace. For more than a millennium, China controlled our nation. In 939 AD, we finally regained our independence. A number of dynasties followed, until in 1802 the Nguyen dynasty unified our nation.

Our independence was threatened again when Napoleon III decided to invade our country in 1857. After battling the French for thirty years, we at last succumbed and became a French territory. Although Japan occupied our land during World War II, France again fought us for control after the war. In 1954, the French were finally ousted, but our country was split into two separate states: North and South Vietnam.

From the moment of separation, we longed for reunification. But debate over how we should reunite led to the terrible war that many Americans will forever associate with our country, even though it ended over thirty years ago.

Known to the rest of the world as the Vietnam War, the "American War," as we call it, killed nearly sixty thousand Americans and perhaps up to three million Vietnamese. We knew we would win the war: millennia of fighting for independence had made us resolute and resourceful. American troops withdrew from our country in 1973, and three years later Vietnam was reunited as a Communist state.

After reunification, we tried to build our nation's economy with a state-run collectivist plan—but the results were not impressive. In 1986 we instituted our *doi moi* ("renovation") policy that introduced market reforms and greatly improved our economy. Our gross domestic product grew at an average of almost 7 percent between 1997 and 2004—substantial growth, especially as it occurred during the worst of the Asian economic crisis. We have become the world's second-largest rice exporter (we once had to import our food), and our agricultural production has doubled. Our domestic savings rate is at 30 percent.

This growth has benefited our people immensely, especially our children. For example, our infant mortality rate has dropped by nearly 75 percent since 1960, and nearly all our children are enrolled in primary schools.

Our political stability has attracted foreign investment and boosted our economic development. Over the last twenty years, foreign investment has tripled. In January 2007 we became members of the World Trade Organization. Our leaders have pledged to pursue legal reform and economic integration, and to fight government corruption.

> In July 2005, Prime Minister Phan Van Khai went to Washington, the first time a Vietnamese leader had visited the United States since the Vietnam War. Most Vietnamese today are eager for their country to reconcile with the United States. More than half the population was born after the war, and most welcome Americans and American companies.

We still have problems to solve. Despite our economic growth, Vietnam is a poor nation. The gap between the rural and urban populations is growing, and our poorest people live in remote areas that are difficult to reach and improve. Although we have improved access to safe water and sanitation, only about one-third of rural Vietnamese have access to adequate sanitation systems. Our government may be stable, but many citizens believe it restricts too many liberties. Many Vietnamese are working for more political freedom and freedom of information, including full Internet access.

Despite its challenges, Vietnam is a delightful place for work or play. Our landscape is breathtaking, our cities are vibrant (especially their nightlife), and our people are warm, friendly, and ready to greet you.

Vital Statistics

Population	84,402,966
Capital	Hanoi
Area	127,244 square miles, slightly larger than New Mexico
Government	Communist state
Living Standard	GDP = US $790 per capita
Natural Resources	Phosphates, coal, manganese, bauxite, chromate, offshore oil and gas deposits, forests, hydropower
Agriculture	Paddy rice, coffee, rubber, cotton, tea, pepper, soybeans, cashews, sugarcane, peanuts, bananas, poultry, fish, seafood

Vital Statistics (*cont.*)

Industries	Food processing, garments, shoes, machine building, mining, coal, steel, cement, chemical fertilizer, glass, tires, oil, paper
Climate	Tropical in south; monsoonal in north with hot, rainy season (May to September) and warm, dry season (October to March)
Currency	Dong (VND)

The People

Correct Name	noun: Vietnamese (singular and plural)
	adjective: Vietnamese
Ethnic Makeup	Kinh (Viet) 86.2%, Tay 1.9%, Thai 1.7%, Muong 1.5%, Khome 1.4%, Hoa 1.1%, Nun 1.1%, Hmong 1%, others 4.1%
Languages	Vietnamese (official); English (increasingly favored as a second language); some French, Chinese, and Khmer; mountain area languages (Mon-Khmer and Malayo-Polynesian)
Religions	Buddhist 9.3%, Catholic 6.7%, Hoa Hao 1.5%, Cao Dai 1.1%, Protestant 0.5%, Muslim 0.1%, none 80.8%

Meeting and Greeting

- The Vietnamese generally shake hands as a greeting and a farewell. They use the free hand to cover the handshake, and bow their heads slightly to show respect.

- Traditionally, the Vietnamese greeted one another by pressing their palms together in front of themselves and bowing slightly (similar to the *wai* in Thailand). Today, only Buddhist monks and nuns give this greeting. If someone greets you this way, respond in kind.

- Elderly people may not shake hands. Bow slightly to those who don't extend a hand.

- Some Vietnamese, especially women, may be shy upon meeting strangers. To show respect, they may not smile and will just give a nod.

- Outside of business settings, Vietnamese women usually bow instead of shaking hands.

- Some women may hug relatives and close friends as a greeting.

Names and Titles

- Name order is last name (surname) + middle name + first name (given name).
- There are only about a couple hundred different surnames for the over eighty million ethnic Vietnamese. For this reason, people address one another by courtesy or professional title + first name.
- The Vietnamese commonly address foreigners by courtesy title + first name.
- Men's middle names may be generational; that is, all male siblings may have the same middle name. Common middle names are Van, Huu, Duc, Dinh, Xuan, Ngoc, Quang, and Cong.
- Less so today than a generation ago, women may include *Thi* (or *thi*) as a traditional second middle name (or as the only middle name).

    Example: Nguyen Thi Kim Phuong
- Vietnamese women don't take their husbands' last names after marrying. In social situations, especially with Westerners, a woman may introduce herself as Mrs. (husband's first name), but she uses her own name in business.

    Example: Nguyen Thi Kim Phuong is married to Le Doan Hop. She uses her own name in business, but may introduce herself as Mrs. Hop at a party.
- Relatives may address one another by their relationship (for example, "my brother" or "my nephew"). To show respect, close friends may address one another by these terms as well.

English	Vietnamese	Pronunciation
Sir	*Ong*	(um)
Madam	*Ba*	(bah)
Miss	*Co*	(coh)

Language

Vietnamese is a tonal language with six distinct tones. That is, a word's meaning depends not only on pronunciation, but also on pitch. Speakers in north, south, and central Vietnam each have their own accent.

Vietnamese was written in characters until the seventeenth century, when Catholic missionaries devised a system for writing the language in Roman characters. The alphabet includes diacritical marks that dictate word intonation and vowel pronunciation.

English is the most popular foreign language studied among Vietnamese high-school students. Older businesspeople aren't likely to speak English well, but younger ones may. Many older Vietnamese speak French, and some speak Russian. Many ethnic minorities speak their own languages.

Conversation

- To Americans, the Vietnamese may appear shy and reserved. They dread losing face and thus will avoid conflict at nearly any cost. They consider bluntness vulgar, and they prefer using indirect language. They avoid giving negative answers and may even give positive ones just to avoid embarrassment.
- The Vietnamese have an excellent sense of humor, but they often need to establish a relationship before showing it.
- In Vietnam, age gives status, and the Vietnamese may ask how old you are. Answer truthfully. If you'd rather not give an answer, say, "In my country, that would be a strange question."
- Don't brag to the Vietnamese. Bragging is offensive because it emphasizes the individual, not the group. It also may cause another person to lose face.

> Families are the foundation of Vietnamese society, and family ties can transcend economic and political differences. The Vietnamese worship their ancestors and revere elders. Especially in rural areas, several generations may live under one roof.
>
> With that said, the Vietnamese no longer arrange marriages and are older when they marry, largely due to urbanization and increased education and work opportunities.

Acceptable topics

- Family: Ask about a person's parents, spouse, and children.
- Local cuisine
- Vietnam's natural beauty, especially its beautiful, clean seashores: Once the vacation spots of French colonists, today they're largely frequented by locals.
- Travel

Unacceptable topics

- Politics: The Communist party is the only legal political party.
- Deaths or accidents (considered unlucky to discuss)
- Vietnam's environmental problems, including deforestation, soil degradation, water pollution, and contaminated groundwater (all consequences of industrialization)
- Ethnic and religious minorities in Vietnam: Both face discrimination and even persecution.

> When in Hanoi and when talking to government or party officials, refer to Ho Chi Minh City as such—don't use the name Saigon. When talking with locals of the city, however, you may use Saigon. Local people prefer that name to Ho Chi Minh City, which the Hanoi government imposed in 1976.

Topics that require sensitivity

- Religion
- History, especially regional history: The Vietnamese likely have a notably different perspective than Americans have.

Body Language

- The Vietnamese frown upon public displays of affection between men and women.
- As a sign of friendship, people of the same sex may hold hands or link pinkies while walking.

> Much to the dismay of the Vietnamese government and the older generation, young people in cities are kissing, hugging, and holding hands in public.
>
> Curiously (to most Americans), it's perfectly acceptable for men to urinate on street curbs.

- Eye contact between strangers or even acquaintances is uncommon.
- The Vietnamese consider the foot unclean because it's the lowest part of the body. Never point your sole at anyone, and never move an object with your foot.
- Because foreigners are still relatively uncommon in Vietnam, locals (especially children) may stare at them.
- The Vietnamese believe slouching and bad posture show disrespect.
- In the north, nodding and saying "yes" conveys understanding, not agreement. In the south, however, these actions convey approval.

The following phrases are only approximations. (The complexities of Vietnamese pronunciation are beyond the scope of this book.) Your Vietnamese colleagues will appreciate any attempt you make to speak a few words of the language. You'll pick up the nuances of common words' pronunciations by listening carefully and practicing at every opportunity. If you want to learn how to speak Vietnamese more accurately, use audio language sources or a comprehensive phrase book.

English	Vietnamese	Pronunciation
Hello/goodbye (informal)	*Chao*	(chow)
(said to a man)	*Chao ong*	(CHOW um)
(said to a woman)	*Chao ba*	(CHOW bah)
(said to a young woman)	*Chao co*	(CHOW coh)
Hello/goodbye (formal, used to express respect and in correspondence)		
(said to a man)	*Xin chao ong*	(seen CHOW um)
(said to a woman)	*Xin chao ba*	(seen CHOW bah)
(said to a young woman)	*Xin chao co*	(seen CHOW coh)
Do you have good health? (polite inquiry after greeting)		
(in the north)	*Co manh gioi khong?*	(gaw mahn ZHOI cum)
(in the south)	*Co manh gioi khong?*	(gaw mahn YOY cum)
Please	*Xin*	(seen)
	Xin moi	(SEEN moy)
Thank you	*Cam on*	(KAM un)
You're welcome	*Khong co chi*	(CUM gaw chee)
Yes	*Co*	(gaw)
No	*Khong*	(kong)
Excuse me	*Xin loi*	(seen low-OY)
Pleased to meet you	*Han hanh gap ban*	(huhn hanh GAHP bahn)
How are you?	*Bahn ko-eh kong*	(bahn koh-EH kong)

Dining

Influenced by French and Chinese cuisines, Vietnamese fare is among the world's tastiest.

- Rice is a staple dish, served at every meal but breakfast.
- A soup called *pho* with beef (*bo*), chicken (*ga*), or pork (*heo*) is virtually the national dish, commonly served for breakfast.
- *Nuoc mam*, a fermented fish sauce, is the primary seasoning of Vietnamese cuisine.
- The Vietnamese use chopsticks to eat noodles, meat, and vegetables, and use flat spoons (held in the left hand) to eat broth. See page 41 for information on chopstick etiquette.
- For most occasions, hosts place serving dishes on the center of the table and invite guests to help themselves. If the meal is particularly formal, hosts don't let guests serve themselves. They make sure guests have enough food.
- Vietnamese dining is a social occasion. Be prepared for constant interaction and lively conversation between hosts and guests.
- Street-side dining is everywhere; local markets sell king cobras alongside noodle stands.

> Vietnam nobility once followed detailed chopstick etiquette. Even today, many Vietnamese can determine another's education and upbringing by the way he or she handles chopsticks.
>
> The Vietnamese don't expect foreigners to know all the intricacies of chopstick etiquette, but they do expect visitors to heed two rules: Never lay your chopsticks across a bowl (doing so symbolizes death), and never use your chopsticks to point or gesture at others.

Drinking

- At receptions and meetings, the Vietnamese serve strong tea in tiny cups as part of a hospitality ritual. Never refuse a cup.
- The Vietnamese serve tea, coffee, mineral water, soft drinks, and beer at meals.
- 333 (pronounced "bah-bah-bah") is Vietnam's most famous beer. Tiger Beer and Heineken are the most popular imports.
- Brandy and whiskey are the most popular spirits.

- Although drinking alcohol in public is less a social stigma for women than it once was, many Vietnamese disapprove of women who drink together in public.

  The Vietnamese don't have a problem with Western women who consume alcohol in public (in a group or not), but women should take care not to get drunk. While drunkenness is somewhat acceptable in men, it's not approved behavior in women.

Toasting

In Vietnam, toasts commonly occur before and during meals and at bars.
- Toasting procedure is as follows: Someone fills every person's glass, then proposes a toast. Before drinking, everyone clinks glasses with everyone else, which may mean people must walk around to accomplish the task.
- During toasts, hold your glass in your right hand, and have your left hand support your right forearm.
- If the recipient of a toast, be sure give a reciprocal toast at some point during the event or meal.
- Suitable toasts include:
  * *Xin can ly* (seen kahn lee), which means "bottoms up!"
  * *A votre santé* (ah VO-truh sahn-TAY), which means "to your health."
  * Short stories and toasts in English
- Women may propose toasts, but to avoid making a social gaffe, a woman should make toasts only if other women in the group do so (and the group receives the toasts warmly).

Tipping

Tipping is always optional in Vietnam, and tips are generally much smaller than in the United States. Never tip more than the equivalent of US $4.
- Restaurants: The bill often includes a service charge. If the bill doesn't include a service charge, tip the equivalent of US $1.
- For all other services, including taxis: No tip is necessary or tip at your discretion. (The equivalent of US $1 is common.)

Manners

- Never visit a Vietnamese home without an invitation. The Vietnamese believe they can't offer suitable hospitality if unprepared.

- In informal situations, take small helpings. Use the spoon in the dish as a guide: one spoonful is an appropriate amount. Don't take a second helping of one dish until you've tried every dish. Never take the last serving of meat. Meat is the most important (and the most costly) ingredient in any Vietnamese meal.
- Compliment the cook on each dish after tasting it.
- Nod when accepting or receiving a dish.
- Never refuse a second or third helping; doing so is an insult. At the first serving, begin commenting how full you are, then reluctantly accept additional helpings and try to eat all the food (helpings are thankfully small).
- Hold your rice bowl in your hand. The Vietnamese believe eating from a rice bowl that's on the table is a sign of laziness.
- At restaurants, the person who extended the invitation pays the bill.
- Cover your mouth when using a toothpick.
- Beckon someone of lower status only. Extend your arm (palm down) then curl and extend your fingers together. Never beckon with your index finger. (Only bosses use this gesture.)
- Always use both hands when giving or receiving an item.
- Many Vietnamese smoke, and it's polite to offer cigarettes to others if you're smoking.
- Vietnamese women rarely smoke or drink in public. Foreign women who smoke in public may attract unwanted attention.

Punctuality

The Vietnamese are generally punctual for business and expect foreigners to be on time; however, they're flexible and accommodating when situations occur that are beyond anyone's control (a traffic jam, for example).

The Vietnamese aren't punctual for most social events. Foreigners should always be on time for a banquet or a dinner party, but they may arrive "fashionably late" (fifteen to thirty minutes) for other events.

Dress

Because of the warm climate, the Vietnamese wear mostly cotton clothing and sandals. In the north, most men and women wear black trousers with white or black buttons tightly buttoned. People in the south wear trousers, too, but they also wear Western styles, especially men.

Vietnamese women sometimes wear the traditional ao dai, a long tunic slit on the sides and worn over satin trousers. Western women should ask a knowledgeable person to help them choose an ao dai appropriate for their age and marital status.

In general, Western women should dress conservatively in Vietnam. The Vietnamese view women who wear heavy makeup and revealing clothing as prostitutes.

- For business occasions, men wear conservative, lightweight suits and ties at initial meetings and appointments with senior government officials. At other occasions, jackets aren't necessary. Women wear conservative dresses or tailored blouses and pants.
- Most restaurants don't have dress codes, and casual attire is suitable at almost every establishment. But to be safe, ask for the recommended attire before dining at an establishment. If the meal is for business, men should wear jackets and ties if their colleagues do. Women should wear dresses or dressy cotton shirts and pants.
- For casual occasions, men wear cotton shirts and pants. Women wear slacks and cotton or knit blouses.
- Wear shorts only at the beach. Only children wear shorts off the beach.

Gifts

- The Vietnamese don't open gifts in front of the giver. They set aside the gift to open later.
- Always have gifts wrapped in colorful paper. Don't use black or white gift-wrap (colors symbolize death). Wrap business gifts in red or gold gift-wrap (colors symbolize success and luck). Wrap New Year's and Christmas gifts in red gift-wrap, and use gold (not yellow) gift-wrap to wrap wedding gifts.
- Like the Chinese, the Vietnamese give "red envelopes" (see page 58).

Hostess Gifts

Always bring a gift when visiting a Vietnamese home. The family will also appreciate small gifts for any children and for elderly parents.

Consider giving
- Designer soap or cosmetics
- Home accessories like lamps or framed pictures
- Sweets
- High-quality tea or coffee
- Flowers, except white flowers (white is the color of mourning)—*Note:* Only men give women flowers, and women usually don't give them to men.

Don't give

- Clocks (associated with death)
- Crystal items (bad luck if they break)
- Personal or religious items
- Handkerchiefs (symbolize a sad farewell): Most Asians consider it disgusting to use a handkerchief and return it to your pocket.

Business Gifts

- The Vietnamese generally don't exchange business gifts.
- Give a gift to an individual only when alone with that person. Give a group gift only when alone with that group.
- Try to give a business gift at a colleague's home, not at an office. If you give a gift in a business setting, the Vietnamese may interpret it as a bribe.

Consider giving

- Whiskey or cognac
- Carton of cigarettes (given from a man to a man and only if the recipient smokes)
- Small items that feature your company logo

Don't give

- Clocks (associated with death)
- Crystal items (bad luck if they break)
- Personal or religious items
- Handkerchiefs (symbolize a sad farewell): Most Asians consider it disgusting to use a handkerchief and return it to your pocket.

Helpful Hints

- If you don't know what to do in a situation, just ask someone. The Vietnamese are happy to help strangers. As long as you're polite, you won't lose face by not knowing what to do.
- Clearing customs is a longer and more unfriendly process in Vietnam than elsewhere in Asia. Always allow a lot of time when entering and leaving the country.
- Always pack extra passport and visa photos, as well as copies of your visa and passport. The government occasionally mislays documents.
- Don't bargain with a shopkeeper or street vendor unless you intend to buy an item.

- Don't take photos of anything that may have military significance.
- The Vietnamese believe that nine is a lucky number and thirteen is unlucky. Unlike in much of Asia, the number four isn't bad luck in Vietnam.

> On city streets, you can find professionals who will clean your ears. For a reasonable fee, they'll scoop out earwax, then wash and dry your ears.

Health and Safety

- In general, Vietnam isn't for people who tire easily or are susceptible to infectious diseases. See the list of resources on page 373 to help you learn about recommended vaccinations and health precautions before visiting Vietnam.
- To avoid contracting malaria, keep skin covered and wear insect repellent when outdoors. To avoid contracting schistosomiasis and other parasitic diseases, wear shoes at all times and avoid swimming in fresh water.
- Avian influenza (bird flu) has claimed several lives in Vietnam. While visitors aren't likely to contract the bird flu, avoid live poultry and poultry feces (on farms or at markets), and eat only fully cooked poultry and eggs.
- Don't drink tap water in Vietnam; drink only bottled or boiled water. Avoid using ice in drinks.
- Make sure food has been thoroughly cooked, and eat only cooked and peeled fruits and vegetables. Hot soup is safe to eat (because it's been boiled), but avoid eating any garnishes like fresh greens.
- Be aware: Smoking is common in Vietnam, and few restaurants have non-smoking sections.
- Medical care in Vietnam is inadequate by international standards. If you become seriously ill, travel immediately to a medical facility in Hong Kong, Singapore, or even Bangkok. Make sure your travel insurance includes evacuation coverage.
- If you use a Vietnamese medical facility, know that providers and hospitals may expect immediate cash payment for services.
- Although serious crimes against visitors are rare, pickpocketing and purse snatching are common. Avoid dark streets at night and back away from confrontations. When walking on streets, always carry your purse or briefcase on the side farthest from the street to avoid drive-by snatchings.

- Don't leave your drink or food unattended. Unscrupulous people may drug the food or beverages of victims, then rob them.
- In Ho Chi Minh City (Saigon), walk purposefully and avoid making eye contact with beggars, homeless people, or street hawkers (people selling gum, candy, newspapers, postcards, and so on). Never patronize street hawkers. If you buy from one, you'll attract other hawkers, who may become angry if you refuse to buy from them.
- Don't drive in Vietnam. Streets are crowded, traffic is chaotic (especially in Ho Chi Minh City), drivers disregard road rules, and accidents are all too frequent. Furthermore, public transportation in cities may be crowded and uncomfortable. Have your hotel call you a reputable taxi or hire a driver to get you around in cities. Between cities, take a train.
- Be wary of traveling to rural regions. Ethnic groups and government troops in remote areas have clashed, and the government may require travelers to obtain official authorization before entering the areas.
- Don't bring anything into Vietnam that authorities may construe as pornographic, political, or religious. They may seize the materials and fine the carrier. They may even detain people for religious or political proselytizing.

Corporate Culture

The Vietnamese are enthusiastic about the rapid development of their new "socialist market economy." They're eager to have American participation. They respect American technology and love American popular culture.

Structure

The Vietnamese government has worked to end central business planning, but it's still involved in all areas of business. In fact, the army or other government ministries own many newly "privatized" companies.

In 2000, the government passed a law to streamline regulations to set up small businesses. In two years, more than fifty thousand new companies were formed. Although these small firms must compete against the large state-owned enterprises to get capital and rent land (the state owns all land in Vietnam), the law represents an important move toward economic liberalism.

Foreigners who want to do business in Vietnam will have to deal with government officials. Before traveling to the country, find out exactly what agencies and ministries must approve your company's application and who the responsible individuals are and where they are located. For example, if you want to do business in Ho Chi Minh City (Saigon), the officials ultimately responsible may be in Hanoi. Keep continual, direct contact with the ministry officials responsible for granting or approving your permits and licenses.

Be aware that any one of the approving agencies may have veto power. You may encounter troubles if one official refuses to honor an agreement granted by another.

Legal structures are still evolving as Vietnam becomes more of a market economy, and the transition may be awkward for foreign companies trying to invest there.

Companies make most decisions by committee; no individual holds absolute power. For these reasons, connections are less important in Vietnam than in other Asian countries.

Meetings

- More so than other Asians, the Vietnamese get down to business quickly at meetings. They're also more pragmatic and explicit than some other Asians.
- The Vietnamese are wary of foreign exploitation, so it's essential that your proposals and presentations emphasize the benefits that working with your company will yield Vietnam.

Appointments

- Regular business hours are 8:00 AM to 4:30 PM, Monday through Saturday. Most businesses close at noon for one hour. Shops close for two hours at lunchtime and are open until 7:00 or 8:00 PM.
- Avoid scheduling appointments for the week before and the week after Tet (Vietnamese lunar new year).

> In 1999, the Vietnamese government implemented a forty-hour workweek for its employees and those in the state sector. It hoped private businesses would follow suit, but many grumbled that working less meant making less money.

Communication

- Relatively few Vietnamese businesspeople speak English well, so an interpreter is usually necessary. Check whether your host organization will provide one. It usually will, but it may charge the interpreter's fee to you.
- Like other Asians, the Vietnamese want to avoid confrontation and may tell you what they think you want to hear—not what they believe. When

the Vietnamese say "no problem," they likely mean "yes, there is a problem." Double-check all commitments, and then monitor them closely.

- The telecommunications infrastructure in Vietnam isn't modern. Telephone installation is often a lengthy process, and international communications are expensive. Consequently, cell phones are becoming increasingly popular.

    The Vietnamese government has committed to developing the country's telecommunications infrastructure, including in poor rural areas.

Business Cards

- The Vietnamese usually exchange business cards upon first meeting.
- Always give and receive business cards with both hands.
- Have your information printed in English on one side of your card and in Vietnamese on the other side. Print shops in Ho Chi Minh City and Hanoi will print such cards overnight.

Be Aware

- Entrepreneurship is booming, and the United States and China are vying for Vietnam's trade and investment opportunities. In fact, both countries have invested billions in the Vietnamese economy.
- Choose your local contact in Vietnam carefully. Make sure the person is reliable and credible.
- Corruption is widespread in Vietnam. Expect it to affect your costs and cause delays. Some businesses may "request" payoffs, kickbacks, and gifts. Your local contact will know how to honor these requests. Never offer or give a bribe yourself.

> Since the Vietnamese government began implementing economic reforms in 1986, the results have been impressive. Between 1995 and 2005, the nation's poverty rate dropped from two-thirds to one-third of the population.
>
> In 2006, the World Bank praised Vietnam's evenhanded economic growth. Although the gap between the rich and poor exists in the country, it's smaller than the gap in many developing countries.
>
> Amazingly, Vietnam accomplished these goals with minimal foreign aid.

- Introductions are important in Vietnam. When trying to make contacts, have a respected third party introduce you to potential clients or colleagues.
- The Vietnamese want to do business with people who know Vietnamese culture. Before meeting with potential clients and colleagues, learn as

much about the culture as possible. Walk the streets, visit shops and restaurants, and talk to locals.

- You must make a long-term commitment. Many Vietnamese suspect foreigners want only to make a quick buck and then disappear.
- The Vietnamese have a strong cultural identity, but they're willing to adopt foreign ideas and practices when their value is apparent.
- When treated fairly, the Vietnamese are hard workers and quick learners, and they adapt easily to change. They're pragmatic, industrious, and entrepreneurial, especially in the south.

Socializing

- Vietnamese companies require employees to participate in all activities, including entertainment activities.
- Business dinners are for more formal occasions like initial meetings. Business lunches are acceptable for less formal occasions.
- If invited to a meal at a restaurant or a banquet, always reciprocate with an event of equal lavishness (never more or less) before you leave the country.
- The Vietnamese rarely include spouses in business entertaining, unless the occasion is specifically for spouses (for example, a reception followed by dancing).

Especially for Women

Especially in the north, Vietnamese women can't imagine not taking care of a family. Rural families still prefer sons to daughters—sons carry on family traditions and maintain the ancestral altars, which are prominent in many Vietnamese homes. Husbands are the bosses, and wives depend on them financially. Husbands may have mistresses, and wives don't object for fear of divorce.

The Vietnamese government has recognized that empowering women is a key to reducing poverty. With the World Bank, it's training provincial officials to recognize gender issues in the fight against poverty. In 2007, it passed the Law on Gender Equality to improve the legal system's promotion of women's advancement in Vietnam.

In the major cities, women are more equal to men, and they receive equal pay for equal work. Women represent slightly more than half the Vietnamese workforce, and almost one-third of companies are women owned.

- A foreign woman may invite a Vietnamese man to a business dinner, and she should insist on paying for the meal. If the man pays, the woman is obliged to reciprocate with a meal of equal value.

- Vietnam is generally safe for women travelers; however, women may run into problems near cheap hotels where prostitution is common. At night, don't take public transportation or ride in a taxi alone.

Holidays and Festivals

January	New Year's Day (1)
January/ February	Tet (Vietnamese lunar new year)*
February	Founding Day of the Communist Party of Vietnam (3)
April	Saigon Liberation Day (30)
May	International Labor Day (1)
	Ho Chi Minh's Birthday (19)
September	National Day (2)

* The date of this holiday depends on the lunar calendar. Check when it's celebrated for the year you're visiting Vietnam.

AUSTRALIA
COMMONWEALTH OF AUSTRALIA

Greetings from Australia

Greetings from the "land down under." Our country lies entirely below the equator and is the world's smallest continent but the sixth-largest nation.

There's nowhere else on earth like Australia. A trip from our expansive deserts to lush rainforest to cosmopolitan cities to spectacular beaches will take you many thousands of miles.

The Great Barrier Reef off our east coast is the world's largest coral reef ecosystem and is visible from Earth's orbit. Our flora and fauna stand out as the world's most unique, thanks to our continent's isolation. It's so unique, in fact, that Europeans heavily suspected that the first platypus specimens that arrived in Europe around 1800 were hoaxes.

We believe that ours is truly an egalitarian society: "Jack's as good as his master" is an old Australian proverb that we live by. Differences in education or place of residence don't affect workplace relationships, and "pulling rank" never gets anyone anywhere in Australia. We love "cutting down the tall poppy" —that is, taking people who boast or think highly of themselves down a peg.

Many prominent Australians have declined knighthood more than once, including historian and journalist Charles Bean and politician and judge Richard Edward O'Connor.

In the 1980s, our nation undertook economic reforms that paid off handsomely. By 2006, our economy had enjoyed fifteen straight years of growth. The rate of productivity growth reached a record high in the 1990s, more than doubling since the reforms began.

Today, Australia has great openness to trade and investment, and businesses are free of unnecessary regulations. Our financial services sector is one of the world's most groundbreaking and successful.

We look forward to a comfortable future, thanks in part to the compulsory employee retirement savings system, which is projected to have a value of US $600 billion by 2015.

Our enormous geography has daunted some foreign investors. But once someone has seen our country's great potential market, it isn't uncommon for him or her to quickly expand operations.

We welcome visitors enthusiastically, especially Americans. We know a great deal about the United States and are annoyed that Yanks know little more about Australia beyond kangaroos and koalas. We cringe when visitors call us "Crocodile Dundee" or ask us if we hunt crocodiles or box kangaroos. (For heaven's sake, we do neither!)

Don't miss the opportunity to tour our world-renowned Sydney Opera House, drink our delicious wine, and enjoy our wonderfully relaxed atmosphere. Be yourself, but don't try to impress us. Take the time to get to know us; we want to get to know you.

Vital Statistics

Population	20,264,082
Capital	Canberra
Area	2,967,909 square miles, slightly smaller than the United States (excluding Alaska and Hawaii)
Government	Federal parliamentary democracy
Living Standard	GDP = $35,900 per capita
Natural Resources	Bauxite, coal, iron ore, copper, tin, gold, silver, uranium, nickel, tungsten, mineral sands, lead, zinc, diamonds, natural gas, petroleum
Agriculture	Wheat, barley, sugarcane, fruits, cattle, sheep, poultry
Industries	Mining, industrial and transportation equipment, food processing, chemicals, steel
Climate	Generally arid to semiarid; temperate in south and east; tropical in north
Currency	Australian dollar (AUD)

The People

Correct Name	noun: Australian(s)
	adjective: Australian
Ethnic Makeup	Caucasian 92%, Asian 7%, aboriginal and other 1%
Languages	English 79.1%, Chinese 2.1%, Italian 1.9%, other 11.1%, unspecified 5.8%
Religions	Catholic 26.4%, Anglican 20.5%, other Christian 20.5%, Buddhist 1.9%, Muslim 1.5%, other 1.2%, unspecified 12.7%, none 15.3%

Meeting and Greeting

- Australians shake hands firmly upon meeting and leaving.
- Women should extend their hands first. Men shake a woman's hand only if she offers it.
- Female friends may kiss cheeks as a greeting.
- Although "g'day" (good day) is the quintessential Australian greeting, foreigners should never use it—doing so annoys Australians. Instead, they should simply say "hello."

Names and Titles

- Australians downplay their academic and professional titles and expect foreigners to do so as well. To them, titles don't necessarily command respect—people's actions do.
- Generally, Australians prefer to use first names (given names) immediately. But foreigners should wait to use Australians' first names until invited to do so. Until then, address people by courtesy title (Mr., Mrs., Ms., or Miss) + last name (surname).
- Australians refer to people of their sex as "mates." They refer to friends as "my mates."

Language

- English is the national language, and almost all Australians speak it—although they'd argue they speak "Strine" (Australian English), whose grammar and spelling incorporate both British and American English usages.

> Ignorance of a country and its people can be costly. A young North American college graduate once told me he declined a job offer with an Australian company because he didn't want to learn Australian!

- Australians may shorten words and add "-ie" (pronounced "ee") to the ends of them.

  Examples: barbie = barbecue

  mozzie = mosquito

  Aussie = an Australian

Conversation

- Australians are candidly blunt, and they appreciate this trait in others. They may also curse more freely than Americans do. Don't react if politically incorrect statements or coarse language shock you.

- Australians respect people with strong opinions, even if they disagree with them. They consider arguments entertaining and will argue with you openly.

- When conversing with Australians, be genuine and be yourself. Don't gush or be pretentious—and never brag.

- Australians appreciate teasing. When someone teases you, reply in kind with good humor. Doing so will increase an Australian's respect for you.

- While conversing, never interrupt anyone. Doing so is rude.

- Don't call koalas "koala bears." (They're not bears; they're marsupials.)

- The words *rooting* and *stuffed* are vulgar in Australia. Avoid using them.

Acceptable topics

- Your home region
- Your career
- Australia's history and culture: Australians are pleased when foreigners can talk knowledgably about Australia.

> The ramifications of non-native settlers' treatment of aboriginal people still reverberate today. Babies born to aboriginal women are far more likely to have low birth weights than are babies born to other Australian mothers. Life expectancy of aboriginal people is far lower than that of other Australians. Since the 1970s, the government has helped improve the health of aboriginal people, but overall progress has been slow and inconsistent.
>
> But Australians are working to change attitudes and respect diversity. For example, the government promotes aboriginal art and culture. In 2000, Australians proudly watched Cathy Freeman, a runner and aboriginal woman, light the Olympic torch in Sydney.

- Sports, especially Rugby, cricket, and footy (Australian football): Other popular activities include swimming, surfing, sailing, tennis, and auto racing.
- Music, especially country music (both American and Australian)

Unacceptable topics
- Treatment of aboriginal people (correctly called Aboriginal and Torres Strait Islander peoples)
- Comparisons between Australians and Brits or Americans
- Comparisons between Australia and New Zealand
- Someone's accent: Accents often distinguish social class.
- Criticisms of Australia: Although Australians are self-deprecating and may criticize their country, don't join in or even appear to agree.

> Although foreigners should understand common Australian words and phrases, they should never use them. Doing so annoys Australians.

Topics that require sensitivity
- Religion
- Politics

Body Language
- Beyond patting one another on the back, Australian men don't touch one another. They generally consider any further body contact between men unmanly.
- In public, men and women who have close relationships may hold hands or kiss one another on the cheek. Any other touching is unusual and may invite curious looks.
- Never wink at a woman. Doing so is rude.
- Don't make a V with your index and middle fingers and palm toward you. It's a vulgar gesture.
- Maintain eye contact when speaking with someone. Australians consider eye contact important to establishing trust.
- Australians expect the same amount of personal distance between people that Americans do.

Phrases

Don't assume that understanding the language means understanding the culture. Foreigners who mistake the meanings of words and phrases make many gaffes. The following is a sample list of Australian slang. Some Australians believe that because younger people use these words and phrases less often than their parents do, the language is becoming obsolete. Many of the terms are more commonly heard in rural areas than in the cities.

American English	Australian English
Good day	G'day
Good afternoon (very informal)	Arvo (AHR-voh)
Thank you (informal)	Ta (tah)
Yes (emphatic)	Bludioth! (Bloody oath!)
It'll be okay	She'll be right
Right on	Spot on
Your turn to pay	Your shout
Someone or something moving fast	Like a possum up a gum tree
Try something	Give it a burl
No problem	No worries, mate
Across the street	Over the road
Australians	Aussies (AHZ-zies, not AWZ-zies)
English people (derogatory)	Brits Poms or pommies
Americans	Yanks
Young woman (rude)	Sheila
Bad, defective, or ill	Crook
True or genuine	Fair dinkum
Knowledgeable	Full bottle
Car hood	Bonnet
Car trunk	Boot
Fender bender	Bingle
Cookie	Biscuit
French fries	Chips

Twelve-ounce bottle of beer	Stubby
Pharmacy	Chemist
Flashlight	Torch
Garbage	Rubbish
Eraser	Rubber
University	Uni (YOO-nee)
Kindergarten	Kindi (KIN-dee)
Television	Telly or TV

This list is by no means extensive. To learn more common Australian words and phrases, consult a comprehensive phrase book.

Dining

Australian cuisine involves the mixing of completely different ethnic traditions from around the world. Australians pride themselves on the availability and quality of fresh produce.

- Australians eat continental style; that is, after using the knife to cut food and push it onto the fork, they keep the fork in the left hand to eat.
- Here are common meals in Australia:
  * Morning tea = tea and cookies served between 10:00 and 11:00 AM.
  * Tea = light meal served in late afternoon or early evening. Australians use the words *tea* and *dinner* interchangeably.
  * Barbecue ("barbie") = a popular informal get-together. Often the host provides the food, but sometimes the guests bring their own.
- In Australia, the word *entrée* refers to the appetizer, not the main course.
- Hosts generally seat the guest of honor to their right.
- Hosts serve salads with the main course. If you want your salad served first, order it as an entrée.

Vegemite is a strong-smelling spread made of concentrated yeast extract that's high in vitamin B. Just as Americans eat peanut butter, Australians eat Vegemite on bread. There are a surprising number of recipes that use Vegemite (including chicken wings and risotto).

Drinking

- Beer is the most popular alcoholic beverage, and lager is the most common variety. Australians serve it chilled. Foster's is likely the brand Americans know best, but Australians brew many other excellent beers.
- Wine is an integral part of Australian culture. The country's wine industry is large (ranked seventh in the world in 2003); each state and two Australian territories produce wine. Between 1996 and 2004, wine exports quadrupled and Australians' wine consumption increased, largely because local wines are reasonably priced.
- Many Australians enjoy Scotch.
- Australians prefer European-style coffee like espresso and cappuccino; they regard drip-style coffee (the weaker coffee that Americans typically serve) and instant coffee as awful. "White coffee" is coffee with milk.
- Tea is also an important part of Australian culture. Although per capita, tea consumption has declined over the years (as coffee has become more popular), Australians still drink over twenty million cups of tea per day.
- Soft drinks are widely available, although consumption of some carbonated and sugar-based drinks are declining (probably because of increased awareness of their perceived adverse health effects). Bottled water and juices are widely available.
- Never miss your turn to "shout for a round" (buy a round of drinks).

Toasting

Australians don't follow any special toasting customs, although men and women may offer the toast "cheers" or "all the best" at any time.

Tipping

Tipping isn't common in Australia and is always discretionary. People in the service industries are well paid.

- Restaurants: The bill may include a 10 percent service charge. If the bill doesn't include a service charge, tip 10 to 12 percent.
- Taxis: No tip is necessary. For excellent service, round up the fare to the nearest AUD.
- Porters and bellhops: Tip AUD1 per bag handled.
- Hair stylists and barbers: No tip is necessary.

Manners

- Call ahead before visiting someone's home.
- To eat the last spoonfuls of soup, always tip the soup bowl away from you.
- When finished eating, place your knife and fork side by side on the plate so they're at the 5:25 position on a clock (see illustration).
- Always keep your hands and elbows above the table.
- When dining in someone's home, offer to help with the dishes.
- In crowded cafés or fast-food restaurants, feel free to ask someone if you may sit at the table. In more formal restaurants, wait for an available table.
- At restaurants, the person who extended the invitation generally pays the bill, but friends often split the bill.
- To beckon wait staff, quietly motion them with your hand. Never shout or wave furiously.
- Australians don't jump queues (cut in line). Always wait your turn.
- Wave to someone at a distance; never shout a greeting.
- Cover your mouth when yawning, then excuse yourself to finish the yawn.
- Don't sniffle. Blow your nose in private, if possible.
- Don't litter. Australia is a very clean country, and there's a stiff fine for littering.
- Chivalry isn't common. Men don't routinely open doors for women, pull out chairs for them, and so on.

Punctuality

Australians respect punctuality and expect people to be on time. For business appointments, never be late; in fact, try to arrive fifteen minutes early.

For social occasions, don't keep anyone waiting more than ten minutes. Always arrive on time or a few minutes early for a dinner party.

Dress

Australians generally wear casual attire, but it's never dirty or sloppy. To be safe, foreigners should assume that *casual* means "smart casual"—which means a nicely coordinated, stylish, elegant outfit in conservative colors. But it can also mean clean, neat jeans and shorts.

- Check on temperatures in the area you'll be visiting before your trip. Don't forget that when it's winter in North America, it's summer in Australia (and vice versa).
- If visiting in the winter, wear layers of warm clothing. Many homes in Sydney don't have central heating and rely instead on space heaters.
- For business occasions, men wear conservative jackets and ties. They may remove the jackets in the summer. (Foreigners should follow their hosts' lead.) Women wear dresses or skirts with blouses.
- In formal restaurants, men wear jackets and ties. Women wear dresses or blouses with skirts or dress pants. In less formal restaurants, casual attire is acceptable.
- At most beaches, any attire (or lack thereof) is acceptable. Most permit topless bathing, and some beaches allow total nudity.

> If visiting during the summer months, protect yourself from the strong Australian sunshine by following simple precautions. Always wear a hat with a broad brim and keep your skin covered with clothing or sunscreen. Try to avoid the midday sun, when the ultraviolet rays are at their strongest.

Gifts

Australians are relaxed about gift giving, and they generally open gifts upon receipt. If you give an inappropriate gift, they'll laugh and tell you why it's unsuitable!

Hostess Gifts

Consider giving
- Flowers
- Chocolates
- Books about your home region
- High-quality wine or beer: Ask a liquor store clerk for recommendations.

Don't give
- Personal items like perfume or clothing

Business Gifts

Australians don't expect business gifts but, as a gesture of friendship, visitors may give gifts at initial meetings or after the successful conclusion of negotiations.

Consider giving
- New, unique gadgets
- Specialty food items, artwork, or arts and crafts from your home region

Don't give
- Expensive or ostentatious items (will embarrass Australians)

Helpful Hints

- Australian men may sit in the front seat of taxis or limousines as a sign of egalitarianism. Women usually sit in the back.
- Be a good sport—win or lose. Australians highly regard good sportsmanship.
- Australia has three time zones: Eastern, Central, and Western.
- Taxis are more numerous in Sydney than elsewhere in Australia, and you can hail a taxi from the street. In most other cities, book taxis by telephone.
- You can rent cars in almost every town and at airports and rail terminals. (Know that Australians drive on the left side of the road.) But public transportation in major cities is frequent and efficient.

Health and Safety

- See the list of resources on page 373 to help you learn about recommended vaccinations and health precautions before visiting Australia.
- Australian medical facilities are world class. Physicians fly to isolated regions to provide care.
- If enjoying Australia's spectacular beaches, swim only at patrolled beaches and only in designated areas to avoid sharp rocks and strong riptides. Between November and April in north Queensland, heed signs warning of poisonous jellyfish.
- The harsh conditions in the outback can be deadly. If you must drive any distance in the outback, leave an itinerary (including your route and departure and arrival times) with someone before you leave. Don't deviate from your plan, and if your vehicle breaks down, stay with it until help finds you. Don't count on your cell phone to get help; it may not work in remote areas.

- Australia has stringent drunk-driving laws, and they're strictly enforced. If your socializing involves alcohol, take a taxi back to your hotel.

Corporate Culture

Australia is an egalitarian society; they treat everyone equally. They make fun of someone who states his or her qualifications, titles, and experience. As businesspeople, Australians are pragmatic, efficient, and profit oriented.

In 2002, the kangaroo industry employed more than four thousand people and had revenues of more than AUD200 million. Eating the national symbol ("chew the roo") has sparked controversy in Australia, but proponents rave about kangaroos' lean meat and venison-like taste.

Foreigners won't have a problem registering with the Australian Securities and Investments Commission, the first step to establishing a business in Australia.

Structure
- Managers make decisions after gathering input from subordinates.
- Most executives at all levels are friendly, approachable, and open to appointments.
- Nearly all workers receive four weeks of paid vacation each year.

Meetings
- Participants shake hands with everyone before and after a meeting.
- Although Australians tend to quickly get down to business, take the time at the beginning of a meeting for some brief personal conversation.
- When speaking to a group, stand tall and use modest gestures. Australians appreciate straightforward, open presentations.
- Negotiations proceed quickly. Australians don't emphasize details; they negotiate major issues.
- Make the proposal you expect Australians to accept. Generally, they don't bargain and there's little room for haggling. Their contracts are detailed and firm.

Appointments
- Regular business hours are 9:00 AM to 5:00 PM, Monday through Friday.
- Make appointments well in advance of your trip (four weeks is reasonable).

- March through November are the best months for business trips.
- Avoid making appointments for the days around Easter and December through February (popular time for vacations).

Communication
- Australians value directness and respect those who stand their ground. If they're dissatisfied, they'll politely tell you so.
- Generally, Australians communicate with good humor.

Business Cards
Like most Americans, Australians exchange business cards at first meetings but they don't follow any special protocol when doing so.

Be Aware
- Connections are necessary for business success in Australia. Take the time to develop relationships.
- The old-boy network is alive among senior executives. Whom you know is vital to business success. Have a well-connected third party initiate business contacts.

Socializing
Australians enjoy entertaining, especially in their homes. Always take the time to dine or party with them.
- Business lunches are common, and business breakfasts are acceptable.
- Australians generally invite visitors for dinner and/or drinks before doing business with them.
- Don't discuss business over drinks unless the host brings up the subject.
- Never miss your turn to "shout for a round" (buy a round of drinks).
- Australians invite spouses to business dinners.

Especially for Women

In 2000, the Australian government implemented the Equal Opportunity for Women in the Workplace Act 1999 to promote equal opportunity in Australian workplaces. By some measures, however, representation of women in corporate leadership in Australia still lags behind that in the United States and the United Kingdom. In 2006, women held 12 percent of executive management positions in the ASX 200 (an index representing the top two hundred Australian companies). Women led just six companies and held less than 10 percent of board directorships.

- Foreign women won't have a problem doing business in Australia.
- A foreign woman may invite an Australian man to a business dinner and will have no problem paying for the meal.

Holidays and Festivals

January	New Year's Day (1)
	Australia Day (often the last Monday)
March/April	Easter (Friday–Monday)
April	Anzac Day (25)
June	Queen's Birthday* (second Monday)
December	Christmas (25)
December	Boxing Day** (26)

* Excludes West Australia

** Excludes South Australia

Note: Each state celebrates additional public holidays. Check what holidays are observed and when they're celebrated in the area you'll be visiting.

NEW ZEALAND*

Greetings from New Zealand

Greetings from *Aotearoa*, which means "long white cloud" in our country's indigenous Maori (MOW-ree) language.

Our land is almost too unique and beautiful for words. We have majestic mountains, glaciers, and fjords, as well as pristine isolated beaches.

The Maori first arrived here from the Polynesian Islands about a thousand years ago. In 1769, Captain James Cook and his crew charted our land, and European missionaries and settlers soon after arrived on our shores and forever changed our culture.

Today, our nation is part of the British Commonwealth, and Queen Elizabeth II is the constitutional head of state. We feel connected to the United Kingdom, and we don't tolerate those who make any flippant remarks about Brits or the British royal family.

Although there are some ethnic tensions among those of European, Asian, and Maori descent, we're proud of the progress we've made to respect all our people, regardless of ethnicity.

For example, Anand Satyanand, who became governor-general of New Zealand in 2006, is of Indian descent. Our Parliament reserves seven seats (about 6 percent) for people of Maori ancestry. Every five years, we adjust this number to reflect the number of registered Maori voters. In 2005, there were twenty-one Maori in Parliament, including the seven reserved seats.

Our nation doesn't have a written constitution, but we nonetheless work to accomplish our goals for peaceful lives. In 1987, our Parliament passed a law that made New Zealand a nuclear-free zone, which lets us concentrate on making and keeping peace.

We're proud of our nation and its values. We value self-reliance and practicality, and we love our homes and gardens. We consider ourselves the nicest people in the world. We like Australians and have a ongoing friendly rivalry with them. But please don't confuse us with Australians and never compare us to them. We're a distinct people with a unique culture.

* This country's name has no conventional long form.

New Zealand is an excellent place to work and play. If you're adventurous, surf along our gorgeous beaches or go bungee jumping (the first commercial bungee site was in Queenstown). See our unbelievable scenery on a "jet boat safari" (a New Zealand farmer invented the jet boat in the 1960s).

If visiting during the sheep-shearing season, take the opportunity to visit a sheep station—although you may have to hunt to find people!

Author Douglas Adams (*The Hitchhiker's Guide to the Galaxy*) once said that southern New Zealand is "one of the most astounding pieces of land anywhere on God's earth, and one's first impulse, standing on a cliff top surveying it all, is simply to burst into spontaneous applause."

In the early 2000s, native New Zealander Peter Jackson showcased his country's stunning vistas—as well as a large share of its people—in his wildly successful film adaptations of J. R. R. Tolkien's Lord of the Rings trilogy.

In 2003, there were twelve sheep for every New Zealander.

There's nowhere else on earth like New Zealand, and there's no one else like us New Zealanders. Come and visit us. We'd love you to get to know us and our wonderfully unique culture.

Vital Statistics	
Population	4,076,140
Capital	Wellington
Area	103,738 square miles, about the size of Colorado
Government	Parliamentary democracy
Living Standard	GDP = US $24,420 per capita
Natural Resources	Natural gas, iron ore, sand, coal, timber, hydropower, gold, limestone
Agriculture	Wheat, barley, potatoes, pulses, fruits, vegetables, wool, beef, lamb and mutton, dairy products, fish
Industries	Food processing, wood and paper products, textiles, machinery, transportation equipment, banking and insurance, tourism, mining
Climate	Temperate with sharp regional contrasts
Currency	New Zealand dollar (NZD)

The People

Correct Name	noun: New Zealander(s), Kiwi(s)
	adjective: New Zealand, Kiwi
Ethnic Makeup	European 69.8%, Maori 7.9%, Asian 5.7%, Pacific Islander 4.4%, other 0.5%, mixed 7.8%, unspecified 3.8%
Languages	English and Maori (both official)
Religions	Anglican 14.9%, Roman Catholic 12.4%, Presbyterian 10.9%, Methodist 2.9%, Pentecostal 1.7%, Baptist 1.3%, other Christian 9.4%, other 3.3%, unspecified 17.2%, none 26%

Meeting and Greeting

- New Zealanders shake hands with everyone upon meeting and leaving. Handshakes are firm with direct eye contact.
- In formal situations, men should shake a woman's hand only if she offers it.
- At formal occasions, New Zealanders greet one another with "how do you do?" or "I am very pleased to meet you." At informal occasions, they say "hello," "hi," or "g'day."
- Only Maori greet one another with the hongi, the traditional greeting in which two people close their eyes, press their noses together, and say "mmm."

Names and Titles

- Generally, New Zealanders prefer to use first names (given names) immediately. But foreigners should wait to use New Zealanders' first names until invited to do so. Until then, address people by courtesy title (Mr., Mrs., or Ms.) + last name (surname).
- Address only a young woman or a waitress as Miss.
- It's acceptable to ask how to pronounce Maori names.

Language

- Almost all New Zealanders speak English.
- New Zealand English has absorbed a few Maori words, like *pakeha* (pah-KEE-hah), which means "white skin" and describes Europeans. If you don't understand a term, feel free to ask.

Conversation

- New Zealanders have a wonderfully sarcastic sense of humor. They often tell ethnic jokes about the Irish. Don't join in.
- Speak quietly. New Zealanders consider loud voices rude.
- Be modest when conversing with New Zealanders. They dislike bragging.
- Never call a New Zealander an Australian, and never mistake an Australian issue with a New Zealand one.

Acceptable topics
- Sports, especially Rugby, cricket, and sailing
- Your home country
- Your reason for visiting New Zealand
- Family (yours and theirs)
- New Zealand sights: Ask about local places to visit.

Unacceptable topics
- New Zealand's antinuclear policy
- Comparisons between New Zealand and any other country, especially Australia: New Zealanders are very proud of their nation.

Topics that require sensitivity
- Maori treaties and rights
- Religion (even though religion doesn't influence many New Zealanders' lives)
- Immigration issues

Because of extensive European immigration and migration in New Zealand, the Maori language (*Te Reo*) had been in decline for more than a hundred years. Since the 1960s, there has been a continual increase in Maori language revitalization efforts.

The government declared 1995 to be *He Taonga Te Reo*, "A Celebration of the Maori Language." Its aims included focusing attention on the status of the Maori language, encouraging New Zealanders to learn and promote the language, and raising awareness and greater understanding of it.

In 2002, a study by the Ministry of Maori Affairs showed that a quarter of Maori speak the language and Maori was no longer in decline. Today, the national anthem is sung in English and Maori.

Although the progress is promising, it's too early to assume the language has been saved.

Body Language

In New Zealand, British customs and gestures are common. Here are some examples:

- New Zealanders don't stand too closely to one another when conversing.
- Foreigners should never initiate hugs with New Zealanders.

> Although foreigners should understand common New Zealand words and phrases, they should never use them.
>
> *Kiwi* is the exception. This informal name for a New Zealander isn't derogatory. The kiwi, a flightless, nocturnal bird, is the national symbol. New Zealanders are proud to be called Kiwis.

- New Zealanders wave as a sign of recognition.
- Don't make a V with your index and middle fingers and palm toward you. It's a vulgar gesture.
- Maintain eye contact when speaking with someone. New Zealanders consider eye contact important to establishing trust.

In addition, friends may pat one another on the back and on the arm when conversing. Foreigners should never initiate this behavior, but may return the gestures if a New Zealander makes them first.

Phrases

Don't assume that understanding the language means understanding the culture. Foreigners who mistake the meanings of words and phrases make many gaffes. Just imagine the misunderstandings that could arise when the meanings of these words and phrases are misunderstood:

American English	New Zealand English
New Zealander	Kiwi
Stuffed	Relates to sexual intercourse
Certify	Commit to a mental hospital
Letter Z	Zed
Cup of coffee or tea	Cuppa
Carbonated beverage	Fizzy
Having a party	Having a do

This list is by no means extensive. To learn more common New Zealand words and phrases, consult a comprehensive phrase book.

If you don't understand someone, or if a word or phrase sounds odd, ask for clarification.

Dining

New Zealand's cuisine draws inspiration from Europe, Asia, and Polynesia—a blend of influences that's created a wide range of flavorful dishes.

Although their diet is similar to that of the British, New Zealanders eat far more mutton per capita than any other nation in the world, and their consumption of beef per capita ranks as one of the world's highest.

- New Zealanders eat continental style; that is, after using the knife to cut food and push it onto the fork, they keep the fork in the left hand to eat.
- Afternoon tea is a mid-afternoon light meal of coffee, tea, soft drinks, finger sandwiches, cakes, and cookies. At a more formal occasion, the meal is more substantial.
- *Supper* is a late evening snack. New Zealanders call the evening meal *dinner*.
- In New Zealand, the word *entrée* isn't the main course; it's the appetizer.
- New Zealand's cheese is world famous, and the country is the world's fifth-largest cheese exporter. Its dairy products account for over a third of the world's dairy trade.

Drinking

- Tea and coffee are popular in New Zealand. People drink tea with milk and sugar. If hosting New Zealanders, serve properly brewed, excellent quality tea (they consider American tea inferior).

  For many years, instant coffee was most common (and people still serve it in some homes and small restaurants), but today high-quality espresso and other European-style coffees are popular. Many New Zealanders believe the special ingredient of their brewed coffee is the added milk and cream from local grass-fed cows.
- New Zealanders brew excellent beer. Steinlager Blue Label and DB are the most popular brands.
- New Zealanders are proud of their domestic wine. In 2004, the country's nearly five hundred wineries exported wine worth over NZD300 million, more than seven times the worth of the 1994 exports. Chardonnay, Pinot Noir, Riesling, Cabernet Sauvignon, and Merlot blends have particularly good reputations.

Toasting

New Zealanders don't follow any special toasting protocol. In informal situations, men and women may offer the toast "cheers." In more formal situations, they may give a small speech, then follow it with "please join me now in toasting...."

Tipping

Tipping isn't common in New Zealand. People in the service industries don't depend on tips as part of their incomes.

- Restaurants: The bill usually doesn't include a service charge, and wait staff don't expect tips. With that said, servers at expensive restaurants or establishments in tourist areas may expect tips. In these cases, tip 5 to 10 percent of the bill.
- Taxis: No tip is necessary. For excellent service, round up the fare to the nearest NZD.
- Hair stylists and barbers: No tip is necessary. For excellent service, tip 5 percent of the bill.

Manners

New Zealanders are formal when first meeting, but they warm up quickly and their manners become open and relaxed. If unsure of proper etiquette, feel free to ask.

- Always keep your hands and elbows above the table.
- When finished eating, place your knife and fork side by side on the plate so they're at the 5:25 position on a clock (see illustration).
- Eat teacakes with your fingers, but eat tarts with a fork.
- Don't talk too much during meals; New Zealanders generally save conversation for after the meal.
- Don't chew gum or use a toothpick in public.
- Cover your mouth when yawning.
- Ask permission before you smoke at the table.
- Gallantry is common. Men routinely open doors for women, pull out chairs for them, and so on.
- Always ask permission before taking a photo, especially of Maoris and Maori objects.

When Dining in Restaurants

- Dinner generally begins around 8:00 PM.
- Wait staff generally don't hurry diners. If you're in a rush, tell the staff.
- Always speak quietly.
- Ask wait staff for the *bill*, not the *check*.

When Visiting Homes

- New Zealanders enjoy having friends in their homes for an afternoon tea, barbecue, or dinner (usually served between 6:00 and 7:00 PM).
- Hosts always offer guests (even repair people) refreshments. It's polite to eat or drink at least a little of the offering.
- When dining in someone's home, offer to help with the dishes.
- Guests should leave about an hour after the meal.

Punctuality

New Zealanders expect punctuality for social occasions and particularly for business occasions.

Arrive a few minutes early for business meetings, if possible.

Dress

New Zealanders wear conservative European and North American fashions. Their dress code is "smart casual"—which means a nicely coordinated, stylish, elegant outfit in conservative colors.

- Check on temperatures in the area you'll be visiting before your trip. New Zealand weather is changeable. Wear layers and don't forget your raincoat. Also don't forget that when it's winter in North America, it's summer in New Zealand (and vice versa).
- For business, men wear suits and ties. Women wear dresses, pantsuits, or blouses and skirts.
- For the theater, men wear suits and ties, and women wear dresses or dressy pantsuits.
- Some restaurants require men to wear coats and ties. If unsure of an establishment's dress code, ask.
- When playing golf, women wear skirts, not pants or shorts.

Gifts

- New Zealanders usually open gifts upon receipt.
- Give modest gifts. New Zealanders don't appreciate ostentation, and expensive gifts will embarrass them.

Hostess Gifts

Always bring a gift when visiting someone's home.

Consider giving
- Whiskey
- Wine (but not Australian)
- Flowers or plants
- Chocolate

Don't give
- Personal items (perfume, clothing, and so on)
- Expensive or ostentatious items

Business Gifts

New Zealanders don't commonly exchange gifts at business meetings; however, as a gesture of friendship, visitors may give small gifts at initial meetings or after the successful conclusion of negotiations.

Consider giving
- Unique food items, artwork, or arts and crafts from your home region

Don't give
- Expensive or ostentatious items

Helpful Hints

- New Zealand has two towns named Waitangi: one in the Bay of Islands and the other in the Chatham Islands. Don't mix them up!
- There are friendly rivalries between North Islanders and South Islanders. Don't worry if they trade insults; they're not serious.

Health and Safety

- If driving in New Zealand, be aware that the mountainous terrain makes for slow-moving traffic (which drives on the left). Also, know that it's illegal to turn on a red light.
- Violent crime against tourists is rare, but theft is common. Be sure to securely lock your vehicle and hotel room.
- Medical care in New Zealand is modern and excellent, but providers and hospitals may expect immediate cash payment for services.
- When swimming in the ocean, swim only between posted warning flags and be aware of powerful riptides and currents.
- If visiting during the summer months, always wear a hat with a broad brim and keep your skin covered with clothing or sunscreen. Try to avoid the midday sun, when the ultraviolet rays are at their strongest.

> New Zealand has several active volcanoes and about fourteen thousand earthquakes each year, two hundred of them significant. Researchers are working to predict tsunami-generating earthquakes.
>
> Don't panic if you feel small tremors during your stay. In the event of a natural disaster, know where to find shelter in your workplace, hotel, or other location. Follow local authorities' directions.

Corporate Culture

- The business pace in New Zealand is slower—and its business atmosphere is more formal—than that in the United States.
- Most employees get three to four weeks' vacation every year.

Structure

- Companies expect managers to be willing to do anything a subordinate does.
- Managers and subordinates freely consult one another for information and feedback.

Meetings

- Hosts serve tea and/or coffee at business meetings. It's polite to accept a cup and take at least a few sips.
- Initial meetings are formal. As the relationship develops, however, subsequent meetings become more relaxed.

Appointments
- Regular business hours are 8:30 AM to 5:00 PM, Monday through Friday. Some businesses and government offices also are open 9:00 AM to noon on Saturday.
- Schedule appointments with senior managers well in advance.
- Avoid scheduling appointments for dates in December and January (Christmas holiday and peak time for summer vacations).

Communication
- English is the main business language in New Zealand.

Business Cards
- Give a business card to each person at initial meetings. Study your counterparts' cards carefully upon receipt.

Be Aware
- New Zealanders value equality more than rank. Education and experience are more important than pedigree. What you know is more important than whom you know or who you are.
- New Zealanders are proud of their ability to overcome obstacles. They highly value ingenuity and creativity.

Socializing
- Business dinners are for socializing, not discussing business.
- New Zealanders discuss business over business lunches. Some businesses host lunch in their offices.
- New Zealanders generally include spouses at business dinners.

Especially for Women

New Zealand is generally conducive to women's equality in society. The country elected Prime Minister Helen Clark in 1999, and in 2005 a third of the members of Parliament were women. In 2001, more than half of all post-secondary students in New Zealand were women, as were nearly half of the country's workforce. Patronizing or sexual comments aren't acceptable in the workplace, although out of a sense of gallantry, some men will open doors for women, pull out their chairs, and so on. Women accept these gestures graciously.

- Foreign women won't have difficulty doing business in New Zealand.
- A foreign woman may invite a New Zealand man to a business dinner. She may pay for the meal, but it's polite to arrange payment with wait staff beforehand.

Holidays and Festivals

January	New Year's Day (1–2)
February	Waitangi Day (6)
March/April	Easter (Friday–Monday)
April	Anzac Day (25)
June	Queen's Birthday (first Monday)
October	Labor Day (fourth Monday)
December	Christmas (25)
	Boxing Day (26)

Note: Each New Zealand town and province observes its own anniversary, celebrated on the Monday closest to the anniversary date.

RESOURCES

The demographic data for the countries I discuss in this book are current as of its publication date. I've included these figures for comparison's sake. The Central Intelligence Agency's (CIA) World Factbook is a free online resource with a wealth of statistical information. To learn the most current information, visit http://www.cia.gov/cia/publications/factbook/index.html before planning a trip.

Before visiting Asia, obtain the addresses and telephone numbers of the American Embassies in the nations you'll be visiting. Here are some other numbers to help you plan your trip:

U.S. Department of State
Hotline for American Travelers: 888-407-4747, 202-501-4444 (from overseas)
http://www.travel.state.gov

Centers for Disease Control and Prevention
Traveler's Health Hotline: 877-FYI-TRIP (877-394-8747)
http://www.cdc.gov/travel

World Health Organization
http://www.who.int/ith/en

INDEX

of Thailand, 312
of Vietnam, 331

D

Dairy products, 60
Dapsang (mountain), 228
Dates, 31
Deforestation, 13
Devanagari alphabet, 156
Dhaka (Bangladesh), 94
Dhaka Ahsania Mission (DAM), 11
Dialects, Chinese, 24, 26, 111, 113-114, 136
Diet. *See also* Food(s); Vegetarianism
  Catholicism and, 85
  Hinduism and, 81-82
  Islam and, 83-84
Dining. *See also* Drinking; Toasting
  in Australia, 353, 355
  in Bangladesh, 99, 100
  banquets and, 38-38
  in China, 117-119, 121
  eating food you'd rather not, 42
  eating styles, 39-40
  general rules on, 36-37
  in Hong Kong, 139, 141-142
  in India, 156-157
  in Indonesia, 175
  in Japan, 194-195, 197
  in Malaysia, 217, 218-219
  in New Zealand, 366
  in Pakistan, 233
  in the Philippines, 249
  in Singapore, 264-266, 267
  in South Korea, 280-281, 282-283
  table manners and, 37-38
  in Taiwan, 300-301, 303
  in Thailand, 317-318
  in Vietnam, 336
Discrimination/prejudice, 14-15
Diseases, 12-13, 60, 179. *See also* Avian
  influenza (Bird Flu)
Disneyland, Hong Kong, 86
Dowries, 166
Dress
  in Australia, 355-356
  in Bangladesh, 101
  in China, 122-123
  general guidelines on, 50-53
  in Hong Kong, 142
  in India, 160-161
  in Indonesia, 177-178
  in Japan, 200-201
  in Malaysia, 220
  of Muslim women, 52
  in New Zealand, 368
  in Pakistan, 235
  in the Philippines, 252-253
  in Singapore, 267-268
  in South Korea, 284
  in Taiwan, 304
  in Thailand, 321
  in Vietnam, 338-339
Drinking
  in Australia, 354
  in Bangladesh, 99
  in China, 119-120
  in Hong Kong, 139-140
  in India, 157
  in Indonesia, 175-176
  in Japan, 195-196, 207
  in Malaysia, 217
  in New Zealand, 366

in Pakistan, 233
in the Philippines, 249-250
in Singapore, 266
in South Korea, 281
in Taiwan, 301
in Thailand, 318-319
in Vietnam, 336-337
Drinking water, 61
  in India, 163
  in Indonesia, 179
  in Malaysia, 222
  in Pakistan, 238
  in the Philippines, 254
  in South Korea, 286
  in Taiwan, 306
  in Thailand, 323
  in Vietnam, 341
Driving. *See also* Traffic congestion
  in Bangladesh, 103-104
  in China, 125
  in Malaysia, 222
  in Pakistan, 237
  safety and, 64
  in Singapore, 269
  in Vietnam, 342
Drug sale/use, 324
Drunkenness
  at banquets, 39
  in China, 119
  general rules on, 42-43
  in Japan, 195
  in Korea, 281
  in the Philippines, 250
  in Thailand, 318
  in Vietnam, 337
Dutch language, 171, 172

E

East Pakistan, 93
Eating. *See* Dining
Eating styles, 39-40
Eating utensils, 39. *See also* Chopsticks; Hands,
  eating with your
  in the Philippines, 249
  in Singapore, 264, 265
  in South Korea, 280
  in Taiwan, 301
  in Thailand, 317
  in Vietnam, 336
Economy
  in Bangladesh, 93
  growth of Asian, ix
  of India, 149
  of Indonesia, 169
  Japanese, 187
  of Malaysia, 211
  of Pakistan, 227-228
  of South Korea, 274
  of Vietnam, 329, 330, 344
Education
  in Bangladesh, 94
  in Pakistan, 228
  in the Philippines, 243
  poverty and, 11
  in Singapore, 259
Eight (number), 114, 143
Elders, respect for, 47
E-mail, in Indonesia, 182
English as a Second Language, 25
English language
  spoken in Australia, 348
  spoken in Bangladesh, 96

spoken in China, 129
spoken in Hong Kong, 135, 136
spoken in India, 151, 154, 163, 164
spoken in Indonesia, 171, 182
spoken in Japan, 191
spoken in Malaysia, 213, 223
spoken in New Zealand, 363
spoken in Pakistan, 229, 231
spoken in Singapore, 261, 262
spoken in South Korea, 275, 288
spoken in Taiwan, 297, 308
spoken in Thailand, 313, 314, 325
spoken in the Philippines, 245, 246
spoken in Vietnam, 331, 333, 343
Environmental problems. *See also* Air pollution
  in China, 110
  in Japan, 203
  in Malaysia, 212
  in the Philippines, 244
Environment, the, 13-14
Ethnic conflict, 14-15
Ethnic makeup/diversity, 9
  in Australia, 348
  in Bangladesh, 95
  in China, 111
  in Hong Kong, 135
  in India, 151
  in Indonesia, 171
  in Japan, 189, 192
  in Malaysia, 212
  in New Zealand, 363
  in Pakistan, 229
  in the Philippines, 245
  in Singapore, 259-260, 261
  in South Korea, 275
  in Taiwan, 295
  in Thailand, 313
  in Vietnam, 331
"Eve-teasing," 166
"Eyebrow flash," 245
Eye contact, 34
  in Bangladesh, 97, 107
  by Muslims, 83
  in Pakistan, 232
  in South Korea, 279

F

Face, saving/losing, 22-23
  in China, 114
  in Malaysia, 223
  in South Korea, 273, 278
  in Vietnam, 333
Fakirs (holy men), 93
Family, the
  in Japan, 187
  in the Philippines, 244
  in South Korea, 277
  in Taiwan, 294, 297
Fatalism, Asian sense of, 49, 50, 94
Feet, 35
Feng shui, 86-87
Ferries, in Bangladesh, 104
Fertility rates, 12
Filipino language, 245, 248-249
Films, South Korean, 278
First impressions, 18
First names, 20, 21-22. *See also* Names and
  titles
Five Chinese Brothers, The (Bishop), 37
Floors, 32
Flower garlands, 159

Salaam, 20, 214
Samsara, 77
Sanskrit, 151
Sari, 101
Sarongs, 51, 177
SARS (severe acute respiratory syndrome), 13, 259
Satyanand, Anand, 361
Saving face. *See* Face, saving/losing
Securities and Exchange Commission of Pakistan, 238
Selamat, 171
Selamat menjamu selera, 218
Sex-based discrimination, 15
Shalwar kameez, 101, 235
Shamanism, 213
Shari'a, 14
Shia Muslims, 227, 229, 238
Shingon Buddhism, 77
Shinto religion, 79-80, 189
Shiva (god), 80
Shoes
    disease prevention and, 61, 163, 307, 343
    not removing, 141
    removing, 51, 100, 159, 176, 198, 218, 234, 251, 267, 303, 319
    wearing clean, 51
Shopping. *See also* Bargaining
    in Pakistan, 236
    in Singapore, 268
    in Thailand, 323
Shopping malls, 131
    in China, 131
    in Indonesia, 170
Sidewalk food stalls, 60
Sikh religion, 151, 213
Sikhs, naming conventions and, 153-154
Silence, 24
    in China, 129
    in Japan, 191, 204
Sindhi language, 151, 229
Singapore, 259-272
    conversation in, 262-263
    dress in, 267-268
    drinking in, 266
    gift giving in, 268
    health and safety in, 269-270
    helpful hints for traveling in, 268
    holidays and festivals in, 272
    land size of, 9
    language spoken in, 262
    manners in, 267
    overview, 259-260
    people of, 261
    punctuality in, 267
    tipping in, 266
    toasting in, 266
    vital statistics on, 260
Singing, 289
Siraiki language, 229
Skin color, 51
Skin-whitening creams, 51
Slametan, 183
Slippers, 198, 199, 303
Slurping, 37, 121, 141, 197
Smiling
    Asian meaning of, 33

    in Bangladesh, 97
    in China, 112
    in Hong Kong, 138
    in Japan, 193
    in Malaysia, 216
    in Thailand, 316
Smoking
    in Bangladesh, 100
    in China, 122, 128
    guidelines on, 47
    in India, 159
    in Malaysia, 219
    in Pakistan, 234
    table manners and, 37
    in Vietnam, 341
    by women, 43
Socialist Republic of Vietnam. *See* Vietnam
Socializing
    in Australia, 359
    in Bangladesh, 106
    in China, 131
    general tips on, 71
    in Hong Kong, 147
    in India, 165
    in Indonesia, 184
    in Japan, 207
    in Malaysia, 224
    in New Zealand, 371
    in Pakistan, 240
    in the Philippines, 257
    in Singapore, 271
    in South Korea, 289-290
    in Taiwan, 309
    in Thailand, 326
    in Vietnam, 345
Soekarnoputri, Megawati, 184
Solana, Javier, 29
South China Mall (Dongguan, China), 131
South Korea, ix, 273-291
    bowing in, 20
    common phrases in, 279-280
    conversation in, 277-278
    corporate culture in, 286-289
    dining in, 280-281
    dress in, 284
    drunkenness in, 42
    gift giving in, 284-285
    helpful hints for traveling in, 285-286
    holidays and festivals in, 291
    language spoken in, 277
    meeting and greetings in, 275-276
    overview, 273-274
    people of, 275
    population in, 12
    punctuality in, 283
    tipping in, 282
    toasting in, 281-282
    vital statistics on, 275
Squat toilets, 62, 200
Standard of living, 10
Standing in lines. *See* Queuing
Starbucks, 281
Staring, 116, 159, 248, 316, 334
Sunni Muslims, 227, 229, 237
Swimming, 61, 163, 324, 357

T

Table manners, 37-38. *See also* Manners
Tagalog language, 245, 246
Taglish language, 246
Tagore, Rabindranath, 96
Taipei, 293

Taiwan, 293-310
    bowing in, 20
    common phrases spoken in, 300
    conversation in, 297-299
    conversing about, in China, 115
    dining in, 300-301
    dress in, 304
    drinking in, 301
    ethnic conflict in, 15
    gift giving in, 304-306
    health and safety in, 306-307
    helpful hints on, 306
    holidays and festivals in, 310
    language in, 297
    meetings and greetings in, 295-296
    names and titles in, 296
    overview, 293-294
    people of, 295
    population in, 12
    punctuality in, 304
    socializing in, 309
    tipping in, 302
    toasting in, 301-302
    vital statistics on, 294-295
    women in, 309-310
Taiwanese language, 295, 297
Tamil dialect, 151, 213, 261, 262
Taoism, 75, 76-77, 111, 213, 261, 295
Tao-te Ching, 76
Taxis
    in Hong Kong, 144
    in Japan, 203
    in Malaysia, 222
    in the Philippines, 254
    in Singapore, 268
    in Thailand, 323
    tipping and, 99, 121, 140, 158, 197, 218
    tips on hiring, 64
Tea, 119, 139, 157, 175, 195, 196, 318-319, 336, 354, 366
Tea ceremony, 195
Telugu, 151, 213
Temples
    attire and, 161
    Buddhist, 78-79
    Hindu, 81
    Sikh, 160
Teochew dialect, 261
Terrorism, 125, 237, 269
Thailand, 311-327
    body language in, 315-316
    bowing in, 20
    Buddhism in, 77
    common phrases spoken in, 316-317
    conversation in, 315
    corporate culture in, 324-326
    dining in, 317-318
    drinking in, 318-319
    eating styles in, 39
    gift giving in, 321-322
    health and safety in, 323-324
    holidays and festivals in, 327
    language in, 314
    last names used in, 21
    meeting and greetings in, 313
    names and titles in, 314
    overview, 311-312
    population in, 12
    punctuality in, 321
    religious conflict in, 14
    socializing in, 326
    tipping in, 319